Anonymous

The Baptist quarterly

Anonymous

The Baptist quarterly

ISBN/EAN: 9783337713591

Printed in Europe, USA, Canada, Australia, Japan

Cover: Foto ©ninafisch / pixelio.de

More available books at **www.hansebooks.com**

Vol. I.   February, 1896.   No. 1.

...The...
Baptist Quarterly.

"AT IT, ALL AT IT, AT IT ALL THE TIME."

Subscription Price 25 Cents per Annum.

PUBLISHED BY THE
BOARD OF MANAGERS OF THE
MISSIONARY AND EDUCATIONAL CONVENTION OF NORTH CAROLINA,

N. F. ROBERTS, Managing Editor,

RALEIGH, - N. C.

RALEIGH:
BARNES BROS., BOOK AND JOB PRINTERS,
1896.

1865   1896

Educational and Missionary Convention of North Carolina.

Officers:

President..........................Rev. N. F. Roberts, D. D.

Vice Presidents:

Rev. J. O. Crosby,	Rev. E. B. Blake,
" Luke Pierce,	" S. W. Dockery,
" J. K. Lamb,	" D. T. Best,
" S. M. Jones,	" Joseph Perry,
" S. Ratliff,	" W. R. Mason,
" T. S. Evans,	" I. Alston,
" W. D. Devane,	" S. Thomas,
" J. D. Dunston,	" D. J. Moore,

J. W. Brewer.

Recording Secretary...............Rev. C. C. Somerville
Corresponding Secretary.........Rev. C. S. Brown, A. M.
Statistical Sec. and Historian...Rev. P. F. Maloy, A. B.
Treasurer...............................Rev. A. Shepard, D. D.
Auditor..................................Rev. G. W. Moore, A. B.

Board of Managers:

N. F. Roberts,	A. Shepard,
J. J. Worlds,	W. A. Patillo,
J. A. Faulk,	R. I. Walden,
C. C. Somerville,	J. O. Crosby,

L. T. Christmas.

Baptist Quarterly.

The Model Sermon.

It should be brief; if lengthy, it will steep
Our hearts in apathy, our eyes in sleep;
The dull will yawn, the chapel-lounger doze.
Attention flag, and memory's portals close.

It should be warm—a living altar coal,
To melt the icy heart and charm the soul
A sapless, dull harangue, however read,
Will never rouse the soul or raise the dead.

It should be simple, practical and clear;
No fine-spun theory to please the ear;
No curious lay to tickle letter'd pride
And leave the poor and plain undefiled.

It should be tender and affectionate,
As his warm theme who wept lost Salem's fate
The fiery laws, with words of love allay'd,
Will sweetly warm and awfully persuade.

It should be manly, just and rational,
Wisely conceived and well expressed withal:
Not stuffed with silly notions, apt to stain
A sacred desk and show a muddy brain.

It should possess a well adapted grace
To situation, audience, time and place;
A serm'n form'd for scholars, statesm'n, lords
With peasants and mechanics ill accords.

It should with evangelic beauties bloom,
Like Paul's at Corinth, Athens or at Rome;
While some Epictetus or Sterne esteem,
A gracious Saviour is the gospel theme.

It should be mixed with many an ardent
    prayer,
To reach the heart and fix and fasten there;
When God and man are mutually addressed,
God grants a blessing, man is truly blessed.

It should be closely, well applied at last.
To make the moral nail securely fast;
Thou art the man, and thou alone, will make
A Felix tremble and a David quake!

          —*The Calporter.*

Gone to Rest.

The sad news reaches us that Rev. Thadeus Wilson, of Bertie County, who, for a long time, has held pastoral care of a number of large churches, has been called "from labor to reward." He passed out of life into that "house not made with hands" on the 18th of January. He was a faithful leader and was sustained by a strong following.

The Tarborough Institute.

This institute began on the 22nd under the direction of brother Whitted, the energetic missionary of the Eastern District. The brethren present became totally absorbed in the questions presented for discussion, and manifested in every way possible their deep appreciation of the efforts of the lecturers.

Rev. L. M. Curtis, of Aulander, and Rev. W. V. Savage, of Tarboro, (both white) rendered valuable assistance as Lecturers. They expressed in the strongest language their hearty approval of the plan of co-operation, and pledged to give the movement their strongest support.

Rev. J. A. Whitted, the district missionary, made a deep impression upon the people. The general missionary was warmly received, and the brethren generally pledged him to rally like men in support of co-operation.

It is but right to acknowledge our profound gratitude to Rev. M. D. Matthewson and Rev. A. C. Tillery, pastors, for the efforts put forth by them to make the institute successful. These brethren acted like true men, like loyal Baptist leaders, and are examples for our brethren in other parts of the State.

An Address.

To the Colored Baptists of North-Carolina, Greeting:

We take this method of conveying to you our hearty congratulations for the hopeful conditions which a gracious and benign Lord has ordered and appointed, under which the great work pertaining to the development of our denominational interests may be executed. Indeed, we are entering upon a new era of church development, religious activity, and aggressive exertion along spiritual lines; and it is hopefully anticipated that an enthusiasm will sweep through our ranks "from the mountains to the seashore" in favor of co-operation, the like of which has never been seen. The fire has already been kindled. It began to blaze at the recent Convention held in Oxford, N. C.; and we are earnestly praying that the blaze may not grow dim until every Baptist heart in the State has been touched, quickened and aroused.

As a denomination, mighty in numerical strength, we have suffered long and grievously because of poor organization, poor management and poor opportunities; but we believe that a brighter day has dawned and that the Church of Christ which we love and support will be able to exert its full measure of strength in the promotion of christian work.

In many respects the recent Oxford Convention enjoys the distinction of being the most important and memorable convocation of colored Baptists ever held in the State; and this distinction is honorably sustained when it is known that in that body of heroes the plan of co-operation in missionary work among the colored people, proposed by and effected between the white Baptists of the North and South and the colored Baptists, was approved and the machinery necessary to operate the plan successfully provided. Those who were present and witnessed the transaction marveled at the wonderful and visible leadings of Providence in this regard. The plan is indeed admirable, and every Baptist should secure a copy and become familiar with its contents.

The State was divided into three missionary districts—Eastern, Central and Western. The line separating the Eastern from the Central begins at Weldon and runs the Atlantic Coast Railway to Fayetteville, thence down the Cape Fear river to the ocean. The line dividing the Central from the Western begins at Danville and runs the Southern Railway to the Yadkin river, thence down said river to the South Carolina line. Three missionaries were elected: for the Eastern district, Rev. J. A. Whitted; Central, Rev. A. B. Vincent; Western, Rev. P. F. Maloy—to begin labor November 1st, 1895. These gentlemen are true, trusty and tried Baptists, and able to do excellent work. In addition to these district appointments, Rev. C. S. Brown was made general State Missionary to supervise the missionary work and to aid in pushing vigorously the various objects specified in the plan of co-operation. It is conceded by all that the brethren chosen to do this work are eminently qualified and deserve the hearty support of every loyal Baptist in the state.

We, therefore, issue this appeal and call upon you to aid this great movement in every way possible in order that the result may not fall below our anticipations. Talk about it in your homes and on the streets. Let the people know the blessed news. We must reach the people. The Lord is truly at work in Israel. The work is yours; may the Lord interest you to do your part to make the movement a success. We also appeal to you, ministers, pastors and loyal church-loving Baptists, to help us to raise during this conventional year for the extenson of this great work FIVE THOUSAND dollars. Will you help us by bringing this matter before your churches, union meetings and associations, and securing donations? We need your help, your co-operation in the promotion of the Baptist cause in the State. Will you stand like men and help us?

We close this appeal by praying that the benedictions of God may rest upon the work and bring success to the glory of His name. As members of the Board of Managers, we beg to subscribe our names as your faithful servants in the work of the Lord,

N. F. ROBERTS, *Pres.*
C. C. SOMERVILLE, *Sec.*
A. SHEPARD.
J. O. CROSBY.
L. T. CHRISTMAS.
W. A. PATILLO.
J. J. WORLDS.
J. A. FAULK.
R. I. WADDEN.

☞ Address all communications and make all your remittances to Rev. C. S. Brown, Corresponding Secretary, Winton, Hertford Co., N. C.

The New Era Institute.

This institute, which is a prominent feature in the new plan of co-operation, is intended not simply for ministers and deacons, but for all members of our churches. Two institutes will be held in the same locality every year. There will be a progresssive course of lectures for six of these institutes during a period of three years. A great amount of valuable and interesting information will be imparted. There will be 12 lectures at each institute (unless special circumstances prevent), and 72 lectures for the entire course. The subjects will include Biblical Theology, Church History, The Ministry, Christian Education, Missions, The Church and its Work, and other practical matters. It will be a kind of a Theological School brought nigh to the people. The best of available talent, both white and colored, will be secured for lecturers.

Everybody is invited. Every minister should attend every institute. It will be of great value to him. It is proposed to publish a "Roll of Honor" of ministers who pursue the entire course of lectures. We look to the pastors to lead the people by word and by example in this new movement that promises so much for our cause in this State. Come, pastors, and bring with you as many of your people as you can.

This first institute will begin at 9:30 a. m. promptly, and continue three days.

Each lecture will be followed by a discussion, for about 45 minutes, when members of the conference may ask questions and present their views on the subject.

The following is the outline of lectures at the first institute:

BIBLICAL THEOLOGY.

1. *God.* Human misconception of God: polytheism; idolatry; right views fundamental to all else; His character; power; dominion, etc.

2. *A Divine Revelation.* Need of it; partial revelation in creation; in man's moral nature; in human history; direct revelation in Scriptures; in Christ.

3. *A Divine Revelation.* The Scriptures; stages in revelation; how God communicated His will to men; Bible revelation; complete, authoritative, the final standard.

4. *The Scriptures.* Books of the Old Testament; their great divisions; objects for which written; New Testament; divisions; uses of the Old and New Testaments.

CHURCH HISTORY.

1. *Spread of the Gospel in the first century.* Judaism; persecution. Spread in Palestine; in Asia Minor, Rome, Africa; heathen religion in these countries; triumphs of the Gospel.

2. *Paul, the Missionary to the Gentiles.* His calling; extent of his labors; difficulties and persecutions encountered; his self-sacrifices; his evangelistic work; his constructive work as shown in the Epistles; general estimate of Paul's character and influence.

THE GOSPEL MINISTRY.

1. *A call to the Ministry.* Men called of God in the Old Testament times. Christ's call to his disciples. Paul. What now constitutes a call to preach? Erroneous views on the subject. Personal ambition and the ministry. A solemn and responsible work.

CHRISTIAN MISSIONS.

1. *Missionary work for the Negroes in the days of slavery.* White preachers. Branch churches and Negro preachers; men of mark among them. Success of this work. Number of colored Baptists in 1860.

2. *Missionary work for the colored people since the war.* Beginnings and progress of the work by Northern Baptists. Work by Southern Baptists. Religious activity of the colored Baptists themselves. Remarkable growth. The new era of co-operation in this work. The objects and methods.

CHRISTIAN EDUCATION.

1. *Define education.* Object of Christian education, right character and proper discipline of one's powers. Man the thinker. Training necessary to correct thinking and expression. Knowledge is power. Difference between educated and uneducated people. Intellect a power for Christ.

CHURCH WORK AND THE FAMILY.

1 *The prayer meeting.* Do churches generally have a weekly prayer meeting? Prayer meetings mentioned in the New Testament. Value of church prayer meetings. The Word of God in the prayer meeting. How to conduct the meeting.

2. *Personal and family religion.* The christian family life should be a model. What a christian home should be. Home life, its influence on children. Teachings of scripture about duties of husbands and wives; parents and children. Family devotions. Daily reading of the Bible.

This will be a feast of good things. Come one! Come all!

Fraternally yours,
C. S. BROWN, Winton,
General Missionary.
J. A. WHITTED, Goldsboro,
District Missionary.

Institutes.

FIRST DISTRICT—Rev. J. A. Whitted, Missionary.

1. Winton, Jan. 2-4.
2. Tarboro, Jan. 22-24.
3. Goldsboro, Feb. 12-14.
4. Elizabeth City, Mar. 4-7.
5. Plymouth, March, 25-27.
6. Scotland Neck, April 15-17.
7. Newbern, May 4-7.
8. Wilmington, May 27-29.

SECOND DISTRICT—Rev. A. B. Vincent, Missionary.

1. Lumberton, Jan. 8-11.
2. Laurinburg, Jan. 29-31.
3. Fayetteville, Feb. 19-21.
4. Oxford, March 11-13.
5. Raleigh, April, 1-3.
6. Franklinton, April 22, 23.
7. Warrenton, May 13-16.
8. Chapel Hill, June 3-7.

THIRD DISTRICT—Rev. P. F. Maloy, Missionary.

1. Reidsville, Jan. 15-17.
2. Winston, Feb. 5-7.
3. Salisbury, Feb. 26-27.
4. Charlotte, March 18-21.
5. Monroe, April 8-11.
6. Dallas, April 29, May 1.

7. Asheville, May 20–22.
8. Waynesville, June 10–12.

The first date indicates the opening day, and the second date the closing day.

The pastors in the towns in which these meetings are to be held will please announce these dates, and urge a full attendance and make all necessary arrangements for the accommodation of those who attend.

For programmes and detailed information concerning these institutes, write to

C. S. BROWN,
Winton, N. C.

Notes of Interest.

Dr. Morehouse wisely recommends as our motto in this co-operation work the following: "At it; all at it; and always at it."

Rev. A. H. Thompson, Moderator of Lumber River Association, says: "Co-operation is a grand thing, and the institute work is the grand blessing that has come to the colored Baptists since the war."

Co-operation is taking like wild fire in a stubble field. White and colored leaders of the church are enthusiastic over the outlook and predict wonderful results.

Dracon W. D. Mitchell, Filmore, N. C., writes: "I thank God for this great movement of Baptist forces. I attended the institute at Lumberton and was more than delighted. It is impossible to estimate the good that was done to enlighten the people."

Miss Letcy L. Moore, one of our most enterprising young lady workers, attended our Lumberton institute and expressed her delight over the success of the meetings.

The Moderators of five associations were present at our Lumberton institute, viz: Rev. S. W. Dockery, of Pee Dee; Rev. A. H. Thomson, of the Lumber River; Rev. Geo. Williams, of the Hominy Creek; Rev. D. J. Moore, of the Lake Waccamaw; Rev. H. S. McDonald, of the Union.

E. K. Proctor, Esq., (white) of Lumberton, attended all our meetings, took part freely in the discussions, and rendered valuable assistance otherwise in making the institute successful. We are especially indebted to him for the hospitality extended to our white lecturers.

The heartiness in which our white brethren take hold of this work is to many a great surprise; but it only emphasises the fact that a new era has begun and that the Lord is in it.

The Lord is at work in Israel and a combined effort is being put forth to develop and strengthen the colored Baptist forces in the State.

Hurrah for co-operation! Brethren, it is now in order to sing "The year of Jubilee has come."

Dr. J. O Crosby, President of the A. & M. College, Greensboro, attended the institute at Reidsville, and lectured on "Christian Education." He has consented to meet us at Winston and deliver a course of lectures. Dr. Crosby promises to give co-operation his hearty influence.

Pastor C. C. Somerville, of Reidsville, did his full duty to make the institute a success. He is, in fact, one of the best pastors in the State and does not propose to be classed in the second rank when it comes to devotion and loyalty to Baptist interests.

A Baptist preacher is a man that preaches solid gospel truth, that advocates Baptist Doctrine, that works for Baptist interests, that talks of Baptist schools, that attends the Baptist State Convention, and arranges for "New Era" institutes.

In order to reach our Baptist forces in the extreme western portion of the State, it has been thought advisable to change the institute to be held in Greensboro May 20th, to Waynesville; and to conduct the institute appointed for June 10th at Asheville.

We must cultivate confidence in each other as brethren in Christ. No part of the great Baptist body should say to any other: "I have no need of thee; nor care for thee." Let this be our watchword: *Close up ranks! Shoulder to shoulder! Forward, march!*—H. L. Morehouse, D. D.

We have received a very encouraging letter from Rev. R. I. Walden, D. D. He states that he heartily endorses the co-operation plan and will do all in his power to push forward the work. Dr. Walden is one of our foremost ministers and we shall hope to secure his services in the institute work.

Rev. John E. White, Corresponding Secretary of the white Baptist State Convention, has consented to lecture in our institutes to be held in Plymouth, Goldsboro, Wilmington and Raleigh. He also informs us that the amount pledged by the white convention toward co-operation has been appropriated by the board. These brethren mean business.

We learn with pleasure that Rev. S. V. Vass, formerly of this State, has been promoted to the position of District Secretary of the American Baptist Publication Society for the Southern States. The appointment recieves the heartiest approval of the Baptist leaders of our State. Rev. Vass is capable, earnest, aggressive and will fill the position with credit to himself and profit to the organization.

Please notify the Corresponding Secretary, Rev. C. S. Brown, Winton, N. C., when any important Baptist meeting is to be held in your community, and let each secretary send him a copy of the minutes of his Association.

Dr. Morehouse, preached at Pleasant Plains at eleven o'clock, on the 5th Sunday morning and at Jordan's Grove church in Winton, at 7 p. m. The congregations were large and appreciative.

The Colored Baptists in many sections of the State are "simply amazed" as well as "delighted" over co-operation. To them it appears to be a special providence sent to quicken and stimulate Baptist influence. The applause and rejoicing is practically unanimous in favor of the new movement. The incredulous are being rapidly converted like souls on the day of pentecost. Why should any one oppose it? A brother well says, "It can do the denomination no harm. It must do good. It will do good."

Emancipation Day, January 1st, was grandly celebrated at Waters Institute, Winton, N. C. The crowd was very large. Addresses were delivered by Rev. J. A. Whitted and Dr. H. L. Morehouse. A collection was taken for the school, which amounted to $216.00.

We learn that a certain brother whom the Convention endorsed several years ago as an evangelist, is using this office to the detriment of co-operation. He is reported as denouncing the plan as a "humbug" and discouraging the institute work. We learn also that he reports himself as a financial agent of the Convention. We desire to say to this brother that we have him "spotted" and shall give the loyal Baptists of the State a full history of his doings unless he discontinues his pernicious work. He is no financial agent of the Convention and has not been authorized to represent the convention in any particular. Beware of him. He is a usurper, if the reports which have reached us be true.

It is strange that in some sections we will find brethren divided by associational lines and hesitate to join in cordially with other brethren in institute work, because they do not belong to the Association within whose territory an institute happens to be held Don't be so narrow brethren. We are laboring to uplift the Baptist Church throughout the entire State.

Rev. Joseph Perry and Rev. M. C. Ransom have been appointed by the American Baptist Publication Society, as Sunday School Missionaries, in the State. They have an important mission in rallying our Sunday School forces, and we feel sure they will prove equal to the task. We wish them all possible success in their new field of labor.

Pray for Your Minister.

No sincere and earnest Christian will neglect to pray for his or her minister. Professing Christians who do not pray for their pastors need not flatter themselves that they are really religious, because such cannot be the case. If your minister is wise and strong, he needs your prayers. If he is weak and inefficient, he needs them greatly. If he is destitute of preaching power, and has not upon his heart the burden of souls, or is unsound in his experience or doctrine, then he ought to be converted or removed, and so much the more does he need the daily earnest prayers of the church. Earnest Christians will pray for their pastors in the public congregation when it is proper to do so, but especially will they remember this duty in secret. Some professing Christians seem to think that the church belongs to them. I suppose they don't pray much for the church or the pastor. It is to be greatly feared that many of our people who attend the preaching of the gospel do so without prayer. When this is the case, they will grow harder and blinder, instead of wiser and better. It is the settled habit at many of our country churches for many of the leading members to assemble in front of the church and engage in prayerless and worldly conversation until the moment when the services are begun. Then they hasten in and take their seats, but if an angel direct from the throne of God were in the pulpit, they could never be reached or profited while continueing such a course.—Selected.

A Special Example.

The work of co-operation was presented to the West Roanoke Union meeting, which convened at Pleasant Plains, Hertford county, on Friday and Saturday before the 5th Sunday in last month, and a motion was immediately adopted approving the same and donating twenty-seven dollars toward running the first institute which was to be held in Winton. A motion was also approved requesting the churches to raise one cent per member for the extension of the work and report the same to the meeting which will be held at Rich Square, in March.

This is a worthy example. We are on trial before the world, and let us not be negligent in expressing our fullest appreciation of the philanthropy and aid offered us to improve our denomination and people.

Dr. Morehouse, honored the meeting with his presence on Saturday and gave an address on the plan of co-operation. It is needless to insert that the brethren were proud to see him and hear him.

The Institute at Goldsboro.

The meetings were held in the African Baptist Church, formerly pastored by the sainted A. Williams, now called to rest. Rev. J. W. Dew, the present pastor, a congenial and splendid man, did his best to entertain the brethren, and he succeeded admirably. Among the many pastors who attended we were delighted to meet our staunch and venerable friend, Rev. Thomas Parker, Rev. S. M. Jones, (who is as true to the church as the needle to the pole) Rev. R. H. Harper, and others whose labors have made them honorable in the church.

Rev. James Long, of Goldsboro, Rev. B. W. Spilman, of Kinston, Hon. John C. Scarborough, State Superintendent of Puplic Instructions, represented the white Baptist Convention as lecturers. Their discourses and addresses were of a very high order, and duly appreciated by all who heard them. Rev. J. A. Whitted, the efficient district missionary, performed his duties with great credit to the denomination and himself. Rev. A. L. Sumner, the able principal of the State Normal School, took an active part in the discussions and displayed increasing interest in co-operation.

As usual, the brethren were highly pleased and edified, and left the institute greatly benefitted. They universally regretted the absence of those who refused to come to the meeting and seemed to think they lost a great deal.

Action was taken to create a Baptist Publishing Company, to see that a good denominational paper is given to the people of the State. We heartily approve the effort, and trust that the movement will meet with general endorsement.

The institute work is moving on grandly and the future will indicate great improvement in the State.

The Lumberton Institute.

The second institute was held in the Baptist church at Lumberton, in Rev. A. B. Vincent's district. The meetings which began January 8th had been thoroughly advertised, and ministers, deacons, and Sunday School workers came to it for fifty miles around. The attendance was surprisingly large, and much credit is due the district missionary for the excellent work done by him in securing the presence of so large a number of leaders. The events and lectures of the entire three days were a series of delightful surprises and the whole formed a magnificent feast of good things.

As at Winton, the general missionary presided and had the pleasure of introducing the lecturers.

Dr. Morehouse was present and took an active part in the meetings. The brethren were proud of his presence. Rev. W. B. Oliver, (white) of the First Baptist Church, Wilmington, delivered three very able and interesting lectures.

Rev. M. L. Kesler, (white) of Red Springs, discussed in four lectures "Biblical Theology." He rendered the topics plain and interested deeply all who heard him.

Other lectures were given by the general missionary, and district missionary Vincent. The people were thoroughly convinced that co-operation is a good thing. Two sermons were preached; one by Rev. C. S. Brown and the other by Rev. M. L. Kesler.

President Meserve, of Shaw University, closed the institute with an able address on "Christian Education." Grateful mention must be made of E. K. Proctor, (white) of Lumberton, for the active interest shown in the meetings and for aid rendered. The country was greatly stirred, and sixty paeenchers and deacons rose and pledged to do their best to make co-operation a success in the State. They say the next semi-annual meeting should be more largely patronized than this was. May the good work go on.

To the Baptist Quarterly.

REIDSVILLE, N. C.,
January 17, 1896.

DEAR BRETHREN:

Concerning the co-operative work of our denomination in the State, as enunciated by the State Convention in its last session, I desire to express my approval of what has already been done under the plan, and my sincere hope of the future.

The first institute in Bro. Maloy's district is being held with our church now. Bro. Brown, General Missionary, is in attendance and is rendering invaluable service.

Last night (Wednesday) the church was crowded with the best

people in the city. Bros. Brown and Maloy lectured on the "Missionary work among the Colored People before the war," which subject was discussed to the apparent satisfaction of all present, white and colored. A great many truths were revealed as they traced the foot-prints of God, leading our people through the dark days of slavery. I wish to remark especially that not once did they treat the subject in that way which would invite criticism or provoke antagonism from any fair-minded person.

The Institute has already done a good work for our people and our church, and the community will be the reapers of the good seed sown for days to come.

Every church in the State where these meetings are to be held, should make the most extensive preparations for them, while the others should do all they could to encourage attendance.

Dr. C. A. Rominger a very prominent dentist of the city and member of the white Baptist church, has consented to lecture tonight on "Bible Chronology," the pastor not being in the city.

This is to be the *magnum jubilum annum Deo*, and with Brown, Whitted, Vincent and Maloy as pioneers, the 140,000 Baptists as followers, the white Baptist church co-operation, we must go forward proclaiming at every step, North Carolina for Christ.

C. C. SOMERVILLE,
Past. 1st Bap. Church.

⁂

We are glad to report decided progress in the matter of co-operation with Southern Baptists in work for the colored people. The plan approved by the Home Mission Society and the Home Mission Board of the Southern Baptist Convention has been submitted to the white Baptist Conventions of Alabama, South Carolina and North Carolina, all of which with hearty unanimity, voted to enter into co-operation with us and with the colored Baptist Convention of these States, each of the four co-operating bodies bearing its share of the expense. Our colored brethren in these States, also enter most heartily and hopefully into this new arrangement. In other States there is a strong desire for co-operation as soon as practicable. We have entered upon a new era in our work for the colored people of the South. The Society believes it is now following the leadings of Providence as truly as it did when the work was first undertaken, and that now as then, the means for this advance will in some way be provided. Are there not those who will make a thank-offering to be used by the Society in the extension of this plan of co-operation throughout the entire South? For this, as well as for other purposes, the Society is sorely in need of funds.—From Home Mission Monthly for January.

⁂

The Winton Institute.

The co-operative work of the Northern and Southern Baptists in favor of the colored people seems to be tending towards sure bases.

The Baptists in Eastern North Carolina, white and colored, hail with joy the new plan, and seem to be very much moved in favor of its successful operation.

The new Era Institute which is a prominent feature in the new plan of co-operation in something in which they take special delight. They say, that through this special feature of the work, they can see the intellectual and spiritual growth of the churches in this section, if the Institute is carried out according to the plan adopted.

The plan is admirable, since it affords a kind of theological school in which, not only the pastors, but the deacons and members may receive a systematic course of lectures on Biblical Theology, Church History and Christian Education.

We are are proud to say that we have the honor of having the first of these Institutes held in our midsts at Waters Normal Institute, Winton, N. C., conducted by Rev. C. S. Brown, Superintendent Baptist Missions for the State, and Rev. J. A. Whitted, Missionary for the Eastern division.

The Institute was largely attended, over 40 ministers and pastors were present, also a large number of deacons and members represent the most of the churches in the immediate section.

Able lectures were given by the following distinguished white Baptist, viz: Rev. W. C. Scarborough, Murfreesboro, N. C., on "A call to the ministry," Prof. C. B. Williams, Principal, Winton Academy, Winton, N. C., on "Divine Revelation," and Dr. H. L. Morehouse, Secretary of the Baptist Home Missionary Society, New York, on the "Missionary work among the colored people of the South before and since the war;" also by Prof. J. A. Whitted, on "Church work and the Family," and Prof. C. S. Brown, on "Paul, Missionary to the Gentiles." Dr. Morehouse, also gave a lecture on the "Spread of the Gospel in the First Century."

The lectures were ably delivered and in a very impressive manner. All were highly delighted and seemed to realize fully the great importance of the work through the new plan.

I read from the expression of the faces of the ministers and brethren present while these lectures were being given, that they were beginning to see the responsibilities of their missions in a different light from that they had seen before, and many were their expressed determinations to return to their fields of labor for the fuller prosecution of their labors than ever before.

The discussions made by the brethren on the topics that come before them portray quite a representative body in point of intelligence and Christian devotion, and their liberal donations made during the Institute bespoke a sincere determination for the furtherance of this special work over this section of our State.

I can safely say, that should there not be another such Institute held in this section, the one already held is well worthy of the money and labor given in its behalf, for its good effects have been indellibly impressed upon the hearts of our people.

In closing, permit me to say that the labors of Profs. Brown and Whitted in making this Institute a success are worthy of much commendation, for they spared no pains whatever in impressing our churches with the importance of the New Era Institute.

Respectfully yours,
John W. Pope.

The New Era Institute at Lumberton.

From Biblical Recorder.

The Northern Home Mission Society, our Home Board, our State Convention, and the Colored Baptist Convention, unite in this work, a part of which is a series of theological institutes to cover a course of three years. There will be two rounds of these each year. The State is divided into three districts with a missionary for each. The plan is to have several white pastors to deliver lectures at each of these institutes. Bro. W. B. Oliver and I were asked to help in the institute at Lumberton. Bro. E. K. Procter laid aside his pressing law business enough to attend almost every session, and gave very practical help on many of the subjects discussed. Dr. H. L. Morehouse, Field Secretary of American Baptist Home Mission Society, who had much to do in bringing about this plan of co-operation, was there. His lectures on missionary work among the colored people before and since the war were very fine. He spoke in high terms of the work done by Christian slave owners before the war. He is a man of fine spirit, and brimful of practical suggestions. Prest. Meserve of Shaw University was there the last night and delivered an address on education, practical and well adapted to the needs of the colored people.

I was very favorably impressed with the colored leaders present. Rev. C. S. Brown, Corresponding Secretary of their Convention, is a man of real power, and speaks in no uncertain sound of the needs of his people, of their follies and their weaknesses. Rev. A. B. Vincent, the missionary of the central district, deserves great praise for the interest he worked up in the first institute. He impresses me as a man of refinement and intelligence, and of an humble Christian spirit.

The preachers who attended were enthusiastic. About seventy ministers and deacons were present. They were in their places every time, and with knotted brows they tried to understand what was said, and many of them seemed to take in the thoughts given them. They want to learn. The meetings were made practical as well as theoretical. Bro. Oliver's lecture on "A Call to the Ministry" was a bomb in the camp. The sentiment among them is strong to put the unworthy preacher out. There are many really genuine men among them.

The crowds that gathered, in their conduct at the church and on their way home, would do credit to any community of white people. The Negroes are delighted. They say the "year of jubilee has come." They thanked us over and over again for coming to their help.

I have high hopes for this work. An opportunity is at our doors to do the work we ought to have done long ago. The Negro must be reached from his religious side.

The colored preachers hold the destiny of their race in their hands. The issue of many moral questions that come up in almost every community depends largely on what the colored preacher can do with his people. Let me urge the white pastors over the State to take an interest in this work. The effort to instruct these preachers will help you in power gained to adapt yourself to every grade of human need. M. L. KESLER.

Red Springs, Jan. 13, 1896.

The Laurinburg Institute.

Missionary Vincent achieved great success in working up this institute. The pastors of the Pee Dee Association were out in full force and seemed to appreciate the exercises throughout. They were unstinted in their praise for co-operation, and pledged to do their part in raising money to advance the cause. The interest in the institute was wide-spread, and many who attended the meetings at Lumberton were present as anxious participants.

Rev. M. L. Kesler, of Red Springs, who rendered such able assistance at Lumberton, was present as a lecturer, re-inforced by Rev. J. J. Blaylock, of Rockingham. These brethren evidenced great interest in co-operation by cordial expressions and splendid discourses on the subjects assigned. In fact, they impressed us that our white brethren of the South had taken hold of the work in good faith.

The criticism had been made that the subjects for the lectures were beyond the grasp of the ordinary colored preacher, but the fact is they understand readily and receive eagerly the remarks made. They drink in great truths until they are "full." There were more than twenty ministers present during the sessions. The community-at-large was stirred up, and the people came from far and near to see what those "Baptist Preachers" were doing. The revival is sweeping over the State; and in the language of another, "co-operation is co-operating everywhere."

Gone to Rest.

Hon. Elijah Shaw, of Wales, Mass., the distinguished founder of Shaw University, departed this life on the 28th of January. He was a true and ardent friend of the colored people, and regarded the sacrifice made to plant Shaw as the crowning act of his life. For years he made annual visits to the school, and took no little pleasure in watching the development of a work which was destined to become the pride of the South. He has gone to his reward, gone to join his life-long friend, the immortal Tupper. How well he lived? He built a monument that will never die. Hundreds and even thousands of young men and women scattered almost all over the face of the earth, who have received training at Shaw, will mourn to hear of the death of this benefactor and friend.

The Baptist denomination sustains a serious loss in the great fire which occurred in Philadelphia on the 14th of February, and which destroyed the great publishing house of the American Baptist Publication Society. The estimated loss is $400,000. The valuable collection of the American Baptist Historical Society was also consumed. The financial loss was not half so great as the loss of literary productions which cannot be replaced.

Our Wertern North Carolina Field.

P. F. MALOY, DIST. MISSIONARY.

The work of co-operation under our new era model is indeed spreading like forest fires all over the western district. Our pastors and churches hail the new era institute and all the co-operation plan with unmeasured enthusiasm. Our white brethren, I am glad to say, are to the front in this grand work. They say co-operation must not fail if their assistance and encouragement will hold it up. One of our white brethren said he wanted to see the work of the colored Baptist on as strong a basis as that of the white. Rev. C. C. Somerville, of the First Baptist Church, Reidsville, made the crooked way straight for our first institute, which was held at his special request at his church. He had stirred up the whole community to the interest of the institute and its far-reaching benefits and results. The people of Reidsville welcomed the new plan of missions adopted by our convention and did what they could to enlarge the work by their contributions. There were only eight or ten ministers present, as the weather was inclement and the road leading to the town quite muddy. Though the rain drenched the earth the people of Reidsville crowded out to the lectures and shared the benefits and good results of the meetings.

Our first institute at Reidsville closed with a most hopeful prospect for the blessed plan of co-operation in Western North Carolina.

From Reidsville we next turned our face toward Winston, the selected place of our second institute. Here we found Rev. G. W. Holland, the founder and father of the Baptist history in our famous and only twin-city, busily erecting a monument, sacred to the memory of colored Baptists in this State, but really after helping to begin our new and best history, co-operation, to give himself, family, congregation and people to the success of the institute held at his church, on February 5th.

Revs. Holland and Johnson have lead Baptist principles to success in Winston. The institute here did great good. The lectures given by Dr. J. O. Crosby, Dr. Witherspoon, Dr. H. H. Brown of the white Baptist church, and Rev. C. S. Brown, our general missionary and secretary, seems to have doubled the hold of Baptists on this great manufacturing city, and inspired the pastors, ministers, deacons and churches of the city, to undertake and do a greater work for the Master than ever before. We opened the roll of honor at each institute and allowed special contributions to the work. The pastor, licensed ministers and deacons felt that the institute was too short, and requested that we hold another before long. There were fourteen pastors and ministers present and seventeen deacons. These men thanked God daily that such a glorious work had begun and prayed for its continuance. Our congregations during the institute averaged from about three to five hundred.

The roll of honor and the Baptist Quarterly were not discarded at the Winston institute, but the love which God reserved for the cheerful giver was fully manifested at Winston as well as at Reidsville.

A long list of names follow who put after their signatures amounts that assure their determination to give life and permanence to this our "New plan and paper."

The following is the roll of honor at Reidsville:

Rev. C. C. Somerville	25
Rev. E. F. Parham	25
Mr. Thomas Williams	25
W. H. Terry	25
Mrs. Anis McGeehee	25
Mr. Mills Evans	25
Mr. Morris (white)	50

There were others who pledged amounts but we leave them off this list. "He that giveth liberally shall be rewarded bountifully.—*Bible*.

The roll of honor for Winston is as follows:

Rev. G. W. Holland	} 50
Mrs. Holland	
Rev. H. H. Brown (white)	25
Mr. Samuel Toliver	25
Dr. Jones	50
Dea. H. Pendleton	25
Miss Addie Morris	25
W. T. Christian	25
J. H. Sessoms	25
J. L. Howard	25
Lee Foy	25
William Minyard	25
H. W. Foster	25
Three white gentlemen	75
Rev. W. L. Bethel (Pres.)	25
John H. Goings	25
Robert Goings	25
J. S. Fitts, L. B.	25
A. R. Bridges, L. B.	25
Dr. H. H. Hall	25
Mrs. Nancy Gibson	25
Mrs. Mary Preston	25
T. E. Setzer	25
Lewis F. Guinn	25
J. S. Lanier, L. B.	25
Miss Mary L. Brown	25
Miss Georgia Brown	25
Mr. Robert Butler	25
Miss Mary Pickett	25

This is not to be understood to be the full influence of this roll, for large amounts were pledged by those who were out of employment, but who will soon fill their places in the factories.

The following persons ordered the Baptist Quarterly, our new journal, to make its first appearance in the month of February: Miss Mary L. Brown, of the colored Winston Graded School; Mr. Lee Foy, Winston; Miss Addie Morris, 202 east Sixth street, at mission rooms, Winston; Mrs. Emma Simmons, 202 east Sixth street, Winston.

The money for the Quarterly has been paid in and they now anxiously await its appearance. God bless the work of our first Quarter and give zeal and enlarged results for the next.

ITEMIZED CONTRIBUTIONS FOR THE FIRST QUARTER.

Providence Bapt. Church, Greensboro	$ 1 30
Institute at First Baptist Ch Reidsville	7 25
An Individual	36
Mt. Zion Bapt. Ch. Winston	2 55
1st Bap. S. S. Winston	2 10
West End Baptist Mission	65
Shiloh Bap. Ch. n.e. Winston	1 15
1st Bap. Ch. Winston	2 04
Bethel Mission	2 00
	$19 40

FEB. COLLECTIONS UP TO 11TH.

Union Baptist Church, Lexington	$ 1 80
Institute at Winston Feb. 5-8	15 06
North Winston Mission	77

M. E. Church............ ... 2 50

$20 13

Yours for Christ,
P. F. MALOY.
P. S.

Our next institute will be at Salisbury, held at the Dixonville or 1st Baptist Church. Dr. Lewis has written us that he intends that the institute at Salisbury shall be a grand thing. Rev. File also said that he would do all in his power to make the Salisbury institute a grand success. The institute will be on Feb. 26th, at which time we anticipate a grand and glorious meeting. Let all Baptists fall in line and reap the great harvest.

CONTRIBUTIONS FROM CHURCHES—
CENTRAL DISTRICT.

St. Luke church, Hasty, Rev
J. J. Hines,.................... $1 50
The following persons of Rev. Hines' church gave 25 cents each: Emma Ross, J. B. Brasville, Sally Hasty, A. J. McKinnon.
Institute, Laurinburg, Jan.
29th.................. ....$23 38
The following gave 25 cents each; Revs. W. H. Woodard, A. Covington, Jane Covington, W. P. Evans, Simuel Deberry, H. I. Quick, D. M. Jackson, T. A. Lomax, J. J. Hines, G. B. Mason, G. W. Covington, R. I. Wall, Wm. Cobb, Tom Gilchrist, Willy Oats, Martha Plunket, E. W. Andrews, T. M. Jones, Mr. Reoels, Amanda J. Beatie, T. D. McLauchlin, J. Grimes, Roberta A. J. Beattie, Fannie McNeil, A. M. Leach, David Ellebee, Eliza Dobbins, Sarah M. Roper, J. P. McNair, J. M. McLauchlin, D. W. Monroe, Corney Hunty, Jane Covington.

C. B. Harris, 50, Charles Dobbins, 50, Miss D. B. Zack 33, Martha and Jno. Sinclair 35, Mary J. Woodward Prof. W. G. Quackenbush 50, Deala Everett 26, Hon. H. C. Dockery, 50.
Poplar Springs Church,
Rev. T. A. Lomax............$2 01
The following gave 25 cts. each: Samuel Ingram, W. H. Leak, Anthony Ratliffe, A. Everett, Daniel Brower, Jno. McRae, F. T. Townsend, F. C. Covington, Lizzie Simmons.
Red Springs church, John
Williams and wife,..............35
St. John church, Rev. H. C. McDonald................$2 15
The following gave 25 cts. each: Henry Smith, Sarah Williams, Herry Johnson, W. H. McEachen, Kennie Patterson, W. S. Smith, Martha McEachen, Sandy A. Ausley.
Shiloh church Rev. W. H. Andrews,............................52
Albert Crawfort................25
Pleasant Grove church, Rev.
H. C. McDonald............$ 4 50
The following gave 25 cts. each: Frank McLean, Alfred McMillan, Prince Curry, Lewis Howell, Sandy McMillan, Patience Smith, Jack King, Nelson McMillan, Adam Humphrey, Leary Smith, Lewis Howell Peter Glover, Alfred Crawford, Rev. J. D. Harrell, St. Paul, N. C.
New Light church,..............49
Mrs. Dora Spearman,..........25
Respectfully submitted,
A. B. VINCENT,
Central District Missionary.

FINANCIAL STATEMENT OF CENTRAL
DISTRICT MISSIONARY.

Total receipts from the Central

District since Nov. 1, 1895, to Feb. 1, 1896, was $86.02.

Salary and expenses..... $ 46 91
Paid Cor. Secretary, C. S. Brown........................ 23 91
Paid for lectures in two Institutes..................... 15 20

Total for 3 months, $ 86 02

A. B. VINCENT,
Missionary Cent'l. Dis't.

The co-operation work is loyally and heroically supported by Rev. S. W. Dockery, moderator, Pee Dee Association; Rev. D. J. Moor, moderator, Lake Waccamaw Association; Rev. George Williams, moderator, Hammond's Creek Association; Rev. H. C. McDonald, of the Union Association; Rev. Geo. W. Moore, of New Hope Association; Rev. Stephen Atkins, of Lumber River Association, and a large number of aggressive Baptists like Rev. W. H. Woodward, D. M. Jackson, J. J. Hines, E. W. Andrews, T. A. Lomax, C. B. Harris, J. A. Spaulding, A. H., and E. H. Thompson, J. D. Harrell, B. W. Williams, T. M. Jones, H. Gore, A. Covington and others.

The brethren of Robeson, Columbus, Bladen, Richmond and Cumberland counties are thoroughly aroused, and are willing to make great sacrifices for the success of the New Era Institutes.

Some of the more prominent brethren, like Rev. S. W. Dockery, have been following the Institutes up from place to place. The Missionary of the Central District can never forget the kindness and devotion of the noble brethren of this section of the State.

MISSIONARY
of Central District.

CONTRIBUTIONS TAKEN BY A. B. VINCENT.

Lumber River Association..$ 5 00
Bryant Swamp Church......   40
Pleasant Hill Church........ 2 08
Little Wheel of Hope........ 1 50
Lake Waccamaw.............. 1 65
Sandy Plains................... 2 00
New Hope Church Bladen.. 1 25
                                                1 75
Baptist Church, Youngsviile 2 50
Greystone, Brookston Ch... 1 25
Fayetteville St. Ral. Mis.... 1 08

COLLECTIONS NOV. AND DEC. 1895.

Pee Dee Ministers' Union...$ 5 00
Providence Ch., Rock'gham 3 18
Sharper Powell.................   25
J. M. Ingram....................   25
Samuel Ross....................   25
W. W. Dovet...................   25
Miss Bettie Stancell..........   25
  " Annie Ross................   25
Rev. W. H. Scott..............   25
Sandy Grove, Maxton........ 1 15
Alex. Pouncer and wife.....   50
Church, Laurinburg........... 1 60
James D. Ellerbee.............   25
A. J. McCall....................   25
Esther Watkins.................   25
Mrs. A. J. Harris...............   25
Nashville Baptist Church... 1 85
Miss Martha Steward........   25
  " M. A. McNeil.............   25
  " Margaret Monro.........   25

LUMBERTON INSTITUTE TOTAL $20.

J. C. Jerman...................   25
W. C. Pope.....................   25
W. M. Cobb....................   25
Rev. Stephen Atkins..........   25
  " Geo. Williams............   50
J. S. McKoy....................   25
Mt. Olive Church..............   33
Rev. E. M. Thompson......   50
  " N. W. Woodward......   25
  " B. W. Williams..........   25
  " D. J. Moore..............   25
Alex. Pouncer..................   50

George Maloy	25
Major Pope	25
R. W. Williams	25
Ervin McKeller	25
Rev. M. Morrison	25
M. Lewis	25
A. H. Thompson	50
I. H. Kinar	25
Whiteville Sunday School	25
Pierce Powell	25
Rev. W. B. Oliver	1 00
D. Powell	25
James Walker	25
A. D. Thompson	25
Esther Moore	50
J. A. Spaulding	25
J. D. Harrell	25
D. R. McCloud	25
G. W. McQueen	25
Isaac Moore	25
T. D. McNeil	25
R. Griffin	25
George Maloy	25
Spring Branch Church	6 00
Henry Gilchrist	25
B. F. McLauchlin	25
Miss Lucy Blanks	25
Samuel Shaw	50
Miss Hattie McLauchlin	25
George G. Love	50
Miss Susie McLean	25
J. P. Shaw	25
Miss Cora McLauchlin	25
" Caroline McNeil	25
" Julia McNeil	25
Grant Armstrong	25
Buffalo Springs Church	1 05
Charles Dobbins	25
Miss M. J. Purcell	25
" E. L. Robinson	25

Co-operation and Missionary Work in Eastern North Carolina.

Upon entering this work we did not expect such a hearty endorsement from all sources, but everywhere co-operation is looked upon with implicit confidence, through it the people expect a great change in North Carolina.

While they admire the work in full, but special features are to them peculiarly hopeful.

First, the improvement in the ministry of North Carolina. One cannot imagine how the people long for a better ministry; while we are proud of many of our men in the ministry in North Carolina, still of a great many we are ashamed, not because they may happen to be more ignorant than some of their brethren, but many of them are not by far as upright and as good as they know. They often appeal to the weakness of their still more ignorant brethren of the laity, and instead of doing the people good they are doing them considerable harm. If co-operation can effect a better ministry, a united ministry for us, be assured our greatest hopes will be realized.

There is a tendency on the part of some of our brethren to think our Institute work is intended to show up their ignorance, but we would have this thought corrected. They are intended to enlighten and benefit. All our ministers, whatever age, or condition will be treated courteously and kindly. It is not a place therefore for them to feel strained, but free and easy, just as if in their pulpits or at their homes.

Quite a number of our brethren have been thus gladly surprised, and feel it to be just the thing for them. We hope the time will soon come when every minister who means to do anything or be anything, will avail himself of this God given opportunity, and attend every

Institute in his reach. The brethren whom we secure, colored and white, to conduct these Institutes are men in full sympathy, and are deeply interested in the elevation of our ministry.

It is a bright day dawning in the North Carolina ministry when we realize that for every day in this year a minister's Institute will be conducted somewhere in the State. A white friend in one of our meetings said every Baptist in North Carolina should give five dollars annually to this work.

Another very commendable feature in the minds of the people is the writing of our forces, especially the young of our race, the strength of the future church.

Everywhere it is hoped a halt may be called, and our young people will begin to realize their possibilities as individuals.

To accomplish what the people are hoping for, no one can afford to stand idly, and ask what good co-operation will do, but each and all will give his means, his prayers, his influence and all will fully recognize in this work the hand which has shaped the destinies of every people.

J. A. WHITTED,
Goldsboro. N. C.

The following churches in the eastern district of North Carolina have contributed the amounts opposite their names for co-operation and the Baptist State Convention of N. C:

Halifax church, Halifax	$ 5 36
St. Peter's Weldon	1 20
Bear Swamp, Warsaw	10 11
Pleasant Plains, Winton	3 25
Jordan's Grove, Winton	1 00
South Winton	1 00
Six Run, Turkey	5 65
St. Stephens' Tarboro	5 30
St. Paul's, Tarboro	8 05
Mt. Hope, Jackson	2 00
Shiloh, Whitakers	6 30
Whitakers, Whitakers	1 16
Jarusalem, Whitakers	1 13
Hill's Chapel, Faisons	7 65
Lisbon St. Clinton	1 50
Mt. Olive, Mt. Olive	1 75
Olive Branch, Elizabeth City	6 00
Rich Square, Rich Square	6 15
Murfreesboro, Murfreesboro	7 15
First Baptist Church, Clinton	2 65
New Sawyer's Creek, Belcross	4 00
Mt. Gilead, Mt. Olive	25
First Baptist, Severn	10 00
Middle Ground Union, Chowan	6 55
Eastern Boundary, Belcross	5 00
Minister's Institute, Winton	6 77
	$112.08
Prof. C. F. Meserve	25 00
Mrs. C. F. Meserve	25 00
West Rowan Union	27 36

These amounts do not include pledges which some of the churches have promised to pay.

Very Respectfully,
J. A. WHITTED,
Missionary Eastern N. Carolina.

Sunday School Department.

Baptist State Sunday School Convention of N. C.

OFFICERS:
President,
James H. Young..............Raleigh
Secretary,
Rev. T. O. Fuller......Franklinton
Treasurer,
N. F. Roberts.................Raleigh
Cor. Secretary,
Rev. J. Perry..................Raleigh
Auditor,
S. S. Person..............Franklinton

☞ The next session of the Baptist State Sunday School Convention will be held in Goldsboro, September 23, 1896.

SHAW UNIVERSITY,

RALEIGH, N. C.

Established at Raleigh, December 1st, 1865, was a pioneer in the education of colored young men and young women. Its young ladies' department, formerly known as Estey Seminary, was the first of its kind ever established. All departments have grown better with age, and parents can feel that Shaw is a safe place for their sons and daughters. While a high degree of scholarship is maintained by her students, solid character is insisted upon, and all unwilling to comply with rules and regulations necessary to this end, will not find here a congenial atmosphere.

There are Departments of Law, Medicine, Pharmacy, Music, Missionary Training and Theology, as well as Normal, Scientific and College courses of study. A corps of thirty-two professors, teachers and employees is in charge of the various departments. Excellent opportunities for acquiring a solid education at a trifling cost are presented. Although the times are hard, the attendance is large.

For catalogues and other information,
    Address,
      THE PRESIDENT,
      Shaw University, Raleigh, N. C.

WATER'S NORMAL INSTITUTE.

For Male and Female.

WINTON, Hertford County, N. C.

This Thriving Institution located in the "BAPTIST" belt of the State, offers the following inducements to young Men and Women seeking Educational Advantages:

EASY TERMS:— Board, Lodging, Fuel, Lights and Washing all for Six Dollars ($6.00) per Month. Young Ladies doing their own washing Fve Dollars and Fifty cents. ($5.50)

COMPETENT TEACHERS:— The Instructors have been carefully chosen and are thoroughly capable of doing First-Class work in the School Room.

SPLENDID CURRICULUM:—A good thorough English Course has been adopted and students are specially trained for Teaching and College.

Send for Catalogue. Additional information can be obtained by writing to

REV. C. S. BROWN, A. M.

WINTON, N. C.   President.

➡ NOVEMBER, 1896. ⬅

The Baptist Quarterly.

CONTENTS:

	PAGE.
ANNUAL REPORT OF C. S. BROWN, CORRESPONDING SECRETARY AND GENERAL MISSIONARY.	1
THE TWENTY-NINTH SESSION OF THE BAPTIST EDUCATIONAL AND MISSIONARY CONVENTION OF NORTH CAROLINA	10
CONTRIBUTORS TO CO-OPERATION AND MISSIONS FOR NORTH CAROLINA	25
INSTITUTES	26
LUMBER RIDGE INSTITUTE	27
DURHAM INSTITUTE	27
LUMBER RIDGE INSTITUTE, ST. JOHN'S CHURCH.	28
OXFORD INSTITUTE	29
THIRD COURSE OF LECTURES "NEW ERA" INSTITUTE	30
LETTER FROM L. P. MARTIN	31
EDITORIAL NOTES	32
FROM THE WESTERN DISTRICT	33
BIOGRAPHICAL SKETCH OF HENRY L. MOREHOUSE, D. D.	34
BIOGRAPHICAL SKETCH OF N. F. ROBERTS, D. D.	35

BARNES BROS CO. PRINTERS AND BINDERS, RALEIGH.

HENRY L. MOREHOUSE, D. D.

Baptist Quarterly.

Annual Report of Rev. C. S. Brown, Corresponding Secretary and General Missionary.

To the President and Members of the Board of Managers:

I have the honor to submit for your consideration and approval my annual report which, by circumstances, is of a dual nature, embracing the financial record for the conventional year, and also the labor performed under the plan of co-operation by the several missionaries on the field. I beg to state that the report is in many respects incomplete and unsatisfactory, as your humble servant, after diligent effort, failed to secure sufficient data and information to make the report more complete.

It is with peculiar pride, however, that I bear to you this message, setting forth the achievements of this conventional year, and rejoice to assure you that more general enthusiasm has been created in our work than has ever existed before. The Baptist forces, widely scattered and poorly organized, have been greatly aroused to the importance of union and concerted action along missionary and educational lines. The demoralization of our forces, produced and fostered by selfish leadership, is gradually giving away, and the general tendency is toward reformation and progress. The outlook is truly hopeful. We need only to increase our efforts, to work, to pray and to hope.

The work as outlined by you has gone on smoothly and successfully with HARMONY ALL ALONG THE LINE. Our pastors have been generally enthusiastic, loyal and helpful, and have opened their church doors wide to welcome your servants and grant collections for the work. The west and the east have met upon the high plane of fraternity, and are now ready as an invincible army to take North Carolina for Christ. We have met the brethren in the villages and on the hills, and everywhere they seem to be of one accord respecting our great missionary work, which is the paramount issue before us ; and we feel safe in asserting that the great majority of our pastors stand ready to endorse and aid in the execution of any plan which has for its object the extension of missions and the more liberal support of our educational work. The time is fully ripe for action, and the field white for harvest.

We have, during the year, exerted our best efforts to the

DEVELOPMENT OF CO-OPERATION,

and I need not consume the time to explain the wonderful success which has marked its progress from month to month. The great work done is known throughout the State and country. It has been discussed in newspapers and magazines, and from rostrum and pulpit. The year's work has been full of interest. Co-operation has proven to be a most practical thing, touching us where the most good could be done, and in a way most gratifying and congenial to all parties concerned. The whole scheme appears more like a divine conception than an invention of purely human ingenuity.

We are pleased to report that the co-operating bodies have sustained toward each other the most cordial relationship, and have striven conjointly to carry out to the letter the great contract for the spiritual uplifting of the colored people.

We desire further to express officially our gratitude to the white brethren of the State for their generous aid and valuable assistance in our institute work. They have cheerfully offered their service, and kindly and promptly responded to our invitations to deliver lectures.

In this capacity, sixty-three of the best men, broad in soul and liberal in knowledge and experience, generous, pious, fraternal, have associated with us to the delight of our brethren. We have been benefited by their contact with us. If co-operation has done no more it deserves commendation for bringing the white and the colored Baptists into closer relationship to each other.

THE FIELD REVIEWED.

As prescribed in our list of duties, we have striven to secure complete statistics of the denomination in the State; and thus far we have been able to secure the Minutes of only twenty-nine Associations, leaving eleven unheard from.

From the digest of these Minutes given below you will observe that the number of churches equal nearly a thousand, with an aggregate membersip of a hundred thousand. By further reference to the table you will see that the great mass of Baptists lie east of Raleigh, and in the great west, our representation is quite small. It might be well to add, however, that the Associations not represented in this table lie chiefly west of Raleigh. It would add greatly to the dignity of our work if we could come in touch with all these Associations, so that accurate statistics could be sent out to the world through this Convention.

I would be grateful for any information concerning the following Associations: Gold Hill, Catawba, Bakersville, Berean, Burnt Swamp, Cape Fear, French Broad, Gray's Creek, Ivy, Lumber River, Reedy Creek, Toisnot, Western, White Oak and Yadkin.

I beg now your consideration of the facts gleaned from the Minutes of the Associations which have come into my possession:

Year.	Name of Association.	No. of Churches.	Total Membership.	Number Ministers.	Total Collections.
1896	Roanoke	80	12,038	705/70	$202.84
1896	West Roanoke	57	11,000	32/52	139.55
	Neuse River	67	11,170	53/60	192.87
	Middle District	37	3,072	20/17	73.00
	Zion	26	2,087	24/30	60.55
	Middle	13	2,014	21/11	41.50
	Old Eastern	51	4,801	30/37	77.02
	Union	20	1,384	10/8	51.77
	Bear Creek	30	1,603	15/15	111.17
	New Hope	34	3,540	18/20	110.86
	Lumber River	23	1,810	27/1	102.18
	Johnston District	26	1,810	24/28	71.30
	Kenansville	45	5,800	31/30	84.30
	Newbern Eastern	40	5,208	24/27	92.94
	Hammon's Creek	11	354	13/7	15.71
	Pee Dee	26	2,403	14/21	135.50
	Ebenezer	23	1,381	11/1	25.01
	Lane's Creek	10	495	15/7	53.34
	Lake Waccamaw	7	400	7/2	17.60
	Cedar Grove	40	5,311	10/32	87.02
	Shiloh Baptist	53	5,830	13/37	247.30
	Yakin Valley	13	375	10/5	18.85
	Mud Creek	10	703	9	11.20
	Rowan Baptist	47	5,627	23/1	129.89
	Wake Baptist	30	1,702	28/11	170.23
	French Broad	12	660	14	41.21
	Shiloh (Western)	15	701	5/1	18.50
1894	Oakey Grove	27	503	15/18	47.60
1891	High Point	22	197	11	10.44
		914	96,495	670/550	$2,379.44

*The left hand figures represent the ordained ministers, and the right hand the licensed preachers.

OUR EDUCATIONAL WORK.

Our educational work demands more than passing notice. In fact, the Baptists lead in the general education of the masses, and many of our ministers have achieved notoriety as educators. Shaw University, under the capable leadership of President Meserve, is doing an immense work as the leading institution in the State, and has a great claim upon us; and we should do more for that magnificent enterprise than pass a resolution of endorsement. It is now time that the Convention was petitioned to consider the advisibility of supporting the Chair of Theology. Ministerial education is our supreme need, and the opportunity ought to be given our young men to secure theological instruction in our own State school.

We regret not having sufficient data on hand to give you complete information regarding our schools in the State.

MISSION WORK IN DETAIL.

Your attention is next solicited to consider the work in detail done by the several missionaries on the field whose year of service expires November 1, 1896.

SYNOPSIS OF THE WORK DONE BY THE MISSIONARIES IN NORTH CAROLINA UNDER THE PLAN OF CO-OPERATION FOR THE YEAR ENDING OCTOBER 31, 1896.

NAMES	DISTRICT	Weeks of Service.	Institutes Attended.	Sermons Preached.	Lectures Given.	Candidates received and baptized.	Churches Organized.	Churches Visited.	Miles Traveled.
J. A. Brown, Winton	General Miss	52	25	122	127	72		23	13,878
J. A. Whitted, Goldsboro	Eastern	52	23	117	170	6		96	9,264
J. B. Vincent, Raleigh	Central	52	13	187	270			91	6,524
P. F. Malor, Greensboro	Western	44	15	95	114	24		72	6,640
Totals		200	76	431	616	102	2	282	24,306

Letters and postal cards written, 2,096; newspaper articles prepared, 143; pamphlets distributed, 11,800; pages, 168,000; Institutes held, 34; number of lectures, 187; ministers and licentiate preachers enrolled, 743.

To obtain an accurate idea of the work done by the missionaries, we must consider the number of churches visited, aided in building, and the number of pastors settled. They have spent no little time looking up our young people and advising them to attend our Baptist institutions of learning; and in various other directions, they have employed themselves in the interest of our church and people.

We have spent but little time in organization of new churches, thinking it better to strengthen old weak ones rather than multiplying more of the same character. Missionary Maloy has, however, succeeded in the organization of two churches in the suburbs of Winston, and placed under the leadership of our esteemed Bro. Joshua Perry, who reports great progress. Reference will be more definitely made to these mission churches later on.

To stimulate the work of the Convention and co-operation, we have written 2,086 letters and postal cards, 143 newspaper articles, and issued 11,800 pamphlets, making 108,000 printed pages. This includes the three issue of the BAPTIST QUARTERLY, published by order of the Board, under the management of our esteemed President, Dr. N. F. Roberts.

THE WEST A MISSION FIELD.

As previously intimated, Rev. Joshua Perry has been employed as local missionary, or missionary pastor by the Board at a salary of $50.00 for the year, to be paid direct from our treasury. From the monthly reports which has come to us, we commend our brother for his faithfulness, and for the success which has attended his labors.

The entire west, rapidly developing in population, presents an inviting field for missionary adventure, and we recommend that steps be taken without delay to plant mission churches in every town unoccupied by a Baptist church.

In the far west, beyond the Blue Ridge, and in co-operation with the Western Convention, a sub-missionary might be appointed and do effective work at little cost to our Convention. It is a field favored by Nature with scenery of unsurpassed beauty and grandeur—now being thronged with hundreds and thousands of health seekers. Let us plant upon those magnificent hills temples of our Lord Jesus Christ. The brethren of that section, though "few and far between," are hopeful and solicitous, and under the great plan of co-operation, anticipate great results for their long-neglected territory. Let us not be slow in our determination to help them.

The missionaries have gone over mountains and through valleys, seeking our brethren, preaching union and co-operation; and we rejoice to note that their struggles and sacrifices have not been wholly barren of results. We bespeak new life for the Baptist cause in the mountain regions.

We invite your attention to the institutes held during the year:

Institutes Held.	Lecturers White	Lecturers Col'd	Ministers in Attendance
Winton	3	2	25
Lumberton	4	3	34
Reidsville	1	4	9
Tarboro	2	2	18
Laurinburge	3	2	21
Winston	1	4	19
Goldsbo No. 1	3	3	22
Fayetteville	3	3	22
Salisbury	2	4	14
Elizabeth City	2	3	25
Oxford	4	3	30
Charlotte	1	4	11
Plymouth	3	2	31
Raleigh	6	5	55
Monroe	2	2	23
Scotland Neck	2	3	25
Franklinton	5	3	33
Dallas	2	3	11
New Berne	4	2	27
Warrenton	2	3	16
Asheville No. 1	2	2	25
Magnolia		3	21
Lake Waccamaw	2	4	18
Rocky Mount		3	18
High Point	4	5	12
Near Maxton		3	18
Rich Square		3	21
Chapel Hill	4	4	20
Hendersonville	2	5	10
Waynesville		3	1
Winston No. 2	2	3	17
Mount Airy	1	1	4
Asheville No. 2	1	4	13
Durham	2	4	12
Hertford		3	13
Goldsboro No. 2		7	26
Wilmington	1	4	24
34 Institutes.	75	122	743

From the above table it will be seen that, in the ten months of institute work, or forty weeks, we have held thirty-four institutes, an average of nearly one a week, as the plan contemplated. An institute each week could not be carried out, owing to the exigencies arising in localities where certain institutes were appointed, which prevented the holding of the same at the designated times. In a few cases, too, the pastors used their influence against co-operation, and caused the churches to close their doors against the institute. These cases were, however, exceedingly rare.

It is noteworthy to observe the army of lecturers (187) which gave instruction in this movable Theological Seminary, and also the large number of ministers that crowded in for knowledge.

FINANCIAL REPORT FOR THE YEAR ENDING OCTOBER 31, 1866.

Receipts—(Condensed.)

On hand Oct. 25, 1895	$ 196 54
Total collected by C. S. Brown	136 76
" " " J. A. Whitted	728 89
" " " A. B. Vincent	610 25
" " " P. F. Maloy	352 49
Total	$ 2,024 93

Disbursements—(For Co-operation.)

To C. S. Brown, General missionary, salary and expenses	$ 190 06
To J. A. Whitted, missionary, salary and expenses	256 74
To A. B. Vincent, missionary, salary and expenses	204 50
To P. F. Maloy, missionary, salary and expenses	162 56
To Joshua Perry, salary local mis	50 00
Total traveling expenses special lecturers, $222.25, and one forth paid by Convention	44 48

General Items.

Oct. 24, 1895,	A. L. Summer	$	12 00
" "	J. A. Fuller		5 00
" "	J. A. Faulk		5 00
" "	F. R. Howell		10 56
" "	M. E. Hall		25 44
" "	Sandy Kittrell (superannuated)		2 00
" "	A. Buck (superanuated)		2 00
" "	H. Cowan (superanuated)		2 00
" "	A. J. Jackson (superannuated)		2 00
" "	N. F. Roberts, printing		15 00
" "	P. F. Maloy, State Secretary		5 00
" "	Oxford Orphan Asylum		10 00
" "	Baptist Church, Oxford		5 00
" "	Recording Secretary		15 10
" "	Sexton		2 00

Oct. 24, 1895, Printing Minutes	80 00
" " " Corresponding Sec'y.	50 00
Nov. 8, '96, Painting circulars	8 00
" " " J. A. Whitted	25 00
" " " Vincent	25 00
" " " Maloy	25 00
Feb. 11, '96, Printing QUARTERLY.	36 00
" 11, " W. A. Pattilo	2 90
Mar. 13, " " "	2 90
Ap'l 3, " " " Barnes Bros printers	7 00
May 20, '96, Printing QUARTERLY and mailing	38 10
" " " Stationery	4 20
" " " Postage, etc	3 60
July 19, '96, Expenses of the Board (Goldsboro)	33 55
" 31, " Postage	3 25
" " " Soliciting envelopes	1 00
Sept. 23, '96, W. A. Pattilo	2 00
" " " Printing and distributing QUARTERLY.	49 05
" " " J. O. Hayes	29 00
	$1,484 20

Collections Acknowledged by C. S. Brown, General Missionary.

1895.

Nov. 1, C. F. Meserve	25 00
Mrs. C. Meserve	25 00
Dec. 31, West Roanoke Union	27 36
Mar. 31, " " "	17 40
" " " " "	15 25

1896.

Sept. 30, New Hope Ch., Gates	8 25
" 14, Mt. Moriah, Ch., Hertford.	9 25
" 24, Pleasant Plains, Hertford,	5 00
Oct. 12, Phillippi Church	3 25
	$ 136 76

It will be observed that no money or contributions was sent up for the various objects of the Convention voluntarily; but what was collected came through the personal solicitation of some one of the missionaries, saving the contributions from President Meserve and wife. Contributions, however, were made by local organizations for Foreign Missions, but no credit is given, since the amounts were not remitted through the regular channel.

EASTERN DISTRICT,

J. A. Whitted, Missionary.

First Baptist, Goldsboro, N. C.	$ 20 00
Eastern Baptist, Goldsboro	10 00
St. John's Baptist, Battleboro	$ 5 00
Morning Star, Battleboro.	2 05
Sandy Point, Windsor	5 00
Zion Bethlehem, "	8 65
St. Elmore, Windsor	5 90
Indian Woods, Windsor	10 00
Spring Hill, Lewiston	7 00
First Baptist, Plymouth	35 25
Olive Branch, Elizabeth City.	20 00
New Haven, Murfreesboro	7 00
Mt. Moriah, Winton	12 25
Zoar, Margerettsville	10 10
First Baptist, Weldon	6 65
Wilson County S. S. Convention	4 00
Cedar Grove, New Berne.	20 00
Phillippi, Tunis	5 00
Waynesville Baptist, Waynesville, Va.,	10 00
Roanoke Baptist Association	25 00
Gale's Street Edenton, N. C.	6 00
Manolia Baptist Church, Magnolia	15 15
Adoram, Wallace	6 30
Creswell Baptist Church, Creswell	16 00
First Baptist Church, Kenansville	8 12
Wilson's Chapel	3 00
New Hope, Gatesville	7 00
Cedar Landing	10 00
Mt. Pleasant, Goldsboro	1 75
Cape Fear S. S. Union	8 19
Central Baptist, Wilmington	3 00
Ebenezer Baptist, Wilmington	2 00
St. John's, New Berne	2 00
James City	40
New Era Institute, Hertford.	12 00
New Ahoskie, Ahoskie	1 00
Joppa, Gates county	3 86
Washington Union	75
Middle Ground Union	5 00
Hertford Institute	13 00
Wilmington Institute	22 00
Roanoke, Salem	5 00
West Roanoke Association.	15 00
Neuse River "	13 00
Old Eastern "	16 08
Magnolia	4 50
Bear Creek Association	7 00
Middle District	10 00
Women's Missionary Society	8 00
Weldon	90
Halifax Baptist Church, Halifax	5 36
St. Peter's, Welcon	1 50
Bear Swamp, Warsaw	10 11
First Baptist, Severn	10 10
Mt. Zion, Rocky Mount	25 50
Pleasant Plains, Wynton	3 85
Jordan s Grove, Winton	1 00
Six Run, Turkey	6 65
St. Stephen's, Tarboro	3 44
St. Paul's, Tarboro	13 37
Mt. Hope, Jackson	2 00
Shiloh, Whitaker's	6 30
Whitaker's, Whitaker's	1 16
Jerusalem, Whitaker's	1 13
Hill's Chapel, Faison	10 90
Mt. Gilead, Mt. Olive	25
Mt. Olive, Mt. Olive	1 30

First Baptist, Clinton	$ 2 65	Baptist Church, Lake Waccamaw	$ 1 00
Lisbon Street, Clinton	1 50	Sandy Plains	2 56
Ebenezer, LaGrange	2 65	New Hope Church, Bladen County	1 25
Rouse's Chapel, LaGrange	5 00	Baptist Church, Youngsville	2 75
First Baptist, Rich Square	20 15	Brookston Church, Greystone	1 25
Murfreesboro	7 15	Fayetteville Street Baptist Church,	
New Sawyer's Creek, Belcross	1 00	Raleigh	1 08
Middle Ground Union	22 00	Pee Dee Ministers' Union	5 00
Eastern Boundary Union	6 55	Providence Church, Rockingham	3 11
New Era Institute, Winton	6 77	Sandy Grove Church, Maxton	1 60
Fi st African Baptist, Kinston	3 00	Baptist Church, Laurinburg	1 60
Kinston Chapel, Kinston	2 05	Baptist Church, Nashville	1 85
Gallilee, Tillery's	7 50	Lumberton Institute, Sandy Grove	
Scotland Neck	27 05	Church	20 00
Magnolia	4 68	St. Luke's Church, Hasty	1 50
Rocky Point	3 05	Laurinburg Institute, Baptist Church,	53 80
Williamson	75	Poplar Springs	2 01
Edenton	5 00	Baptist Church, Red Springs	35
Kenansville Eastern Association	15 00	St. John's, Lumber Bridge	2 16
		Shiloh Church	77
RECEIPTS FROM CENTRAL DISTRICT NOT OTHERWISE REPORTED—4TH QUARTER.		Pleasant Grove	4 58
		New Light	1 00
		Institute, Fayetteville	9 40
August.		Baptist Church, Smithfield	4 00
James and Amanda Cook	$ 30	Olive Grove, Granville	1 35
First Baptist Sunday school, Oberlin, (Rev. B. P. Peterson)	1 00	First Baptist Church, Henderson	2 21
		Baptist Church, Apex	68
Sophia Battle	25	Holly Springs Church	2 02
P. A. Crocker	25	Nut Bush Church	2 75
		Liberty Church	50
September.		Mt. Leull Church	3 00
Institute White Rock Church, Durham, (Rev. A. P. Eaton)	$ 1 40	Stovall Chapel	3 30
		Antioch Church	2 08
Belton Creek Church (Rev. T. O. Fuller)	3 24	Huntsville Church	1 13
		New Light Church	5 00
		White Pond	3 35
October.		Oxford Institute	20 30
Betsy McCadon (New Light Ch	$ 25	Institute, First Baptist Church, Raleigh	52 46
Church at Keyser (Rev. J. J. Hinet, pastor)	50	Institute, First Baptist Ch., Franklinton	31 99
Mrs. Patience Holland (Rev. P. T. Hall, pastor)	50	Manasas Chapel	2 50
Mrs. Esther Page, Apex	25	Flat Chreek Church, Williamsboro	2 64
Dr. J E. Dellinger, Greensboro	25	Spring Green, Warrenton	5 16
Rev. G. W. Johnson, Winston	25	Baptist Church, Warrenton	4 00
Wakefield Church, Rev. George M. Perry	1 51	Greenwood Baptist Church	1 45
		Woman's North Bound Missionary Union	5 00
Bryant Swamp Church	1 50	Baptist Church, Louisburg	1 35
Institute St. John's Church, Lumber Bridge, Rev. H. C. McDonald	37 00	Wilson's Mills	59
		Malaby's Cross Roads	1 61
Pleasant Grove Church (Rev. H. C. McDonald	1 75	Riley Hill	2 23
		Sunday-school, Greystone	8 00
Total receipts for last quarter	175 24	Missionary Society, Greystone	2 30
Respectfully,		Sandy Plain Church	1 05
A. B. VINCENT.		Little Wheel of Hope	3 50
		Lake Waccamaw Union	2 00
FINANCIAL REPORT—CENTRAL DISTRICT,		White Pond Church	3 35
From November 1, 1896, to November 1, 1895.		*For the Quarter February, March and April.*	
Lumber River Association	$ 5 00		
Bryant Swamp Church	40	Institute, Warrenton	15 01
Pleasant Hill Church	2 08	Sandy Plain	4 30
Little Wheel of Hope, Columbus to Rev J. M	4 50	New Light Church	75

Mt. Olive Church	$ 7 65	Mt. Zion, Winston	$ 2 55
Piney Grove Church	5 00	First Baptist, Winston	2 04
Riley Hill	75	First Baptist Sunday school, Winston	2 10
Brookston, Greystone	6 30	West End Mission, Winston	65
Piney Grove Church	5 00	Shiloh, Winston	1 15
Social Union, Hilliardston	1 00		
Swift Creek	4 31	*February 4.*	
Laurinburg Church	1 25	Union Church, Lexington	1 80
New Hope	75	Winston, Institute	15 06
Social Union, Hilliardston	2 50	North Winston Mission	77
Little Wheel of Hope, Lake Waccamaw	1 66	M. E. Church, Winston	2 50
		Mt. Carmel, Charlotte	50
White Pond Church	1 15	Ebenezer, Charlotte	2 05
Welch's Chapel Church	2 10	Friendship Church	1 15
Laurinburg Church	1 87	First Baptist, Salisbury	1 71
Allen's Chapel	1 16	First Baptist S. S., Salisbury	1 38
Clarkton Church	50	Zion Baptist Church, Salisbury	1 55
Pilgrim's Hill	52	Woman's Missionary Society, Zion Church	1 55
Institute, First Baptist Ch., Chapel Hill	10 00	Institute, Salisbury	12 32
Institute, Lake Waccamaw	30 92		
Bethlehem Church, Maxton	3 52	*March 1.*	
Baptist Church, Lumberton	10 00		
First Baptist Church Fayetteville	4 26	Mt. Pleasant, Winston	4 00
Holly Grove, Richmond		West End Mission, Winston	2 00
Baptist Church, Whiteville	5 00	New Bethel	2 12
Mount Moriah Baptist	5 60	Summer Hill, Lexington	2 00
Spring Branch Institute	21 71	Summer Hill, Lexington	2 00
		Summer Hill S. S., Lexington	87
Fourth Quarter.		First Baptist Church, Charlotte	5 17
		Institute, "	9 95
Women's Home Mission Society, Piney Grove Church	5 00	Friendship, "	3 35
Social Union, Hilliardston	1 00	Ebenezer Church, "	2 05
Nelson's Chapel	4 80	First Baptist S. S., "	87
Wake Chapel		Union Meeting, Mint Hill	2 00
First Sunday-school, Oberlin	1 00	Mt. Moriah, Matthews	1 00
Shiloh Association	10 00		
Pee Dee Association	10 00	*April 4.*	
Union Association	5 06	Elizabeth Church, Monroe	2 42
Wake Association	15 00	Nicy Grove Church, Ames	1 65
Baptist Church at Method	1 15	Nicy Grove S. S., Ames	1 07
Middle Association	5 00	Institute, Monroe	11 43
Mt. Vernon Baptist Church	1 00	Flint Ridge, Marshville	3 50
Wake Missionary Union	10 00	Flint Ridge S. S., Marshville	2 56
Graham Church	1 85	Piney Grove, Marshville	1 56
St. Matthew's Church	1 75	First Baptist Church, Dallas	2 67
Wake Chapel	3 25		
Baptist Church, Kittrell	3 00	ITEMIZED STATEMENT FOR THE YEAR 1896 UP TO OCTOBER, 1896.	
Institute, Durham	13 15		
Belton Creek Church	3 25	St. James Chapel, Bessemer City	25
Institute, Oxford	17 56	Golden Grove, King's Mountain	1 75
New Hope Association	13 17	Shiloh Church, Shelby	2 05
Johnson District Association	5 00	Shiloh S. S., Shelby	1 00
Baptist Church, Rolesville	6 00	Providence Church Lincolnton	65
Sunday-school, Youngsville	1 50	Institute, Dallas	1 75
WESTERN DISTRICT—P. F. MALOY, MISSIONARY.		*May 4.*	
		First Baptist Church, Asheville	6 05
January.		Mt. Zion Church, Asheville	3 95
		New Hope, Asheville	40
Providence, Greensboro	$ 1 30	Institute, First Baptist Church	13 39
Reidsville Church	1 17	First Baptist Church, Hendersonville	3 10
Reidsville Sunday-school	80	First Baptist S. S., Hendersonville	50
Reidsville Institute	5 28	Mud Creek, Flat Rock	1 30

Providence Church, Greensboro	$ 2 27
Providence Sunday-school	1 32
June 5.	
Mt. Cavalry, Mt. Airy	1 65
Mt. Calvary S. S., Mt. Airy	80
Institute, Mt. Airy	3 13
West End Mission, Winston	3 00
New Bethel, Winston	55
Institute, Providence Church, Greensboro	9 02
First Baptist Church, High Point	5 28
Mt. Pleasant, Church, Winston	5 00
Baptist Church, Kernersville	76
July 5.	
Liberty Grove Church, Trinity	1 60
Liberty Grove S. S., Trinity	55
Baptist Church, Thomasville	20
Jerusalem Blade, Trinity	1 25
Jerusalem Blade S. S., Trinity	35
Institute, High Point	25 51
First Baptist, Winston	5 00
Institute, Winston	12 56
First Baptist Church, Waynesville	1 30
M. E. Church, Waynesville	50
Institute, Webster	7 75
August.	
Baptist Church, Hendersonville	10 25
Baptist Church, Waynesville	3 13
Institute, Waynesville	9 51
Mud Creek Association	7 51
Rowan Association	10 00
Mt. Zion Church, Asheville	3 12
Institute, Asheville } Mt. Zion Church, Asheville }	7 77
First Baptist Church	4 25
September.	
Waynesville Association, Murphy	10 61
Shiloh Baptist Church, Greensboro	5 05
Bethel, Mt. Holly	8 00
Shiloh, Charlotte	75
First Baptist, Charlotte	5 50
Institute, Friendship Ch., Charlotte	1 44
Western Baptist Convention	10 00
Brevard Mission	2 05
Waynesville Church	75
Pine Grove Church	1 50
Pine Grove Sunday-school	55
Institute, Franklin	12 35
Ebenezer Association	10 00
Mt. Moriah Mission	2 75

OUR FOREIGN WORK.

We regret no little to announce that scarcely anything has been done for foreign missions. The total receipts for this purpose has not equaled a hundred dollars. Can it be possible that the great army of Baptist leaders in this great and favored State have not once during the year made mention in their pulpits the heathen world? Has Rev. J. O. Hayes, our missionary in Africa, been entirely forgotten? Could we not have gathered up some "crumbs" to have relieved the wants of his suffering family? Brethren, reflect.

By inspecting our Associational Minutes, it will be seen that about four hundred dollars have been paid out to moderators, clerks, treasurers and other officials, for their services during the annual meetings, and nothing for Africa. This ought not to be so.

Again, we ought to agree to urge our Associations to forward all moneys to the Corresponding Secretary of this Convention.

BOARD MEETINGS.

Only one important meeting of the Board has been held, the work being supervised by the Executive Committee. The Board convened August 29th, in the town of Goldsboro. The general missionary offered his resignation, which was accepted to take effect September 1, but finally the date was changed to November 1st.

The Board proceeded to nominate a gentleman to fill the vacancy, and Rev. J. A. Whitted received the unanimous endorsement.

Rev. R. I. Walden, D. D., was endowed to occupy the position of District Missionary for the Eastern District.

I submit the within as our annual report, and beg your charitable consideration of all imperfections which may appear.

Fraternally yours,
C. S. BROWN.

The 29th Annual Session of the Baptist Educational and Missionary Convention of N. C.

GREENSBORO, N. C., Oct. 20, '96.

Pursuant to adjournment of the previous session held with the First Baptist church of Oxford, N. C., in 1895, this Convention met in its 29th annual session with the Providence Baptist church of Greensboro, N. C., Rev. N. F. Roberts, D. D., presiding.

The president, on taking the chair, appointed Revs. D. J. Moore and Wm Devaughn to conduct devotional exercises.

The choir sang a voluntary, "Let us Praise Him," No. 395.

Scripture lesson 2d chapter Acts.

The choir again sang with great animation hymn No. 368, "Come Gracious Lord." At this juncture the pastor, Rev. S. H. Witherspoon was introduced to the body and delivered the welcome address on behalf of the church. He said it was a source of great pleasure to him to welcome the brethren to the church, for he welcomed them not as men who had come to discuss 16 to 1, but because we feel that you have come to discuss graver matters, questions that pertain to the Kingdom of God, a coming that will promote the interest of the great Baptist family of the State, numbering more than 160,000 souls. We hope your deliberations will reflect credit upon you, upon your church and upon the Baptists of the State.

We welcome you because we feel that your coming will be an inspiration to the Christians of this city; we welcome you because your coming is not so much for the pleasure that may be found in the Society of our ladies and friends, enjoyment you may have at our tables, but because what you say and do in this Convention will give emphasis to this Bible truth: "One Lord, one faith, one baptism." We welcome you, yea, thrice welcome you to this church and the hospitality of our people, the latch string of whose doors hangs on the outside.

The Mayor of the city had been invited to welcome the Convention on behalf of Greensboro, but not being accustomed to public speaking, sent an excuse for not being present, which was accepted. Rev J. J. Worlds, pastor of the First Baptist church of Raleigh, delivered a felicitous response. He had been a member of this body he said for 22 years, and as he looked upon it now he found it very different to what it was then in its personel. We cordially thank our brother for his welcome. We have gathered from the different parts of the State to bring a report of the work done; we are in this magnificent church which is much finer than any edifice belonging to us at this time. Let us put Christ in the best places in our hearts, in our homes and we shall have occasion for rejoicing.

The choir sang a voluntary.

The President introduced Rev. T. O. Fuller of the Girls' Training School of Franklinton, N. C., to preach the annual sermon. Brother Fuller selected for his text the 20th verse of the 5th Psalm, "We shall rejoice in thy salvation, and in the name of our God we will set up our banner." Theme—"Salvation chief joy of the church now, and the mainspring of its future life and activity." He preached an able and forceful sermon, clear and pointed, filled with much information concerning the numerical strength and growth of our denomination within the last thirty years. The sermon was well received.

Rev. C. L. Davis, pastor Ebenezer Baptist church, of Charlotte invoked divine blessings.

The following distinguished persons were introduced to the body and made welcome to seats:

Mr. J. W. Bailey, of the *Biblical Recorder*, Prof. J. H. Scott, Theologial department of Shaw University; Miss Miller, Missionary, Training School, Shaw University; Prof. J. D. Chavis, President Bennett College; Rev. S. L. Moore, late of S. C., Prof. S. N. Vass, District Missionary of the American Bap. Pub. Society; Rev. B. F. Hemphill leader of the Baptists of Western North Carolina; President Nelson of Asheville; Nunnally, of Hendersonville, N. C.; and Christmas of Warrenton.

A collection of $6.29 was taken.

The President made his announcements and appointed Revs. Dockery and Christmas to conduct praise service from 9:30 to 10 o'clock on Wednesday morning.

On motion, Prof. Vass was requested to address the Convention his work at 4 o'clock Wednesday afternoon.

Adjourned with the benediction by Rev. T. O. Fuller.

WEDNESDAY—MORNING SESSION.

Praise meeting was conducted by Bros. S. W. Dockery and M. G. Christmas.

Scripture lesson, 1st Psalm.

Warm and fervent prayers were offered by the brethren.

The Convention was called to order by the President.

The minutes of the previous session were read and adopted.

Dr. H. L. Moorehouse was introduced to the body.

A committee on the hours of meeting was appointed, viz: P. F. Maloy, L. W. Wood, S. S. Henderson, who made the following report, which was adopted:

Meet at 9:30 p. m.; adjourn at 12:30 p. m.; meet at 2:30, p. m.; adjourn at pleasure.

On motion, a committee of five be appointed to confer with Prof Scott in regard to a short term of theology at Shaw. Committee.— L. T. Christmas, A. Shepard, H. Pair, C. Johnson, H. L. Moorehouse, B. F. Hemphill, W. T. Minter.

Prof. J. B. Dudley, Pres. of the A. & M. College, Rev. A. J. Tate, pastor of the Presbyterian church, and Rev. L. Johnson, pastor of the white Baptist church were introduced to the body.

While the Committee on Nomination of Officers were out, the following brethren made pointed and timely remarks on co-operation: Revs. T. S. Evans, B. F. Hemphill, J. A. Spaulding, Wm. Devaughan, D. T. Best, T. J. Floyd, S. M. Moore, W. T. Minter.

Committee on Officers made the following report, which was adopted:

For President, Dr N. F. Roberts; Vice Presidents, J. O Crosby, Luke Pierce, H. C. Hodgers, E. M. Croom, S. Ratcliffe, T. S Evans, Wm. Devaughan, J. H. Dunston, E. B. Blake, S. W. Dockery, D T. Best, Jos. Perry, W. R. Mason, J. Alston, S. Thomas J. A Spaulding, M. W. Brewer; Recording Secretary, C. C. Somerville; Corresponding Secretary, ————; Statistical Secretary, P. F. Malloy; Treasurer, A. W. Pegues; Auditor, G. W Moore; Board of Managers, N. F. Roberts, C. C. Somerville, A. W. Pegues, J. J. Worlds, C.

S. Brown, A. Shepard, W. A. Pattillo, D. J. Moore, L. T. Christmas,
J. W. Moore,
J. W. Wood,
W. B. F. Kornegay,
S. H. Witherspoon,
A. P. Eaton,
M. T. Hawkins,
J. R. Nelson,
J. W. Dew,
D. J. Moore,
J. Spells,
Committee.

Mr. J. W. Bailey, editor of the *Biblical Recorder*, was invited to address the body. He said as he came forward:

"My love for the colored people is largely inherited. My father, in the dark days of slavery, sought to preach to the co'ored people in preference to the white; because, he said, they seemed to appreciate his sermons more, having come more to hear and imbibe the message than to criticise it. History fails to reveal a race of people more loyal than the colored people. When the sons of the Confederacy were fighting to keep them in bondage, they themselves were at home defending their wives, children and fireside.

"As to a newspaper, I would suggest that you need a good denominational paper of your own, that will tell the world what you are doing—will be moulding sentiment. I want to say that it is charged that the majority of the white people do not recognize the fact that the colored man is his brother. While I admit that for argument's sake, I want to say that in a very broad sense of the word the colored man does not realize that *he* is the colored man's brother—brother of the poor, the needy, the infirm. I warn you, my brethren, against the Roman Catholic Church, which is making a desperate effort to capture and bring into its church the colored man of the South. I put you on guard, that you may not be deceived.

"As to the Presbyterian Church, I am frank to confess that I never saw a colored Presbyterian in my life. The *Biblical Recorder* is a liberal friend of the colored people, and always stands ready to offer aid and advice. The price is $2.00 per year, but to any colored minister $1.00, or 50 cents for six months."

Dr. J. O. Crosby, of Salisbury, followed the gentleman, and very substantially endorsed every word said by Mr. Bailey. He said Dr. Bailey did more to harmonize the feelings between the races than any man in North Carolina. He secured from Wake Forest the degree of D. D. for the late Dr. Tupper.

Rev. W. R. Mason made extended remarks.

Rev. T. O. Fuller was elected Reporter from this body to the *Daily Record*.

On motion, Miss Miller, of the Woman's Training School of Shaw University, was allowed thirty minutes this afternoon to present her work.

The Convention adjourned, with prayer by Rev. J. Perry.

AFTERNOON SESSION.

Promptly at 2:30 the Convention was called to order, Dr Roberts presiding. Rev. A. P. Eaton offered prayer. The minutes of the previous session were read and adopted.

The following communication was read to the body:

DEEP CREEK, N. C.,
Oct 20, 1896.

Dear Brethren of the Convention:—Being unable to meet you this session, I pray the blessings of God upon you, hoping the God of heaven will be your moderator, and may this be the greatest sitting in the history of the Convention. I ask an interest in your prayers.

Yours truly,
JOSEPH RATCLIFFE.

Rev. J. E. White, Corresponding Secretary of the white Baptist Convention, was introduced to the body and promised to speak to-night.

The Corresponding Secretary, Rev. C. S. Brown, read an exhaustive report of the work done by the missionaries, and showed that besides arousing a general interest throughout the State for the "co-operative work," that they had actually collected from the field $2,063.24. The report was unanimously adopted.

Dr. H. L. Moorehouse, of the American Baptist Home Mission Society, was requested to address the body. He said in part:

"I congratulate you upon your appearance, and I must confess unbounded satisfaction in the report read by your Corresponding Secretary. The reports made to Dr. Tichenor, Bro. White and myself are identical, and show great harmony in the plan of operation. I feel that each missionary has been doing his very best, but as I said, his success will depend largely upon his own personality, and his grasp upon the people. We are extremely careful in the selection of these men, for we wanted less of politics and more of religion. The work at first was wholly experimental, and many in the North, as well as in the South, doubted its practicability.

"When first I met you brethren at Warrenton, N. C., many of you plied me with curious and suspicious questions People are wonderfully afraid of ghosts and spooks, and imagine that they see them when there are no spooks around. Rudyard Kipling's description of a ship when making its trial trip bears a striking illustration to our work along this line. He said the parts—boiler, engine, rods—were all new, and nobody could tell whether each part would do its duty when needed, or whether all the parts would run without friction, but when the steam was applied, and all the parts brought into harmonious action, it presented one grand whole, with all the parts at work; just so with the co-operation work in North Carolina. Institute work is revealing to men this deficiency, and helping them to improve themselves.

"This work tends to unification, for previously many of you felt that you were alone, like the Psalmist said: 'No man cared for my soul;' but now you feel that a bond of union has been established between you and the brethren all over the State. A Baptist church standing alone in certain sections does not impress the people of the strength or work of the denomination, but these institutes will do it. Some people haven't got much rootage, and are easily capsized. We need not only more denominational rootage, but we need denominational character and fruitage as well. My prediction of the relation of the two races of the Baptist Church of this State have been already fulfilled. You brethren have misunderstood the white brethren, and they have misunderstood you; *we are brethren in the Lord*. I would be glad to see your co-operation with the *Biblical Recorder*, such as would give you two or three columns in that paper, and one of your members the editor.

"The plans of co-operation give us insight into the responsibility of boards, etc. When I was in Switzerland a year ago I had the pleasure of climbing some very high mountains, and the higher I ascended the grander and more sublime became the scenery. You came to the Convention out of the valley and dales of your churches and homes, to take a broader view of the work. The co-operation enlarges.

"Dr. Taylor, of Wake Forest, said one of the institutes was worth a hundred dollars to him. I am gratified at the growth of benevolence. Last year the collection was about $800, now it is over $2,000, and I predict that next year will take it to $3,000. Paul said: 'Let this grace be in you'—the grace of giving liberally, the want of it disgrace.

"I again congratulate you upon your success, and the harmony of your meeting. The co-operating bodies will stand by you."

At the conclusion of this magnificent address, the following resolution was adopted:

Resolved 1. That this Convention heartily endorse and commend the work of co-operation as has been carried out during the past conventional year. No effort heretofore put forth has so widely and effectively reached and helped our ministers and churches.

2. While we and the denomination generally, North and South, are in the midst of a financial stringency, yet we cannot afford at this time, without much injury, part from our present plan of work and the number of workers. The Convention therefore asks the co-operating bodies, viz: American Baptist Home Mission Society, the Southern Baptist Convention and the Baptists of North Carolina, the Educational and Missionary Convention—to employ at least the same number of missionaries and under the present arrangements, as entered upon one year ago. A. W. PEGUES.

Miss Miller, of the Training School, being introduced, said, among other things:

"The Woman's Home Mission Society was first organized to send missionaries to your people, though it is broad enough to extend its help to all the races. Just now it is helping ten nationalities. Our motto is: 'Christ in every home.' There are ten thousand in the industrial schools, to whom the missionaries talk every week. The missionary work touches every department of the church work. In speaking of heroines and great women, I can safely say that no woman in the world is more honored, or has done more for your people, than Miss Joanna P. Moore.

"A word about our school-room work: The work is begun in the morning with prayer service, and closes with the same in the afternoon. I usually lead the morning service, but have some of the girls to assist in closing, always using Bible selections. We have five or six exercises daily. First period, Normal Bible study; second, Old Testament; third, New Testament; fourth, Lectures.

"I have received aid from many of the white ministers, who have very generously consented to lecture on Bible subjects. Besides, some members of the medical faculty have promised to deliver lectures on the treatment of diseases. We want to bring the practical work of a woman's field right home to our young women. I appeal to you to send your daughters and members of your church to this Training School. Boarding students $8.00 per month, which practically covers all expenses. We want young women twenty-one years old and of a good moral character."

The address was quite gladly received. Miss Miller always impresses you as one whose heart is thoroughly in the work, and that all she does is done with an eye single to the glory of God.

The Convention sang verses of a lively hymn, after which the President introduced Prof. S. N. Vass, District Secretary of the American Baptist Publication Society. Bro. Vass said:

"The colored Baptists are a great conservatism of power, and with their united forces can accomplish almost anything. As to the society which I have the honor of representing, it is doing untold good in scattering literature—the printed page. We, as Baptists, ought to contribute to the society, it has done so much for us. The society comes to you to ask you to have but one publication society, and to rally to its support. Because of this lack we have been forced to pay more for some of our books than other denominations have to pay for similar books from their publication society.

"Dr. Rowland has decided for the coming year to reduce our literature 25 per cent. The society's missionary work has been largely neglected by our own people. North Carolina has sent less money to the society than any other State, I regret to say. Some of the States have sent as much as $500.

"But we feel proud of this State, for in it we recognize American manhood.

"The fire last February destroyed all the society's property in Philadelphia, but so efficient was its body of officers that it did not cease to issue its periodicals regularly, which alone ought to make you rally to its support. The young people of this State are more progressive and intelligent than I have found them elsewhere, which is largely due to the indefatigable labors of the great veteran, Dr. Shepard, whose constitution is now giving away from the effects of his labors. The society is now $140,000 behind."

Prof. Vass made a splendid speech.

On motion, offered by Rev. J. A. Whitted, we heartily endorsed the appointment of Prof. Vass as District Missionary.

A collection for the work of the American Mission Baptist Publication Society, to be paid to Prof. S. M. Vass, which amounted to $6.35, was taken up.

On motion, the collection of last night was ordered to supplement this collection, the whole amount being $12.64.

Mr. Bailey, in bidding adieu, said he wanted to leave one motto with you: "One Lord, one faith, one baptism, one brotherhood in North Carolina."

Doxology. Benediction by Prof. Vass.

NIGHT SESSION.

The Convention met at 7:30. Rev. H. Cowan led in prayer. The choir sang a voluntary. Rev. H. M. Maloy invoked Divine blessing.

The President announced that the Board of Managers would meet to-morrow in the basement of the church.

The President introduced Rev. J. C. White, Corresponding Secretary of the Home Mission Board of the Southern Baptist Convention. He said among other things:

"*Dear Brethren:*—I congratulate you upon your achievements. You are getting where you can see the light. In the third chapter of Ephesians you will find a record of Paul's prayer, in which he praises them for their excellencies; but especially does he pray that they may be filled with the fullness of God. Before, my brethren, you can be filled with the fullness of God, you must think as God thinks. My intercourse with your missionaries has been most pleasant, indeed. It must have taken a great deal of grace to prevent Bro. Brown from being a politician. Bro. Whitted is the highest type of your race, and Bro. Vincent has all the parts of a theological professor, while Bro. Malloy is a giant in song and speech. These men have accomplished more for your people under God than all the politicians and every legislature since the war. What is the power of education? It may be illustrated by the story of an Irishman and a Dutchman who decided to divide a piece of meat they had found with their teeth. The one getting the larger piece should be entitled to the meat; so when they had gotten to the point the Irishman cried out, 'Are you ready?' and the Dutchman sucked it right in.

"It is a fact that keen wit and sharpened intellect will come out on top. Education can be measured by cents and dollars. Scientists say 80 per cent. of our coal goes out of the chimney in the combustion; doctors say 60 per cent. of our food is wasted in improper cooking; the agriculturists say 40 per cent. of our soil is never utilized, all of which shows the lack of education. A ton of iron ore in the crude state is worth $20, made into horse shoes is worth $90, and into watch springs $3,000. Moloy, the great French painter, took 40 cents worth of material, and with a skilful hand put it on canvas, produced a picture that he sold for $150,000.

"I believe in an education for every man, woman and child. I believe in the best quality of education for the colored people. But people do not need an education to make a living; they want an education that teaches how to make a life. The matter of institutes, as contemplated by co-operation, teaches us first to know about God. A creature never finds himself until he finds God, and God finds him. There are two kinds of education—religious and secular. The secular undertakes to teach that all we know about God is imagination; that there is nothing real and tangible about God. This plan provides that we shall study the Bible, for without a knowledge of God's revealed will, no man can attain to the higher Christian life. Co-operation provides for the study of man. If God did not make man, then I don't care if the devil gets him. Before God, men are equal.

"Why is a certain kind of education called Christian education? Because Christ was the first teacher; he taught that all men had a common ancestry. He organized the first college with twelve members. Christian education looks deeper than the skin, it looks at the true man within. No truth is more potent than that "a man for others." Educated homes—No great people ever came from bad homes. This kind of education makes better citizens. Every man should try to make himself the best citizen possible. He who cannot see God's hand in the history has no right to true citizenship. We want Christian citizens who shall pray how they shall vote. The time is coming when men who know how to pray will be called upon to save this country. Co-operation teaches missions. The man who knows nothing of missions knows nothing of God. You can measure a man's religion by the good he means to do to the heathen. I believe it with all my heart, that God intends that the Baptist shall evangelize North Carolina. The Baptist of this State do not live in cities, but in the country, but I thank God they have no other creed but the New Testament.

This government was founded upon the principles of liberty as taught by Thomas Jefferson, who caught the spirit of liberty from the Baptist church, the enthusiasm and spirit which seemed to actuate the brethren in their work for the Master."

Rev. Scott, of Shaw, expressed his delight in being present with the brethren, because this meeting gave him a splendid opportunity to see the needs of the ministers.

On motion, a committee of seven was appointed who would appoint various committees over the State on "Systematic Giving."

Rev. E. B. Blake made some timely remarks in regard to increasing our missionaries in the field.

On motion, a committee of seven be appointed to confer with a similar committee from the Sunday School Convention, relative to a newspaper.

The following are the committee: A. B. Vincent, P. S. Lewis, T. O. Fuller, A. P. Eaton, S. S. Henderson, J. E. Dillinger, E. F. Parham.

On motion, it was ordered that the minutes be printed in connection with the BAPTIST QUARTERLY.

Rev. W. A. Patillo presented the claims of his church to the Convention. His church he said was utterly demolished by a recent storm, and his people were without a place to worship. He made a strong plea for his cause which was spoken to by Eaton and Somerville.

A motion to pay that church $50 was arrested on its passage.

Convention adjourned with the benediction by Rev. E. B. Blake.

THURSDAY—AFTERNOON SESSION.

At 2:30 o'clock the Convention was called to order by Vice-President Evans.

Hymns No. 422 was lined and sung.

N. F. ROBERTS, D. D.

Scripture lesson, 23d Psalm.

Minutes of the morning session were read and adopted.

On motion, the order of business was suspended for 15 minutes to consider the matter of the Oxford church.

On motion, the Board of Managers was asked to appropriate $50 to the Oxford church.

Dr. Pegues offered a substitute that after the legitimate expenses of the body be paid, the Board be asked to contribute as much as they can to the cause.

Substitute adopted.

Mrs. J. E. Wilson, of Lancaster, S. C., representing an orphanage at that place, was introduced to the body.

According to the order of business, the Missionaries were requested to state the condition of their fields.

Rev. J. A. Whitted, representing the Eastern District made a clear and forceful statement of his work, showing that the brethren, wherever he had been were in hearty accord with co-operation.

Prof. A. B. Vincent, of the Middle District made a telling speech, and at once demonstrated the fact that the Convention made no mistake in his appointment.

Rev. P. F. Maloy, the "warrior of the mountains," told in a strong, pathetic and grand style, how, through those everlasting hills he had carried the cross of Christ, as many a sheaf in this great body could abundantly testify.

The Chair announced the following obituary committee; J. O. Crosby, J. W. Wood, W. M. Moore, J. L. Fennell, G. W. Holland.

On motion, Thursday afternoon at 4 o'clock, Mrs. Shepard was allowed to present her work and a collection be taken for the same.

A collection of $.44 for Rev. H. Cowan.

Adjourned with the benediction.

THURSDAY—EVENING SESSION.

The Convention assembled at 8 o'clock, Rev. C. L. Davis conducted devotional exercises.

Hymn 18 was sung by the large congregation. Scripture lesson 52d chapter of Isiah.

Dr. H. L. Morehouse invoked divine blessings.

The congregation again sang a choice selection.

Prof. C. F. Meserve, President of Shaw University, was introduced to the Convention.

On motion, Dr. McVicker will follow Dr. Crosby on the program instead of Dr. Roberts.

On motion, Mrs. J. E. Wilson, of Lancaster, was allowed to present her work to the Convention.

Dr. Crosby said in part, he would not say anything to-night derogatory of the churches and schools, especially those of Greensboro, among whom he has the distinguished pleasure of laboring for the last four years.

The Baptist church, as the other churches ought to educate the idea among its members that we are a great denomination, for unless we have such an opinion of ourselves we will not do our duty.

I teach my children to feel that I am the greatest papa in all the country, and if it does no good it certainly does no harm. As a race we must have our people know and feel that we are a great race; we must have the idea that we represent something. It is a mistaken idea that Shaw University would take your sons and daughters away from you by educating them, instead, it will make them come nearer you, make them more powerful to help you, make them a power for good. It is your school, I make that claim without fear of contradiction, it ought to have not less than a thousand boys and girls in it now. The school has claim upon every Baptist in North Carolina, at its head stands one of the grandest men in this country Prof. Meserve is a great man. I am in hearty accord and sympathy with the school.

At the conclusion of Mr Crosby's address the President introduced Dr. McVicar, Superintendent of the schools of the Home Mission Board located in the South The Dr. Said the reports made by the Missionaries greatly pleased him, indeed, they were highly interesting to say the least. The power of the pulpit is based upon a through training. To preach the Word as it ought to be preached, one ought to be thoroughly trained Thank God I have lived to see the day when the colored women are coming to the front. The standard of all races are measured by their women.

I never knew a race to lift itself by its bootstraps, you cannot educate yourself except as other races have done. We believe that the colored people should have the same advantages of the whites. New England to-day is what its higher institutions have made it. As to Industrial Schools, I would say that at their heads are men of the highest training, and the wisdom of the management shows that even to teach the branches in these schools, college trained men are wanted.

The governor of New York pays his head farmer more than six thousand dollars per annum It is the qualification of the man. The right kind of religion takes in everything. My friends, God is not deaf. It rejoices me that the black man can no more get sympathy on account of their color, that day is gone. Some are complaining because certain places, such as barber shops and hotel waiters have been taken from them and given to white men. I regard it as a blessing, you should know that you ought to fill a higher place. As to the time to procure an education, is takes as long time for you to qualify and equip yourselves as it do's the white man.

The speech of Dr. McVicker was of the highest order and instructive throughout, from beginning to end.

The choir rendered a choice selection.

At this juncture President Roberts introduced Prof. C. F. Meserve, President Shaw University.

Prof. Meserve said he needed to offer an apology to the Woman's Home Mission Convention held at Salisbury. It was a body of able Christian workers.

"Now, I want to say a word about Industrial Education. I was invited to address the colored fair at Durham, but could not on account of being called away Prof. Booker T. Washington made the address, but the one idea advanced, as I caught it from the newspapers, was that the salvation of the race was industrial training. I do not quite agree with him. But I would say to you t at Mr. Washington is a great man, and means well for your people. By skillful management he has been able to get a bill through Congress for some government lands in Alabama which he has been able to sell, and they have brought an endowment of $160,000 to the institution. That is good judgment, that is good sense.

'At a certain place in the State I was invited to deliver an address to a colored school, and when I got there I was waited on by some white gentlemen whose business it was to say to me that "it was against the wishes of the white people for me to speak to negroes," but as soon as I had found out their object I told them that I had not come to discuss that matter, and if that was their object of visitation I would politely ask them to withdraw from the room or I would do so. When they saw that I would hear none of that they desisted. But the beautiful part of the whole affair was, they came out to my meeting that night and heard me for an hour and a half.

"You must know there is no conflict between Shaw and other schools. I am a Baptist brethren alone, by the influence of the Spirit of God, for all my people, mother and father belonged to other churches, and I am, you observe, the only renegate. If we Baptists were as live to the interest of our denomination as the other churches, our schools would soon be filled.

"It gives me pleasure to say that since the establishment of Shaw there has not been a scandal connected with Estey. Do you know that that is the first female seminary for colored women ever established below the Mason and Dixon line? We are not surprised at assaults and attacks, every good thing is attacked. A charge has been made that Shaw is no place for poor students, bless the Lord, no one other but poor students come to us. Your people in the State own about $8,000,000, you may talk about the "golden star" as much as you please, but be sure to get out of the one-room log cabin. In God's name the Bible is the leading text book.

Prof. Meserve, as usual, gave one of those strong and practical addresses that once heard you cannot forget.

At the conclusion of the address Rev. A. P. Eaton, of Durham, addressed the body in regard to his work, he gave a fine description of his new brick church, and renewed his allegiance to the Conventional work.

Mrs. J. E. Wilson, of Lancaster, S. C., was introduced to the body and made a splendid address concerning the colored orphanage of which she was an agent.

A collection of $6.05 was taken for Shaw University.

Benediction by Rev. A. B. Vincent.

FRIDAY—MORNING SESSION.

At 9:30 the Convention was called to order by Vice-President, Rev. Wm. DeVaughan.

Rev. G. W. Moore conducted devotional exercises.

The Committee on Place made the following report:

We your Committee on Place beg leave to report that we meet in the next annual session, with the Ebenezer Baptist Church, at Charlotte, N. C.

WM. DEVAUGHAN,
C. L. DAVIS,
O. B. ALSTON,
Q. C. MIAL,
S. THOMAS,
J. W. DEW,
J. L. NUNNALLY,
JOHN THOMAS,
M. D. MATHERSON.

Rev. J. S Nunnally, of Hendersonville addressed the Convention, and asked the body to send a committee to meet with the Convention in the West, saying it would be helpful to the people over there

On motion, a committee of five was appointed to meet the brethren in the West.

Rev. R. L. Jordan, of Philadelphia, was introduced to the body and made a few remarks.

Rev. C. Johnson reported some interesting facts concerning the Foreign Mission work. He stated that at the last meeting they raised enough money to pay Bros. Hayes and Jackson.

A motion prevailed that thirty days be allowed the delegates from Neuse River Association to send the money required for representation.

West Roanoke Association was allowed fifteen days to send in their representative fee.

Prof. J. B. Dudley, President of the A. & M. College, came before the Convention and invited it to visit the school which invitation was accepted by a vote.

Mr. W. A. Hunter was introduced and represented the Young Mens' Christian Association of which he was Grand Secretary, and showed the organization to be in a prosperous condition.

The Committee appointed to confer with Prof. Scott of Shaw, concerning a short term at the Theological department made their report which was adopted. (See report.)

A resolution was offered by Rev. L. T. Christmas, concerning delegates withholding money which was referred to the Committee on Resolutions.

Adjourned with the benediction by Rev. W. A. Patillo.

AFTERNOON SESSION.

At 3 o'clock the Convention was called to order by the President.

Prayer was offered by Rev. W. T. Minter.

Minutes of the previous session were read and adopted with proper corrections.

The special order according to the program was "The Woman's Work."

Miss Miller, of the Girls' Training School led off. She explained clearly and fully woman's work in the home, and showed the necessity for training in this sphere. There is, she said, a demand for increased missionary work.

We have not fully decided on our plan for future operations, but the matter is receiving prayerful consideration. I shall not be able to visit you at your churches, but if you will cheerfully receive our Missionary we shall send you one.

Miss Addie Morris, of Winston, followed her. She said the training course of the school at Raleigh was more than she could describe. Attending the school there has been of untold benefit to me. My work in Winston has been a success because God was in it.

The Chicago Board has done more for me even than it promised, sending barrels of clothing and things of that kind.

Mrs. Robert Shepard spoke as follows:

"I do n t think it is a w man's work to fill the pulpit as preacher in the church, but we can fill our pulpits around our firesides every day. We had not fully understood the Society's work or we should have received more money this year. We want more missionaries, we must have more. Our children at Oxford are getting on nicely and they are making God's Word a study. We ought to do away with festivals to raise money in our churches, it ought to be raised without such means.

Bro. Hill made a few timely remarks.

Rev. R. Shepard spoke directly

of the Orphan Asylum and was followed by Rev. A. Shepard.

A collection of $10.28 was taken for the cause.

The Woman's Home Mission Society, through its delegate, Mrs. R Shepard, presented the Convention with $15.00 to be paid to the Foreign Mission work.

Secretary Brown read a report of the Board of Managers which was adopted.

Committee on finance made a partial report.

It was ordered that the following statement appear in the Minutes:

Central Baptist Church, Wilmington, N. C., paid to Fuller's Church, 1895,	$ 5 00
Pledged and paid,	5 00
L. T. Christmas and wife pledged and paid to Foreign Missions,	5 00
	$ 15 00
The Sisters' Bible Board of said church paid in 1896 to Orphan Asylum,	$ 1 00

Convention adjourned, with benediction Rev. S. Henderson.

NIGHT SESSION.

The Convention assembled with praise meeting, conducted by Rev. J. Perry. Hymn 245 C. M. was sung. Scripture lesson, Ps. 42. Rev. I. W. Holt invoked Divine blessing.

The President ordered the report of various committees.

Statistical Secretary, P. F. Maloy, made his report. (See Report.)

The Committee on Resolutions made their report, which was spoken to by Brethren Vincent, Somerville, Christmas, Holden, Brown, Williamson, Lewis and Spaulding, and was adopted by a standing vote.

The final financial report was adopted.

The report made by the Committee on Temperance was adopted. (See Report.)

The report made by the Committee on Denominational Paper was referred to the Board of Managers.

Rev. L. G. Jordan made a most eloquent appeal for Foreign Missions, at the conclusion of which the delegation was invited into the basement of Bro. Witherspoon's church, where, with willing hands and loving hearts the ladies of the church had prepared quite a grand banquet.

There was sharp competition for victory, but the great abundance of delicacies made it impossible for any one to achieve much of a victory—all had sufficient.

All honor to the members and friends of the church, who so nobly and royally entertained that great Baptist body.

Thus has passed into history one of the grandest and most representative colored Baptist gatherings that has ever convened in North Carolina.

REV. N. F. ROBERTS,
President.
Rev. C. C. SOMERVILLE,
Secretary.

COMMITTEE ON RESOLUTIONS.

Resolved, That a committee of five be appointed to take into consideration the withholding of funds belonging to the Convention, the same having been voted to the Convention from different sources, and to take such steps as in their judgment may be deemed necessary, and report to this Convention at its next sitting.

L. T. CHRISTMAS.

REPORT OF COMMITTEE OF THEOLOGICAL ACCOMMODATION.

We, your committee, beg leave to submit the following report: We are requested by President Charles F. Meserve to state that all ministerial studies can be accommodated all the session in either preparatory studies to theological training, or the regular theological course, at the same reasonable rates as other students, and that the advantages and opportunities of said department in the future will depend much upon the interest and patronage among the theological students attending this year; and that all can attend as few or as many months as they desire.

Respectfully submitted,
L. T. CHRISTMAS, Chm'n.
A. SHEPARD,
H. PAGE,
C. JOHNSON,
H. L. MOREHOUSE,
B. F. HEMPHILL,
W. T. MINTER.

REPORT OF COMMITTEE ON RESOLUTIONS.

To the President and Convention we would report: 1. That this Convention expresses its continued and renewed interest in Shaw University, and commends the institution to the patronage of the colored Baptists of the State.

2. The Convention again renews its allegiance to the Home Mission and Publication Society. We would also thank the pastor and kind people of this city for their hospitable entertainment of the Convention during our stay. We pray the blessings of God ever to rest upon them and theirs. Also to the newspapers, which have so kindly published the proceedings of this Assembly, as well as the railroads, who so favored us in reduced rates to this meeting.

We have heard from our General Secretary of Foreign Missions, the needs of the field and his plans to raise $10,000, among which is the plan to have a "Cape Town Chapel Day," on Wednesday, November 25; therefore be it

Resolved, That we heartily endorse his efforts along the line mentioned, and that we urge our churches to take hold of the work, and especially the "Cape Town Chapel Day."

Respectfully submitted,
A. W. PEGUES,
W. T. MINTER,
T. S. EVANS,
W. R. MASON,
THOMAS SHARP.

REPORT FROM COMMITTEE ON TEMPERANCE.

WHEREAS, Intemperance is one of the greatest evils in the land, no sin being regarded more popular and destructive in its effects, to all good; and whereas, said "evil" is working untold damage to our people and the nations by consuming their means—the support of their life and support of the greatest cause; and by blighting the prospects of the higher and nobler life, and by demolishing their interests in God's Zion; and because of the speedy growth and the fascinating influence of this monster, intemperance; and whereas, all sin should be denounced, and every evil combatted, especially such gross ungodliness as intemperance, by every child of grace and minister of Divine truth; therefore be it

Resolved 1. That this, our grand old Baptist Educational and Missionary Convention, unanimously endorse the most stringent efforts to destroy intemperance, and to chase the demon from the land.

2. That we recommend that every minister of the Gospel should preach absolute temperance to his flock, and that he countenance nothing less; and that this *example* be required of him ere we recognize him in the ministerial fraternity, deeming one otherwise of so little spiritual appetite and backbone and moral integrity unworthy of the Divine and highest calling of mankind.

3. That we encourage and promote the temperance cause:

(1). By ministering the Word of God, and by keeping all intoxicants, as wine, etc., from our social circles.

(3). By organizing, supporting and building up temperance bands and societies; and also by a prohibition vote, and by any other means by which the Holy Spirit may teach.

Respectfully submitted,
M. G. CHRISTMAS,
H. M. MALOY,
JOSEPH SPELL.

REPORT FROM COMMITTEE ON A PAPER.

Your committee on the question of establishment of and maintenance of an organ published in the interest of the Church in North Carolina submit the following:

1. That such an institution is with us a dire necessity, and one which the cause which we cherish cannot afford to be without.

2. We believe the running of a paper to be in fact a business matter, and if successfully carried on it must conform to the same laws that govern other business enterprises. There must be a monthly investment sufficient to meet the outlay in material, etc., and to pay somebody to edit the paper. This money must come from somewhere. Our previous failures along this line have emphasized the fact more than once. Now, therefore, we recommend that no attempt be made at publishing a paper until the means are in hand, or at least in sight, with which to meet expenses.

But we suggest that the matter be now left with the Board of Managers, with instructions to use their judgment as to the origination of any plan, the making or acceptance of any proposition or suggestion.

Respectfully submitted,
A. B. VINCENT,
P. S. LEWIS,
S. S. HENDERSON,
J. ELMER DILLINGER,
T. O. FULLER,
A. P. EATON,
E. F. PARHAM.

STATISTICAL SECRETARY'S REPORT.

Statistical and Historical Report for the Year Ending October 1, 1896.

With gratitude to God and love to our brethren, we stand together and grasp each other, hand in hand, in another annual session of our Convention, and with deepest interest and hope scan the lines of progress during the year ending October 31, 1896.

The full tide of blessings, enlargement of our work, its accomplishment through the plan of co-operation and the New Era Institute, have far surpassed our most sanguine expectation. The great increase of the number of souls saved during the year, the astonishing increase to church extention, and the renewed energy to build on modern and improved models for houses of worship, all go to confirm the fact that the colored Baptists of this State are contending for the front ranks in the great move of Baptist progress in this country. Never before have we been able to report so many pastors and churches directly interested in the work of the state Convention. The plan of co-operation and the New Era Institute, in which the Baptists of the North have co-operated with the Southern Board at Atlanta, and with the white and colored State Conventions of this and other States, makes a shining page in the history of North Carolina colored Baptists. These imitative "Schools of the Prophets" of olden times have done more to arouse our preachers to more earnest study and a high estimate of the Gospel ministry than Paul's great sermon on Mar's Hill. The history of our denomination will ever be importantly associated with this great plan. Our greatly increased membership over that of last year is a living evidence of the force and need of Baptist faith and principles in our State, and wherever man is found.

We more than doubled our contributions; this year, they are three-fold greater than on any previous year. May we not, with pride, let to the breeze our banner, inscribed, " North Carolina for God and the Baptists ?"

Our report cannot be regarded as strictly accurate, knowing that our churches govern themselves, and not the Bishop, therefore many of them are not connected with our Aasociation; some only report financial members, some fail to give full statistical reports through their letters to the Association, and a number of things, it is reasonable to suppose one could hardly make a true report. My report therefore will be based on facts gathered from the ministers, as far as they could be secured from personal observation and from the year book.

In the State we have two Conventions of churches, the Baptist Educational and Missionary Convention of North Carolina, and the Western Baptist Convention, west of the Blue Ridge Mountains.

The State Convention was organized at Goldsboro, N. C., October, 1867, in what is now known as the First African Baptist Church. The Western Convention has been organized about eighteen years. We have in the State forty Associations, eighteen of which represent annually in the State Convention, and four in the Western Convention, making twenty in all represented this year, just one-half of the whole number. We are doing all we can to have every Association represented, and every Baptist in the State. Our membership in the State by actual census taken during the year by the various missionaries is 160,000, and this is short of the Minutes of one or two Associations. Churches in the State, 1,260; members represented in the State Convention 15,000, not quite half of our church population in the State; churches organized in the Sta'e during the year was 16; preachers and pastors in the State, 1,322; ordained ministers, 977; pastors' salary, $77,000; aggregate expenses, including buildings, repairs, and pastors' salary, $97,322; Sunday-schools in the State, as represented through the State and District Conventions, 765; teachers, 2,347; pupils, 18,713; total number of Associations, white and colored, 91; ordained ministers, 1,113; churches, 2,716; baptisms during the year, 8,300;

total membership, white and colored, in the State, 340,000, an increase during the year, including letters of restoration, experience and baptism, of 14,670; whole number of Sunday-schools in the State, 1,705; whole number of Baptist churches in the United States, 40,064; ministers, 27,771; whole number of Baptists in the United States, 3,720,235.

Let us take courage from what God has done through the great Baptist family, and do more, undertake greater things, and pray and expect even greater things next year.

LIST OF DELEGATES.

Prof. N. F. Roberts, D. D., Raleigh, N. C.
Rev. C. Johnson, Raleigh.
" Joseph Perry, Raleigh.
" J. J. Worlds, Raleigh.
" Wm. Elerbee, Raleigh.
" W. A. Jones, Raleigh.
" Wm. DeVaughan, Wilmington.
" S W. Dockery, Maxton.
" D. J. Moore, Rosindale.
" E. B. Blake, Raleigh.
" O. B. Alston, Enfield.
" G. W. Holland, Winston.
" R. H. Hogans, Asheville.
" H. Pair, Shotwell.
" J. H. Spaulding, Elkin.
" T. S. Evans, Morehead City.
" W. A. Moore, Kerr
" C L. Davis, 612 E 2d St., Charlotte.
" M. F. Hawkins, Ingleside.
" J. L. Nunnally, Hendersonville.
" B. H. Boyd, Mathews.
" T. J. Floyd, Shelby.
" John Thomas, Louisburg.
" Nicholas Moore, Wallace.
" J. H. Holden, Youngsville.
" Joseph Spells, 508, Campbell St., Wilmington.
" H. C. McDonald, Lum. Bridge.
" S. L. Moore, Wilmington.
Prof. J. O. Crosby, Ph. D., Salisbury.
" C. C. Somerville, Reidsville.
" C. S. Brown, A. M., Winton.
" A. W. Pegues, Ph. D., Raleigh.
" J. E. Dellenger, M. D., Greensboro.
" J. A. Whitted, A. M., Goldsboro.
" A. B. Vincent, Raleigh.

Rev. T O. Fuller, Franklinton.
" J. W. Dew, Goldsboro.
" A. B. Wyche, Henderson.
" W. B. F. Kornegay, Willard.
" M G. Christmas, Warrenton.
" H. J. Malloy, Goldsboro.
" Q. C. Mial, Clayton.
" W. T. Minter, B. D, Asheville.
" G. W. Brewer, Monroe.
" Thomas Sharp, Harrisville.
" B. F. Hemphill, Hendersonville.
" Graves, Greensboro.
" S. Thomas, Burlington.
" S. Atkinson, Whiteville.
" J. T. Hill, 106, Lane St. Wilmington.
" W. A. Pitillo, A. B., Henderson.
" S S. Henderson, Greensboro.
" J. R. Nelson, Asheville.
" E. Hemphill, Hendersonville.
" R. H. Hogans, Asheville.
" J. W. Words, Jackson.
" R, I. Walden, D. D., Graysburg.
" M. D. Mathewson, Tarboro.
" W. R. Slade, New Berne.
" L. T. Christmas, A. B., Wilmington.
" W. R. Mason, Boykin, Va.
" A. Shepard, D. D., Charlotte.
" S. H. Witherspoon, Greensboro.
" R. E. Blake, Raleigh.
" C. H. Williams, A. B., 407 S. Myers St., Charlotte.
" M. C. Ransom, Oxford.
" E. F. Parham, Wentworth.
" J. T. Davis, Polkton.
" D. M. Montgomery, Dallas.
" A. H. Thompson, Lumberton.
" P. S. Lewis, B. D., Salisbury.
" J. W. Jones, Winston.
" P. F. Maloy, A. B., Greensboro.
Deacon L. D. Wilson 228, E. Boundary St., Charlotte.
" J. Shore, Greensboro.
" J. D. Ware, Greensboro.

※

Contributors to Co-operation and Missions for North Carolina.

Willis Wilford, Jerry Long, Mrs. Jennie Burke, Mrs. Mary Gordan, Thomas H. Hoffler, John Lassiter, Mrs. Katie Creecy, Mrs. Ann Eason, Isaac Benbury, Claude Harrel, Elisha Dail, Hertford; W. W. Hill, J. B. Hill, James Spicer, Owen Bryant, J. C. Hufham, Fred. Sampson, Simeon Hicks, M. J. Devane, Miss C. C. Bell, H. Hill, G. W. Williams, Howell Hall, Frank Powell, J. D. McClymy, Rocky Point; Rev. J. Spells, Mrs. C. J. Hill, A. F. Wright, Rev. S. L. Moore, Mrs. Wm. H. Moore, James Boney, Mrs. E. H. Thomas, Rosanna Reynolds, Noah Herring, Silas Webboon, W. H. Dudley, H. C. Williams, Wilmington; George W. Tuntle, Oscar O. Martin, David Rooks, John Holland, P. D. Butler, George Hayes, Gaston Langston, J. R. Rooks, Daniel Ballow, W. T. Butler, A. Green, Douglass Collins, H. M. Taylor, C. W. Price, Alexander Dildy, A. Smith, Asbury Reid, Wm. S. Kater, Adoir, N. C.; Rev. I. Arnold, John Gordon, J. W. Faulk, W. H. Taylor, C. E. Burke, Elijah Bryant, O. Bryant, H.L. Robinson, Mrs. Emma Fillon, Angus Reid, Rev. J. Elliot, Rev. A. W. Bufort, Mrs. Ferebee Creecy, Philmore Burke, Charles H. Jenkins, Miss Annie Lassiter, Mrs. Rebecca Skinner, Miss Ellen Creecy, B. F. Sills, Hertford; James A. Johnson, Rev. L. T. Christmas, Niss S. E. Butler, Gaston Hicks, Rev John F. Hill, F G Manly, M. F. Ellison, Mrs. Anna McKoy, Mrs. Phoebe Bouden, Mrs. Nancy Murphy, Rev. L. H. Harris, A. Miller, Rev. C. Spicer, Rev. J. T. Fuller, J. M. Jenkins, D C. Council, Wm. H. Lee, Miss Blanche Dudley, Sampson Isler, Dennis Dixon, Wilmington; K S. Jacobs, Bryantstown; Mrs. Lucy A. Raynor, Windsor; Isham Jacobs, Rich Square; I. S. Priedan, L. F. Sharpe, Peter Linder, Harrellsville; D. P. Mitchell, Miss Lucy Williams, Windsor; R. Merriman, Mrs. F. F. Taylor, Guilford Farrior, Mrs. Hannah Moore, Handy Robinson, Magnolia; Rev. G. E. Freeman, Harrellsville; Rev. Keny Jacobs, Bryantstown; L. H. Lassiter; Richmond Brewer, Rich Square; Right Hollomon, St. John's; W. L. Lassiter, Lassiter; Richmond Peel; J. T. Riddick, Como; Rev. Lype Deloatch, Moherring; Humphrey Smith, Woodward; Mrs. Hannah Barden, Magnonolia; Thadeus King, M. T. Taylor, L. H. Hayes, A. Boone, G. Richardson, Scotland Neck; Abram Peyton, S. H. Hyman, S Smith, Grimesland; W. H. Culley, W. C. Jeannette, Stewart

Hardy, Havelock; D. D Bryant, Grifton, Pitt county; Prof. G. G. Hill, Scotland Neck; J. S. Sills, Tarboro; W R. Mason, Boydton, Va.; W. S. Thompson, Windsor; Frank Madre; W. H. Leath; Humphrey Smithwick, Woodward; A. Franks; W. M. Taylor, Rev. Thos. Sharpe, Windsor; Wright Hollomon, St. John's; K. S Jacobs, Turner Outlaw, E. D. Parker, Mrs Moriah Cherry, Bryantstown; J C. Hollomon, Union; M. P. Etheridge, Coleraine; Isaac Gay, St. John's; Pearce Askew; Rev. A G Thomas, Gary's; Rev. M Brown; Jerry Pittman; F. F. Fenccl, Halifax; Guilford Geo. Weldon; W H. Harden, Enfield; George Spicer; Miss Maggie Mosely; Major Whitley; Wm Hill; Rev. J. Rainsy; Hon. F. D Dancy, S. Jeffrey, C. G. Williams, M. D. Matthewson, Moses Jones, Tarboro; N. C. Rountree, H W Hyman, T. J. Johnson, New Berne; A. R. Robinson, Elias Gayard, W. H Rosebury, Jesse Payton, M. Spruill, W. J. Randtree, Geo. L. Garris, W. T. Garris, Wiley Key, Cainecsland; John W. Newsom, Phillip Garris, C. C. House, Mrs. Bettie Roberts, Mrs. Sarah Davis, Gary's; Mrs. Sarah Vassar; Phoebe J. Key Seaboard; Mrs. Virginia Buffaloe; Caroline Deleatch; Jack Vassar, Gary's; Miss C. B. Ryland, Ginnberry; Wm. Wood. Point Caswell; Rev C. A Carr, Colley; Abram Henry, Ivanhoe; En ch Hansley, Wilmington; A. J. Stanford, Warsaw; G. Stringfield, Harrel's store; G. W. Corbett, Delta; George Bland, Safe; Rev J. M Johnson, Rose Hill; James Enniss, Moore's Creek; Rev. R. Royalls, Kelly's; C. D. Corbett, Kerr; Miss Hettie Jones, Wilmington; Rev. R. A Harper, LaGrange; Mrs. Rosanna Reynolds, 607 Red Cross street, Wilmington; Mrs. Mary E. McKenzie, 317 South Sixth street, Wilmington; Rev. J J Patterson, Falling Creek; B F. Thompson, Saulston; Rev. C. Carroll, Goldsboro; Alex. Johnson; E. P. Pearsall, Lucama; Isiah Pearsall Freemont; Isaac Aycock, Weldon; D. A Staton, Lake Best, G. M. Foust, T. H Hawkins, B. C. Johnson, Goldsboro; Rev. W. C. Cowan, Taylor's Bridge; Allen Moore, C. H. Baggett, H. A. Brewington, Rev. C. B. Underwood, Clinton; J. T. Kerr, Tomahawk; Mrs. R. A. Spears, Castle Hayne; Anthony Curry, Calvin Carlton, Magnolia; D. D McCallister, Long Creek; K E. Edwards, Clinton; M. Robinson, Rock Fish; Simon Wilson; Mrs G. A. Boykin; S. H. Wilson; N. Moore, Wallace; W. H. Ashford, C. T. Underwood, Clinton; Rev W. T Cowan, Taylor's Bridge; G. A. Bizzell, Clinton; Hon. A R. Middleton, Kenansville; Jerry Patterson, Wilmington; A J. Carlton, Mount Olive; C. C. Graham, Dudley Monk, Kenansville; C Taylor; W. H. Bizzell; A. Gellesful; P. A Robinson; H J. Wheeler; D A. Williams, May E. Whitley; Rev. S. C Larkins, Long Creek; Rev. O. D. Holmes, Clinton; Richmond Browd; F C. Mitchell, Robert Cross; T. J. Reynolds; C. Smallwood; Turner Outlaw; W. H. Leath, Windsor; Howard Hall, Gabriel Williams, J. H Hill, Gilbert De Vane, Rocky Point; Rev. P. P. Ward, Scotland Neck; Mrs. Gracie Melchor, Willis S. Peacock, Robert Martin, Mrs. Harriet Brinkley, Mrs. Mary M Armstrong, Fayetteville.

INSTITUTES.

The Institute held with the First Baptist Baptist church of Oxford, Oct. 2-4 was not a whit behind that of previous meetings, when all things are considered. These noble people had just lost their large church edifice by the storm, and while gloom and discouragement hung like a dark cloud over them, the white Babtist church threw open its doors and heartily invited the Institute to hold its session in their old edifice.

Rev. J. S. Hardway, of whom too much cannot be said, because he is one of the grandest men in North Carolina, ever loyal, conscientious, with untiring devotion to the great cause of Christ. He goes at the work with all his might; his lectures are always highly instructive and able.

His sermon on what the Bible teaches on Sanctification and Holiness was a masterly effort, and evidently was a Godsend at that time. We would also make kindly mention of Mayor Royster and Superintendent F. W. Hancock, both of Rev. Hardaway's church, who delivered entertaining and instructive addresses on Sunday-school work and education.

Rev. W. A. Patillo and his good people did well in their support of the meeting. It is always a pleasure to think of the kind and sympathizing friends to the work at Oxford. May these deserving Baptists soon be blessed with another substantial church edifice. Pastor Patillo's labors have been blessed by the addition of about 38 conversions to his church recently.

Lumber Ridge Institute, Oct. 27-30.

This great meeting was a fitting tribute to the closing of the years' work. The Institute was held in St. John's church, the charge of Rev. H. C. McDonald, and from the beginning there were unmistakable evidences of the spirit, and through the whole there was the most encouraging indications that the work was God's work, and the most blessed institution ever inaugurated since emancipation. White and colored ministers were simply enthusiastic in their praise and devotion to the work. The District Missionary was ably assisted by General Missionary J. A. Whitted and Rev. W. M. Jones, of the white church, of Maxton, a recent graduate of the Southern Baptist Theological Seminary. The lectures of brethren, Whitted and Jones were magnificent. We regard Rev. H. C. McDonald as a model in working up and providing for "New Era Institutes." His plans are to say the least, the best yet witnessed. Bro. McDonald never stops until he has excelled, and that means volumes among our Baptist leaders and pastors. Without invidious comparisons, for we would not detract from our noble leaders, as all have done well for the "New Era" meetings in the Central District, but justice suggests that credit be given to whom due, and the credit for the most successful meetings of the year all things considered, must be given to the St. John Baptist church, Robeson county, and its pastor, the Rev. H. C. McDonald. This idea was endorsed by those who have observed the work in every section of the State. Credit is due to the white friends of Lumber Bridge for their liberal support of the meeting from the beginning to the end. We have never witnessed a more harmonious and pleasant meeting. The crowds were simply too large to be accommodated, and the interest was intense from beginning to end.

Durham Institute.

The New Era Institute held in the White Rock Baptist church at Durham, Sept. 16-18 was creditable alike to those who participated and those who entertained. The speeches were of the highest order and made a profound impression upon those who attended.

Judge W. A. Montgomery, of the Supreme Court of North Carolina, delivered two lectures, one on Church History and one on Christian Education. The efforts of this eminent jurist, polished scholar, loyal Baptist and dignified Christian gentleman were simply superb. The unanimous opinion of all was that these two scholarly addresses should be published and put into the hands of our leaders.

Able and instructive lectures were delivered by Rev. W. C. Tyree, of the white Baptist church, and Rev. B. W. Spillman, Sunday School Missionary for the white Baptists of North Carolina. Rev. Joseph Perry, Sunday School Missionary of the American Baptist Publication Society, pastor Rev. A. P. Eaton and Judge R. W. Winston, of Durham, and District Missionary A. B. Vincent. The institute was royally entertained by Rev. A. P. Eaton and the White Rock Baptist church. Bro. Eaton left no stone unturned to make the work a success, his fine choir which so faithfully did their part, left their places in the factories and remained with the meeting through the three days' session.

The church provided at extra expense carriages for eminent visitors who attended. Rev. Eaton deserves great credit for the excellent work done in the erection of one of the most substantial, commodious and tasty edifices in the State.

Rev. W. C. Tyree and the friends of the white churches liberally and kindly entertained white visiting friends as is done everywhere.

We visited the Lumber River Association Nov. 6, in Columbus, and found a noble and warm-hearted delegation waiting to do all possible for co-operation. Special mention might be made of Revs. A. H. Thompson, J. D. Harrell, Stephen A. Gore, E. W. Thompson and Singleton, Mr. T. B. Peacock, W. C. Pope and others who are ever ready to assist in the furtherance of the work.

Lumber Ridge, Robeson County Institute, St. John's Church.

C. P. Meloin, Rennest, (to Quarterly) 25; David McAlister, Volars, 50 cents; David McDonald, Lumber Bridge, 25; W. S. Smith, Rennert, 25; Geo. Boker, Lumber Bridge, 25; David Ausler, Lumber Bridge, 25; R. D. Melvin, Lumber Ridge, 25; Vander McGeacky, Lumber Bridge, 25; S. A. Ausler, Lumber Bridge, 75; Samuel McNeal, Lumber Bridge, 50; Henry Johnson, Lumber Bridge, (Quarterly,) 25; John McNeal, Lumber Bridge, 25; Henry Patterson, Lumber Bridge, 25; Rev. E. W. Pritchard, Lumber Bridge, 25; Miss Maggie Patterson, Lumber Bridge, 25; Mrs. Emeline Patterson, Lumber Bridge, 25, Rev. N. B. Dunham, Cedar, $1.00; Rev. H. C. McDonald, Lumber Bridge, 50; Geo. W. Carver, Shearwood, 50; George Baker, Lumber Bridge, 25; S. A. Ausley, Lumber Bridge, 25; Ned Jones, Shandon, 50; Jeremiah Brown, Cedar, 25; Rev. A. B. Brown, Cedar, 15; Rev. A. R. Pittman, Rennert, 25; Robt. McLauchlin, Bromt 25; T. J. Toler, Rennert, 50; E. S. Ausley, Rennert, 25; W. A. Graham, Rennert, 25; David Curry, Shondon, 25; S. A. Ausley, Lumber Bridge, 25; T. J. Connelly, Lumber Bridge, 25; Rev. W. H. Anders, Idaho, 25; G. R. Smith, Rennert, 25; A. J. McNatt, Hasty, 25; Nelson Shaw, Lumber Bridge, 25; Mrs. Amanda McNeal, Lumber Bridge, 25; H. H. Marley, Shandon, 25; Mrs. Louisa Jones, Shandon, 50; Sarah Wilsow Lumber Bridge, 25; Joe Shaw, 25; Charles McLauchlin, Sherwood, 25, O. Smith, Lumber Bridge, 25 cts.; Hayes Smith, Rennert, 25; J. T. Carver, Rennert, 50; David McDonald, Lumber Bridge, 25; Moses

Brown, Lumber Bridge, 60; Mary J. McDonald, Lumber Bridge, 25; Rev. M. Whitted, Cedar Bladen, 50; Rev. Charles McGugan, Lumber Bridge, 25; Rev. T. J. Honnely, Lumber Bridge, 75; Priscilla McLauchlin, Fontell, (quarterly,) 25; Henry Johnson, Lumber Bridge, 25; Rev. A. F. C. Pittman, Rennert, 25; Amos Council, Tar Heel, 25; Sam'l Smith, Lumber Bridge, 25; A. S. McMillan, St. Paul; 25; Comfort Sinclair, St. Paul, 25; Henry Smith, Rennert, 50; Alexander McEachen, Lumber Bridge, 25; Rev. J. D. Moore, Red Spring, (quarterly) 35; Rev. W. M. Jones, Maxton, 25; Geo. McNeal, 25; W. H. McCathern, 25; Rev. T. M. Council, Cedar, 25; G. R. Richardson, Cedar Bladen, (quarterly,) 25, M. T. Smith, Rennert, 25; Alex Cary, Lumber Bridge, 25; Dan McDesmine, Lumber Bridge, 25.

Cash indicated by names above, $22.20.

Total collections, $14.80.

Total Institute St. John's church, Rev H.C. McDonold pastor, $37.00.

Nelson's Chapel, Rev. P. T. Hall, pastor, Raleigh, 25; Geo. Nicharne, 25; Archer Webb, 25, H. P. Perry, 25; Mittie Mills and Ellen Kittrells, 25; James Cook and Amanda Cook, 30; Nancy Roberts, Louisburg, 25;

Belton Creek, Rev. T. O. Fuller, pastor. Geo. Boyd, Clay, 25.

New Hope Association, D. J. Emerson, Sanford, 25; J. F. Holland, Haywond, 25; Rev. J. L. Barrett, Old Store, 25; G. B. Perry, Durham, 25; Caton Hinton, Raleigh 25; W. H. Stewart (mossey) 50.

Institute Oxford, Oct. 2-3, 1896.

F. W. Hancock, B. F. Taylor, J. L. Lewis and Mrs. Isaac Young each gave 25 cts.; B. S. Royster, Oxford, 50; R. B. Handy, Oxford, 50; Rev. G. C. Shaw, Oxford, 25; Hawkins Curtis, Oxford, 50; Mrs. G. C. Foster, Oxford, 25; Peter Royster, Oxford, 25; William Hester, Oxford, 25; H. H. Eatman, Oxford, 25; Geo. I. Peace, Oxford, 25; J. H. A. Jenkins, Oxford, 25; Mrs. Bettie Jordan, (white,) Oxford, 25; Mrs. Dr. Dalby, (white,) Oxford, 25; Mrs. L. J. Powel, (white,) Oxford, 25; Smith Watkins, 25; Junius Herndon, Oxford, 25; Mr. Taylor, Oxford, 25; collections, 12.56. Total. $17.56.

SUBSCRIPTIONS TO QUARTERLY.

Wake County Missionary Union, (A. B. Flemming,) $10.00. Dr. J. E. Dellinger, Greensboro, 25; Mrs. Esther Page, Apex, 25; Rev. Geo. W. Johnson, Winston 25.

Rolesville Baptist Church, Rev. Geo. W. Perry $6.00.

UNION ASSOCIATION.

S. A. Ausley St. John's, Lumber Bridge, 25; Rev. O. Watkins, Lumber Bridge, 25; Hezekiah Melone, Blounts, 25; A. B. Brown, Cedar, 25; Rev. G. R. Richardson, Cedar, 52; A. J. Counsel, 25; Rev. W. H. Anders, Idaho, N. C., 25; M. T. Calvary, Idaho, N. C., 25; F. S. Council, Populi, 25; R. M. McLauchlin, Bronets, 25; Mrs. Mary Anders, Idaho, 25; Philip Evans, Edonia, 25; Rev. J. M. Whitted, Cedar, 25; Geo. W. Spearman, Cedar, 25; Rev. N. B. Dunham, Cedar, 25; Leary Smith St. Paul, 25; Simpson Brown, Idaho, 25; Rev. J. J. McDonald, Gray's Creek, 25; Daniel Walker, Fayetteville, 25. Total, $5.26.

Baptist church, Method. Wm. Patterson, Method, 50; Samuel Yelloady, Garner, 50.

Peed Dee Association—W. H. Woodard, Rockingham, 25; D. M. Jackson, Rockingham, 25; G W. Covington, Laurinburg 25; Rev. T A. Lomax, Keyser, 25; Philip Chalmers, Cameron, 25; E. W. Andrews, Pike, 25; O. W. Morgan, Powelton, 25; C. B Harris, Laurinburg, 25; Rev. H. T. Carmicheal, Maxton, 25; Alexander Pouncey Maxton, 50; C. A. Watkins, Dockery's Store, 25; James Davis, Roberdell, 50; A. Byrd, Lilesville, 25; O. T. Pankey, Farlow, 25; Nelson Graham, Maxton, 25; Peter McDowell, Maxton, 50; George Malloy, McNair, 25; Thomas Gilchrist, Laurinburg, 50.

Third Course of Lectures "New Era" Institute;"

TIMES AND PLACES—EASTERN DISTRICT REV. C. C. SUMMERVILLE. 1897.

Jan. 5-7,	Aulanda,	N. C.
Jan 26-28,	Granville,	" "
Feb. 16-18,	Eliz. City,	" "
Mar. 9-11,	Rocky Mt.	" "
Mar. 30, Apr. 1	Newbern.	" "
Apr. 20-22,	Wilming'n.	" "
May 11-13,	Edenton.	" "
June 1-3,	Clinton.	" "

CENTRAL DISTRICT—REV. A. B. VINCENT, MISSIONARY.

Jan. 12-14,	Lumberton,	" "
Feb. 2-4,	Rockingh'm.	" "
Feb. 23-25,	Henderson,	" "
Mr. 16-18,	Clayton,	" "
Apr. 6-8,	Raleigh,	" "
Apr. 27-29,	Seaboard,	" "
May 18-20,	Graham,	" "
June 8-10,	Red Springs,	" "

WESTERN DISTRICT—REV. P. F. MALOY MISSIONARY.

Jan. 19-21,	Winston,	" "
Feb 9-11,	High Point,	" "
Mar. 2-4,	Salisbury,	" "
Mar. 23-25,	Charlotte,	N. C.
Apr. 13-15,	Monroe,	" "
May 4-5,	Gastonia,	" "
May 25-27,	Rutherfordton,	" "
Jun 15-17,	Wilkesboro,	" "

In connection with the above mentioned Institutes. Missionary and Educational mass-meetings will be arranged with the General Missionary and the District Missionary at the times and places yet to be announced.

It is sincerely hoped that the brethren, pastors, deacons, and Christian workers will take due notice of these meetings as they come in their Districts, and earnestly co-operate with the District Missionary in securing a full attendance and raising funds for the further prosecution of the work. We will secure our best talent white and colored, as lecturers for all of these meetings.

J. A. WHITTED,
Gen. Missionary.

Biblical Theology.

Redemption. Coming of a Redeemer. Significance of his name. His testimony concerning himself and his mission.

Redemption. Christ as the Light of the World; His teachings; miracles: life

Redemption. The death of Christ: voluntary; His words concerning the purpose of His death. Teachings of the New Testament: the blood of Christ; life for life.

Redemption. His Resurrection; Ascension; Intercession at the right hand of God.

Church History.

Christianity in Europe from 1517. The Roman Catholic Church supreme. Church and State. Worship of images. Purgatory. Indulgences Transubstantiation. Monasticism. Celibacy of the clergy. Capital punishment for heresy.

General character of the middle or "dark ages."

The Great Reformation. Reformers before this. The Walde ses, and Albigenses; Wycliffe, Huss. Luther: a Monk; visit to Rome and co version; his theses; excrement; at diet of Worms; his translation of the B ble; hymns; rapid spread of the new doctrines. Estimate of Luther's character and work.

Pastoral Work. Christ, the Great Shepherd The Church a flock Personal attention t the needs of all; inquirers; wayward members; the sick; funeral services. Paul an example of the faithful pastor.

Christian Missions.

Foreign Mission work of Colored Baptists When begun Total contributions. Number of Missionaries Fields of Labor Results. Obligations for the evangelization of Africa. Great opportunity.

Foreign Mission work of Northern and Southern white Baptists, Their organizations: Fields occupied. Missionaries. Annual receipts. Total receipts. Results Prospects.

Christian Education.

The growing demand for educated men and women among the colored people. As American citizens to know what they should do As ministers of intelligent congregations. As teachers in the Sunday-School and public schools; educated young women needed here. As editors, physicians, professors in higer schools, etc

Special Subjects.

Reception of members by the church. The general custom. Evils of hasty acti n. Relation of their Christian experience, or conversion, What of visions? What are the Scriptural requirements?

Church discipline. Scriptural a thority for it. Necessity both for the offenders good and the honor of the church. Sp rit in which it should be administered. The proper steps to take How personal differences should be adjusted.

NEW BERNE, N. C., Nov. 25, '96.
REV. J. A. WHITED:—Dear Sir. I reply to your letter of the 27th, therefore please accept of the representation for the several churches which lie under my custody. In the next representation, I think that I can bring the extreme East to the light of the Convention, for we are fast developing in the East. Since the Association we have been able to bring in touch with the Convention twenty-five churches out of forty-six, and as the time elapses we shall take the East for God and the Baptists.

I am with Rev. Slade to-day and consolidated on the different points that draws the rays to the East, the people are with us, when we reach the people success attends the future, therefore we solicit your prayerful attention.

Very Respecfully,
L. P. MARTIN.

CHURCHES WHO CONTRIBUTE.

Mt. Shiloh church, Shiloh, N. C., Rev. L. P. Martin pastor, $1.00.

St. John church, New Berne, N. C., Rev. L. P. Martin, pastor, $1.00.

St. Luke's church, James City, N. C., Rev. R. Blount, pastor, $1.00.

Pilgrim's Chapel Baptist Church, James City, N. C, Rev. N. C. Roundtree, pastor $1.00.

Mt. Shiloh, First Baptist church, James City, R. P. Pope deacon, P. J. Lee, Clerk, $1.00.

Rev. J. M. Taylor, Greensboro, 25; Rev. J. H. Lyon, Berea, 25, Rev L. A. Johnson, Durham, 40; Dr. A. M. Moore, 50; Judge Walter A. Montgomery, Raleigh, $2.00; Judge R. W. Winston, Durham, 50; Mr. W. T. O'Bryant, Durham, $5.00; Rev. D. J. Avera, Franklinton, 25; Dr. J. E. Shepherd, Durham, 25;

collections, $6.00. Total, $14.40.

Wakefield Baptist church, Rev. Geo. W. Perry, pastor. Mrs. Lucy Dortch, Wakefield, 25; Branch Hopkins, Wakefield, 50; Oliver Stokes, Wakefield, 25; Miss Annie Merritt, Wakefield, 25; T. B. Ellis, Wakefield, 50; Julia Foster, 25; Theastless Stokes, 25; T. L. Stokes, 25; Jacob High, 25; A. W. Williams, 25; Isaac Hill and Miss Albenetta Thomas 25 cents each.

Graham Baptist Church, Rev. F. A. Long, pastor, Greensboro, 25; Jno. Banes, Mebane, 25; William Long, Graham, 25; C. L. Ruffin, Haw River, 25; Rev. A. Long, Graham, N. C., 25.

Baptist Church, Kittrells, Rev. D. J. Avera, pastor. Mrs. Martha Blacknall, Kittrell, 50; Mrs. Ella Owens, Kittrell, 50; Miss C. L. Crudup, Kittrell, 50; Miss Rebecca Mills, Kittrell, 50; Miss Nannie Scott, Kittrell, 50; Miss Laura Scott, Kittrell.

Pleasant Grove Church, St. Paul, Rev. H. C. McDonald, pastor. Sallie King, Pleasant Grove, St. Paul, 25; Mary H. McMillan, St. Paul, 25; Emeline Sinclair, St. Paul, 25; Sophia Sinclair, St. Paul, 25; Rev. H. C. McDonald, Lumber Bridge, 50.

Middle Association, Neverson Canady, Oxford, 50 cents; Plummer Branch, Watkins, 25; Rev. A. J. Greene, Bobbitts, 25; Phil Marrow, Oxford, 25; Rev. T. B. Hicks, Williamsboro, 25; F. Perry, 25; Wm. Hayes, Adoniram, 25; Paul Turner, Henderson, 25.

Very Respectfully,
L. P MARTIN.

Bro. Buck Perry, 25; J. H. Thorp, Kittrell, N. C., 50; Harris Alston, Bobbit, N. C., 50; Mrs. Auliza Macon, 25; Lorena Dunston, 25; Lee Brooks, Mitchiners, N. C., 25; Wm.

Oliver, Long Ingleside, N. C., 50; Washington Perry, Tetha, N. C., 50; Simon Perry, 25; Mathew Hawkins, 25; Jordan Hayes, 25; Conrad Jones, Moulton, N. C., 50; John Young, Pughs, N. C., 50 cents.

For the past year THE BAPTIST QUARTERLY has been edited by our able manager, Dr. N. F. Roberts. He insisted upon some one else assuming the editorship, and the board unanimously elected their General Missionary and Corresponding Secretary as Managing Editor of THE QUARTERLY.

Much praise is due the Board and former editor of THE QUARTERLY for the able management with which THE QUARTERLY has been edited. We shall feel satisfied if we can carry it on with the same proficiency. We shall greatly depend on the brethren to help us make this organ what it should be.

We shall endeavor as near as possible to secure statistics from all our religious bodies in the State. The Secretaries of our Associations and Conventions are hereby notified to send minutes and reports of all their organizations and meetings so that they may appear in THE QUARTERLY from time to time.

The office of Supervisor is dropped as every licensed preacher has an Elder appointed to assist him.

Southern Pines Christian Normal School will open Dec. 28th, 1896. This school is for the educating of colored boys and girls. For further information address A. A. Bright, B. D., President, Southern Pines, N. C.

EBENEZER BAPTIST CHURCH, CHARLOTTE, N. C.
EXTERIOR

The address of Rev. S. N. Vass, District Secretary for the Southern States of the American Baptist Publication Society, has been changed to Raleigh, N. C., and hereafter he will make his home in Raleigh. Those having business with him in reference to the work of the Society should address him here. He has an office in the same building as Rev. J. A. Whitted, our General Missionary of N. C. In some future edition of THE BAPTIST QUARTERLY we hope to present a short sketch and cut of Rev. Vass, so that our readers can see how changed he is in appearance from his old familiar look while a teacher at Shaw University. He traveled over this State several times in the interest of Shaw and missionary work, and he has many friends who will gladly welcome him back to his old home.

Co-operation in North Carolina has been tested in the past twelve months. Our brethren everywhere seem to be delighted with the work. It is not only expected that we raise money in Institutes and where our Missionaries are present, but our Board will arrange a Mission Day and will announce it in the next issue of THE QUARTERLY.

It gives us pleasure to note the great reduction that has been made by the American Pubication Society in the prices of its literature and also its books. The Society has also wisely decided to issue small and cheap editions of all its valuable popular books at such low prices that even the poor can buy them and thus be benefitted. We hope that our schools and churches will avail themselves of the advantages so that they can do better work the coming year.

We exceedingly regret that our QUARTERLY is so full, we cannot include all our communications but they will appear in the next issue.

The Baptist State Sunday School Convention of N. C., held its annual session with the First African Baptist Church of Goldsboro, of which Rev. J. W. Dew is pastor. The meeting was presided over conservatively and with dignity, profitable and pleasant to the immense crowd of our best talent, males and females assembled from all parts of the State.

The program as supplemented from time to time was quite interesting.

This being the test year of co-operation between the American Baptist Publication Society and the Convention, all were anxious to know of the work done by our Missionaries, Rev. M. C. Ransom and Rev. Joseph Perry.

It was evident a new work was begun, not only in church work in the State, but Sunday-School work as well, from the quanty of money raised and the increased delegation in attendance.

This Convention has been a great factor in many departments of our work, and we have reason to hope for still greater developments.

For the Quarterly.
From the Western District.

I am glad to say to the brethren that the work in this district has every indication of hope and gradual advancement.

The pastors are saying that the State Convention has truly begun its work for the elevation of the entire Baptist hosts of Noth Carolina. The brethren are becoming better acquainted with the Institute work and therefore are attending in larger numbers. We have great responsibilities resting upon us as Baptists, to preach the gospel in western N. Carolina. From Salisbury to Asheville, a distance of 141 miles, with thousands of people living in the villages and towns along the line, we have only three small churches. I am planning to open a mission station at Morganton at an early day. My visit to the white Baptist State Convention at this place was to me "a feast of good things". The work of co-operation had many warm friends and hearty supporters. I was made welcome among the brethren, and knew not my color while enjoying the many handshakes and words of approval to the great work and influence of the plan of co-operation. I would have made a speech, but for the Institute to be held at Wadesboro, N. C., which made my time short at the Convention.

On my way home it was my extreme pleasure to join our very excellent President of Shaw University, who by his whole conversation showed his untiring interest in the uplifting and education of our people as a race, and especially along moral and religious lines. We are at his right arm in the support of Shaw.

The Institute at Wadesboro was the most largely attended of any in my district; more than 45 ministers and deacons were present. The pastors of the Zion, Yadkin and Lane's Creek Association were present.

P. F. MALOY,
Missionary Wes. Dis. N. C.

HENRY L. MOREHOUSE, D. D.

Henry L. Morehouse, D. D., was born in Stanford, Dutchess Co., N. Y., Oct. 2, 1834. Mr. Morehouse was graduated at the University of Rochester in 1858. He entered Rochester Theological Seminary in 1861, and was gradvated in 1864. His first settlement was at East Saginaw, Mich., where he remained from 1864 to 1873, when he was called to the pastorate of the East Avenue Baptist church, in Rochester. Mr. Morehouse was prominently identified with educational and State missionary work in Michigan. He was for some time corresponding and financial agent of the New York Baptist Union for Ministerial Education, which has charge of the Theological Seminary at Rochester. He was elected to that position in 1877. His report in "Vindication of the Beneficiary System" won for him high encomiums from the first educators of the country. He also published several able sermons. He was poet of the alumni of Rochester University in 1874. His racy and very readable contributions to the *Examiner* and *Chronicle* over the signature "Helmo," have earned him a good reputation. His church has greatly prospered under his ministry, and his earnest labors for the Seminary have secured for him the respect of all the friends of ministerial education in the State and in the many States where Rochester is represented. He is now the able corresponding Secretary of the American Baptist Home Missionary Society.

Dr. Morehouse was for a number of years the able Corresponding Secretary of the American Baptist Home Mission Society, and afterward unanimously chosen as the Field Secretary of the same great Baptist organization.

In this great position the efficiency of his labors and his wonderful influence have been felt wherever the Society undertook to labor.

The great plan of co-operation between Baptists, white and colored, North and South, for the prosecution of mission work and ministerial education for the colored people throughout the South is largely due to Dr. Morehouse.

As an organizer he has no superior and few equals in any of the churches. We have no greater Baptist leader North or South.

Prof. N. F. ROBERTS, D. D.

Prof. N. F. Roberts, D. D., principal of the Normal department, and professor of mathematics in the college department of Shaw University, was born in Seaboard, in Northampton county, N. C., Oct. 13, 1849. From early boyhood he was a great lover of books, and eager to grasp and assimilate all the knowledge that could be obtained from them. He was brought up in a farming district, and he was a farmer all the early years of his life. Farming is an exceedinly healthy life for the mind as well as for the body. Not a few great men, not only of the negro race, but of the nation, owe their greatness in a large measure to their life as farmers. There is a certain atmosphere of freedom, a rare opportunity for observation, a wide sphere for studying nature, a pure balmy air, which are not found in cities and towns. Young Roberts was not a careless observer of his environments; they stimulated him to think and study. He was apt to learn and had a special liking for figures: so much so that he was considered a little genius in the neighborhood. He could solve almost any problem in the common school arithmetic before he attended school. This boyhood precosity was only a precursor of what he attained in the mathematical sphere. October, '71, he entered Shaw University (then Shaw Collegiate Institute), Raleigh, N. C. He began in the lowest grades and was rapidly promoted, easily keeping at the head of his class. His whole school life was consistent, his deportment called forth many expressions of commendation from his teachers. May, 1878 he graduated from the college department and received congratulations from students and faculty for his attainments. Mr. Roberts became a Christian in 1872. Being impressed that he was called to preach he was ordained to the work of the gospel ministry, May 20th, 1878. As a preacher he is earnest, able and logical; a deep thinker and an impressive speaker. Since the year of his graduation Rev. Roberts has been professor of mathematics in Shaw University with the exception of one year when he was General Missionary under the American Baptist Home Mission Society, and the Baptist State Convention. Prof. Roberts is not only an adept in mathematics, but he is an apt teacher. Some of his methods of teaching are original, and his students are usually interested in that branch of study.

July, 1882, he was elected pastor of the Blount street Baptist church, and served the church nine years, resignidg August, 1891, because he felt that it was too great a pressure to discharge his duties as teacher, etc., and at the same time perform all the functions of a city pastor. He is popular among the brethren of his State; he is esteemed by them as a man, minister and educator. He has held many positions of honor in the State. For many years he was President of the Baptist State Sunday School Convention, and is now the Treasurer of that body.

For a number of years he was editor of the *African Expositor*, published at Shaw University. For twelve months editor of the BAPTIST QUARTERLY, the organ of co-operation in North Carolina. Several times was Dr. Roberts elected Corresponding Secretary of the Baptist State Convention, several times President, which position he now holds with much dignity and respect.

The history of the Baptist denomination in North Carolina would be minus of many important pages without the labors of Dr. Roberts.

EBENEZER BAPTIST CHURCH, CHARLOTTE, N. C.
(INTERIOR.)

CHURCHES.	PASTORS.	Sabbath Preaching.	Baptized.	Received by Letter.	Restored.
Ashland	C. J. White	2			15
Bethany	Thos. Sharp	4		1	10
First Baptist, Colerain	Isaac Arnold	2	26		7
Second Baptist, Union	W. A. Cobb	1		2	1
First Baptist, Severn	C. M. Cartwright	2	15	2	7
First Baptist, Powellsville	G. E. Freeman	3	12	2	4
Second Baptist, Murfreesboro	Wm. Reid	2	26	1	2
Second Baptist, Aulander	D. W. Early	2	11	1	1
Second Baptist, Potecasie	J. J. Joyner	2	12	3	
Second Baptist, St. John's	Thos. Sharp	2		1	1
First Baptist, Kelford	King Jacobs	2	36	3	2
First Baptist, Rich Square		1	3		1
Conoconary	G. E. Freeman	4	1	4	
Chapel Hill	J. J. Thompson	4		1	30
Cedar Landing	J. A. Faulk	1		4	2
Elm Grove	G. E. Freeman	1			
Harrellsville Chapel	W. P. Sharp	1	21	1	2
Indian Woods	I. J. Thompson	3	20	2	12
Jerusalem	W. A. Cobb	1	5	42	
Jordan's Grove	Wm. Reid	3	14		
Lincoln's Grove	J. C. Williams	2		3	1
Luella	Julius Grant	3	8	1	1
Mt. Sinai	W. A. Cobb	3	10	2	5
Mt. Moriah		3	24		6
Mt. Hermon	J. J. Mitchell	2	12	2	2
Mt. Ararat	B. J. Lenox	3	80		1
Mt. Pleasant	W. P. Sharp	3	26	1	15
Mill Branch	I. J. Thompson	1		3	1
Mill Neck	Wm. Reid	1			2
Menola	W. A. Askew	1	20	6	
Nebo Chapel	J. J. Joyner	1	6		4
New Haven	H. Clemons	2		1	5
New Holly Grove	Thos. Sharp	1	8		2
New Ahoskie	W. P. Sharp	2	7	2	7
Newsom's Grove	E. Reynolds	1	8	8	2
Oxlie Hill	P. H. Holly	1	21	4	1
Mt. Olive	Luke Pierce	1	8	14	6
Piney Woods Chapel	G. E. Freeman	2	4	9	3
Pleasant Oak	C. J. White	4	22		4
Parker's Grove	J. J. Joyner	4	13	2	3
Peterson's Chapel	Geo. W. Bolden	4	46	2	18
Philippi	C. S. Brown	3	19	7	7
Pleasant Plain	C. S. Brown	2	19	2	5
Ross Mizell	R. W. Hoggard	3			
Spring Hill		2	5	15	
St. Luke	C. M. Billup	1		1	1
St. Elmo St.	G. E. Freeman	3	8	8	2
St. Frances	W. Outerbridge	4	11	5	2
St. Matthew	D. W. Early	4			
Sandy Point	L. Pierce	2		2	8
Sandy Branch	C. J. White	3	45	5	15
Weeping Mary	D. W. Early	3	59	4	1
Woodville Plain	W. A. Cobb	4		3	10
Wynn's Grove	W. P. Sharp	4	8		4
St. Paul	A. Cooper	3			
Pleasant Hill	G. W. Bolden	2	12		4
Zion's Grove	W. Reid	4	33	5	3
Zion's Hill	W. D. Norman	3	30	14	10
Zion's Triumph	A. Cooper	4	5	1	
Zion's Bethlehem	C. M. Cartwright	1			

Pleasant Union, P. F. Hare, Pastor, not represented.

TABLE—WEST ROANOKE BAPTIST ASSOCIATION.

	Deaths.	Male.	Female.	Total	Association Fund.	Foreign Missions.	Home Missions.	State Convention.	Orphan Asylum.	Ministerial Education.	W. N.	Institute.	Bertie Academy.	Pastor's Salary.	S. S. Scholars.	CLERKS AND POST-OFFICES
6	2	77	139	216	$1 00	$	$ 20	$ 50	$ 50	$ 05	$	05	$	65 00	50	H. L. Gaskins, Mt. Gould.
23	13	100	207	127	1 00	1 30	30	50	1 00	25		10	1 05	90 00	80	Harrison Jenkins, Powellsville
3	5	62	60	122	1 00	1 30	80	50	1 00	25		10	1 05	75 00	80	A. J. Wilson, Colerain.
2	1	25	48	73	50			50		10				05 00	30	W. S. Askew, Union.
5	5	81	107	188	1 00	25	25	50	50	25		25	1 25	150 00	75	A. J. Lassiter, Severn.
5	5	10	60	100	1 00	50		50	50			50	1 00	100 00	85	
4	1	122	268	390	50	25	50	50	25	50		50		110 00		J. W. Jones, Murfreesboro.
1	1	28	26	51	50	50		50	50				30	18 00	25	G. W. Anderson, Aulander.
		33	33	66	1 00			50						10 00	105	T. H. Edwards, Potecasie.
		39	25	64	25	25			10	25				50 00	30	C. P. McGlaughn, St. John's.
1	2	47	44	91	1 00	10	10	50	10	10		25	50	50 00	35	J. D. Johnson, Roxobel.
2	3	61	80	150	1 00	25		50	50			25	50	100 00		G. G. Magget, Rich Square.
1	1	62	60	122	1 00	20		50	20				60			C. G. White, Powellsville
22	3	144	187	324	1 00	10	10	50	10	10		10	10	125 00	60	R. P. Taylor, Aulander.
4	2	290	380	670	1 00	50		50	25	25		25	1 25			S. S. Webb, Rich Square.
3	3	34	45	79	50	50	25	50	25					05 00	30	W. M. Carter, Windsor.
7	2	72	74	146	1 00	25	50	50	25	25		75	50	75 00	75	Goodman Early, Early.
10	7	236	380	616	1 00	25		50	25	25		25	50		60	Geo. Sessoms, Harrellsville.
	2	54	60	114	1 00			50				25	25	115 00	90	Henry Ruffin, Quitsna.
		186	345	531	1 00	50	25	50	10	15		25	1 00	100 00		E. C. Jones, Winton.
		26	30	56	25			50					25	25 00		J. H. Eason, Woodland.
	1	30	30	60	1 00			50						35 00	40	H. Jones, Harrellsville.
	2	70	80	150	1 00	50	10	50	75				25	200 00	75	C. R. Powell, Aulander.
30	4	162	245	470	1 00	25	25	50	25			50			50	I. J. Cooper, Lola.
		20	11	31	50	05	10	50	05	05		10	05	25 00	50	A. T. Beverly, Winton.
	1	51	59	110	1 00	13		50	02				27	50 00	90	N. G. Speller, Drews.
9		130	170	300	1 00	25	25	50	25			75		120 00	80	G. E. Hendrix, Drews.
	2	36	56	92	1 00	12	12	50	12	12		12	12	50 00	80	W. Sharp, Harrellsville.
10	4	178	221	399	50			50	25	25		25	25	110 00	120	J. H. Boon, Eagletown.
		16	17	33	1 00	25	25	50								J. H. Harden, Como.
		53	83	136	1 00			50						50 00	90	Eli Vincent, Menola.
4		71	113	187	75			50				25	15	100 00	25	M. D. Vaughn, Murfreesboro.
3		30	40	70	1 05		05	50	25	10		05	50	50 00	40	M. Lawrence, Menola.
6	2	137	182	319	25	50	25	50	50	2 00				200 00	50	H. G. Lane, Colerain.
1		20	18	38	50		25	50					50	20 00	50	J. H. Newsom, Ahoskie.
	1	29	62	91		10	10	50	10	15			25	40 00	28	John Peele, Ahoskie.
3	3	110	509	919	1 00	50		50	25				2 25	200 00	200	N. D. Holly, Merry Hill
	2	189	227	416	50	75		50	75				1 50	100 00	150	Noah Cherry, Drews
5		41	75	126	1 00		20	50	25			25	75		6	Geo. R. Freeman, Powellsville.
		45	56	101	20			50				25	20	60 00	2	C. H. Madre, Windsor.
10	7	133	214	347	1 00	25	25	50	50	25			5 00	80 00	75	A. J. Porter, Mapleton.
4	5	128	191	319	1 00	15		50	25	10	1 50			150 00	30	A. T. Wilson, Merry Hill.
6	11	211	334	545	50	50		50	50		2 50		50	200 00	50	Isaac Boon, Tunis.
	3	10	18	28	50	05	05	50	05	05	05		50	20 00	17	R. H. Bizell, Winton.
5	5	224	258	482	1 00	25	15	50	15	13			80		113	G. W. Watford, Rosemead.
3		40	40	80	1 00			50	50					75 00	42	K. S. Smallwood, Lewiston.
1	1	39	84	123	50		05	50	50	13	20		50	75 00	40	B. H. Cooper, Sans Souci
		75	65	140	1 00			50	50				10	80 00	60	A. Robbins, Windsor.
4	1	32	53	85	50			50		25			50	50 00	25	Dennis Dean, Quitsna.
11	7	138	234	372		exe	mp	ted						125 00	54	Monroe Rice, Windsor.
6	3	115	189	304	1 00	05	10	50	25	10	20		25	125 00	50	Thos. J. Rayner, Windsor.
1	1	60	80	140	50	05	10	50		05			25	60 00	40	R. C. Biggs, Kelford.
11	4	61	106	167	50			50					50	140 00	120	P. M. Watson, Lewiston.
4		46	51	97	25			50	25				1 00	60 00	55	W. Wilkins, Lewiston.
					1 00			25	50	25						J. T. Morris, Rosemead
2	1	21	23	44		1 00		25	50	25				30 00		D. Roulline, Windsor.
2	7	144	160	304	25	25		50	25	25	05		50	100 00	75	Jno. T. Gay, St. John's.
10	4	143	238	381	2 50	1 00	1 00	1 00	2 00	50	10	2 60		150 00	75	K. J. Redmain, Colerain
		14	9	23			1 00	25	50	25						W. D. Gillam, Quitsna
							1 00	25	50	25						D. E. Rayner, Windsor.

SHAW UNIVERSITY,
RALEIGH, N. C.

Established at Raleigh, December 1st, 1865, was a pioneer in the education of colored young men and young women. Its young ladies' department, formely known as Estey Seminary, was the first of its kind ever established. All departments have grown better with age, and parents can feel that Shaw is a safe place for their sons and daughters. While a high degree of scholarship is maintained by her students, solid character is insisted upon, and all unwilling to comply with rules and regulations necessary to this end, will not find here a congenial atmosphere.

There are Departments of Law, Medicine, Pharmacy, Music, Missionary Training and Theology, as well as Normal, Scientific and College courses of study. A corps of thirty-two professors, teachers and employees is in charge of the various departments. Excellent opportunities for acquiring a solid education at a trifling cost are presented. Although the times are hard, the attendance is large.

For catalogues and other information,

Address,

THE PRESIDENT,
SHAW UNIVERSITY, Raleigh, N. C.

—MARCH, 1897.—

The Baptist Quarterly.

Edited by Board of Managers Baptist E. and M. Convention,
J. A. WHITTED, Managing Editor,
Box 145, Raleigh, N. C.

CONTENTS:

	PAGE
SOME OF THE PIONEERS OF THE WORK AMONG THE BAPTISTS OF NORTH CAROLINA	1
A MODEL CHURCH	3
FROM THE WESTERN DISTRICT	5
CENTRAL DISTRICT	7
INSTITUTE WORK	8
THEOLOGICAL TRAINING AT SHAW UNIVERSITY	11
SOME OBSERVATIONS ON THE LITERARY STATUS OF SHAW UNIVERSITY	12
INSTITUTES	14
SCHOOLS	22
COMMUNICATIONS	26
A CALL TO DUTY	31
CONTRIBUTIONS	30 and 32

Baptist Educational and Missionary Convention of North Carolina.

Next Session will be Held in Charlotte, N. C., October 21, 1897.

Officers 1896-97.

Rev. N. F. ROBERTS, D. D., President, Raleigh.
Rev. C. S. BROWN, Secretary, Winton.
J. A. WHITTED, Cor. Secretary and General Missionary, Raleigh.
A. W. PEGUES, Ph. D., Treasurer, Raleigh.
Rev. G. W. MOORE, Auditor, Fayetteville.

Missionaries.

J. A. WHITTED, General, Raleigh.
Rev. P. F. MALOY, Western District, Greensboro.
Rev. A. B. VINCENT, Central District, Raleigh.
Rev. C. C. SUMMERVILLE, Eastern District, Rocky Mount.

☞ All communications concerning State Work, New Era Institutes, Co-operation, and the Baptist Quarterly, should be directed to the Corresponding Secretary and General Misssonary at Raleigh.

REV. C. C. SOMERVILLE.

Baptist Quarterly.

SOME OF THE PIONEERS OF THE WORK AMONG THE BAPTISTS OF N. C.

Rev. H. Cowen, of Salisbury, is the oldest Baptist minister in the State, and has done a great work in laying the foundation for Baptist principles and establishing Baptist churches in western North Carolina. He is now in his 85th year, but manifests more direct interest in the general advancement of our State work than many of our young active pastors. He attends the State Convention and his own Association every year; has organized churches all the way from Charlotte to Durham, and from Reidsville across the State to Wadesboro, N. C. His whole life seems fraught with burning zeal and unfailing love for the Master's cause.

***

Rev. G. W. Holland, of Winston, N. C., has planted Baptist churches from Greensboro to Wilksboro, and from the Virginia line to the Yadkin river above Salisbury. He came to Winston from Danville when there was not a single place of worship in the town, for it was only a town then; he began holding prayer meeting and preaching about the place and continued till now. We now have five Baptist churches in that city, all of which are branch churches from the first Baptist church of which he is still pastor, and which is by far the largest and strongest congregation in the city. Mt Zion church, of which Rev. G. W. Johnson is pastor, is a most popular and thriving daughter. Rev. Johnson being a man of quick thought, far sight and well educated, would not rest till his congregation is regarded among the best in the State. Rev. Holland laid hands on Rev. Johnson and consecrated him to that work, and he regards him as his most successful son in the gospel. He also owns a large farm.

***

REV. THOMAS PARKER.

The subject of this sketch, Rev. Thomas Parker, of Warsaw, N. C., has just passed his three score years and six, professing faith in Christ in 1862, he was baptized by Dr. Young and united himself with the white Baptist church, of Wilmington, N. C.

He realized a call to the ministry in 1868, and since it may be said of him, though often at the peril of his life he has preached the word successfully and "with no uncertain sound."

One thousand one hundred and sixty persons have been plunged in the "watery grave" by his hands, and in spite of his years, if he could he would plunge as many more.

No, one who has ever known Rev. Parker doubts his loyalty to the Baptist cause.

Like every leader should be, his "sheep hear his voice" and to have his approval in any measure among his people, means the approval of the entire flock.

REV A. WILBURN, OF TRINITY COLLEGE, N. C.

Rev. Wilburn was born in 1840, he became a member of the Baptist church in 1870, and was ordained a deacon of his church the same day. He was licensed in 1870 and ordained to the gospel ministry in 1872; he was then associated in the ministry with our reverend Father, Rev. Harry Cowan. For twenty-one years he has served the High Point church, Simon's Grove, New Hope, two years, at Lexington; Thomasville, twelve years; Liberty Grove, fourteen years.

Probably no minister of the State has preached more funerals, and many of them persons outside the Baptist church. Rev. Wilburn has baptized one thousand persons, he was Moderator of the High Point Association one year, and Treasurer of the Rowan Association four years, which position he now holds.

What Rev. Wilburn has done for the cause in western North Carolina will be known only when the deeds of mortals are fully revealed. Long may he be spared to the Master's cause.

**

REV. ZION H. BERRY, OF ELIZABETH CITY, N. C.

He was born in Camden county, April 24, 1830, united with the Baptist church in 1848. He felt his call to the gospel ministry in the year of 1860, and was ordained in 1866. He has held charges over the following churches: Corinth, Philadelphia, New Sawyer's Creek, Olive Branch, Union, New Chapel, Hertford, Pool's Grove, Galatia, Corner Stone, Harrell's Creek, Roanoke Island, New Shiloh.

As one of the results or the labors of Rev. Berry, 4,953 persons have been baptized. Rev. Berry has been Moderator of the Roanoke Baptist Missionary Association and holds a very prominent place in the councils of his brethren in eastern North Carolina. He deserves great credit for his push in every effort to lift up his church and his race. He, though passed his three score by six years, is full of energy and as active in the work as if twenty-five.

**

REV. GEORGE W. PERRY, OF RALEIGH, N. C.

The subject of this sketch was born in Franklin county, near Louisburg, in 1833, united with the white Baptist church, of Louisburg, N C., in 1853; ordained to the gospel ministry and held pastoral charge over the following churches:

Assistant pastor, Louisburg. St. Matthews, Rolesville, Wakefield, Macedonia, First Baptist church of Raleigh, for some months after the death of Rev. Wm. A. Greene.

Upward of five hundred persons have been baptized by Rev. Perry in his different pastorates, being the first student of Shaw University, he was afterward chosen to be a trustee.

As a missionary, Rev. Perry has done efficient work in North Caroolina. He was the first Treasurer for the proposed Orphan Asylum nine years and did much in shaping the history of that institution of which we are all so justly proud.

**

REV. CHAS. E. HODGES, LAND OF PROMISE, VA.

Rev. Hodges was born in Princess Ann county, Va., on May 7th, 1819, he was baptized May 4th, 1743, and ordained to the gospel ministry Apr. 1st, 1861. During the years of his ministry he organized the following churches : Union Chapel and Galilee, in Pasquotank county; Readie Grove and Pool's Grove, in Perquimans county; Willow Grove, St. Matthew, Mt. Tabor, St. Pauls, Pleasant Valley, in Norfolk county, Va.; Oak Grove and Piney Grove, in Princess Ann county, Va.; Anders Grove, Chowan county; Chesnut Grove, Halifax county; Pastolich, Brooklyn, N. Y.; Christian Home, Currituck county and others.

Twenty-six brethren, some now holding important churches, have been ordained to the ministry by Rev. Hodges. At one time he was the honored pastor of the First Baptist church of Brooklyn, N. Y. He has held many prominent churches in North Carolina and Virginia. Sixteen hundred and seventy-three persons have been baptized by him.

Several times he has been elected to the important position of Moderator of the Roanoke Baptist Association, which position he now holds. He is greatly loved and respected by his brethren.

A MODEL CHURCH.

According to the almost endless varieties of churches that meet one's gaze in every section of the country, from the antique Dutch chapel with its pigeon hole windows, scarcely large enough for a private residence to the modern handsome church edifice with its large gothic windows and chancel, offering every opportunity to scientific acoustics, and well nigh perfect ventilation, it would be hard to describe a church that would be suited to so many tastes. All churches should be constructed primarily with a view to comfort for all seasons, so that there must be a groundless objection for the disinterested and careless class who are sometimes found in our churches ; besides, the entire architecture ought to display taste and beauty in its mechanism, however simple the design, for that individual must be unusually coarse and vulgar who does not desire beauty even in a church.

While much can be said about a "model church" and with profit, much more can be said about the pastor, officers and members of such a church, for after all a congregation of Christ's baptized disciples constitute the real basis of a New Testament church.

The two first classes alluded to should be progressive, and spiritual. These two qualities go together, for wherever there is a lack of one the other seriously suffers The non-progressive pastor is a positive hindrance to his church. He may not intentionally keep the ox from the hay, but virtually he is playing the same trick. Lest he should become top-heavy for want of ballast, he should abound in the grace of spirituality. "Like priest like prophet" a dead preacher will have a dead congregation—a thing very different from a "model church."

Church officers ought to be intelligent business men of broad and liberal views and of marked piety ; for if they are wanting in these graces they will soon become so narrow and contracted that they will be mere sycophants, whose only office is to serve some selfish end, and not the good of the church and the glory of God.

Indifference in the selection of deacons, or over-anxiety to make a "board" has been the means of writing "Ichabod" over an otherwise prosperous and contented church. The members of the church ought to be plainly taught the grace of "Christian liberty" and given to know that as great a falsehood can be told by willfully refusing to pay your salary as can be told about anything else. Every member of the church should strive to cultivate a fraternal feeling and courtesy in speech to each other, and at all times should be solicitous of the comfort of the visitors and the welfare of the pastor. In all the departments of the church work all parties ought to be cordially in touch with each other—"my brother co-laborers together with God."

Of the interests fostered by a model church, we shall speak first of the Sunday school. Where no Sunday school exists, and where the pastor and deacons are averse to such an agency, you need not be surprised to pass that way in a few years, and musing on the ruins of broken windows, a dilapidated building, a moss-grown walk, you read out in the reflection from every fluttering leaf and solitary songster who may chance to pass that way that preaching used to be held there. The children must be gathered and taught. Whenever practicable a young people's society should be organized and the fires kept burning. A well organized Woman's Home Mission Society, managed and officered by Christian women, who are imbued with the spirit of missions, is an indispensibility. It can do the work for the relief of the poor, the spread of the gospel. Baptist retrenchment, that is not possible for any other seperate agency to perform.

A church that is not alive to missions generally fails of its high calling. The demand for home and foreign missions is as constant as the throbbing of the pulse—"the poor ye have always" is a call to missions as imperative now as when the Saviour spoke it; yet many of our churches neglect the subject until the missionary comes. Africa must not be forgotten. We must provide something for the enlightenmen of the 300,000,000 souls in a comparatively hopeless night. A "model church" has not done its duty unless it provides for its superannuated and disabled members. Unless Christianity comes to the rescue of these unfortunate ones, the church need not be surprised that in proportion as it declines societies will flourish.

The church should be alert to its educational interest. It *does* make a difference where our children are educated, and by whom taught. Sainted Dr. H. M. Tupper, though dead, yet speaketh through the teachers and preachers all over North Carolina who as Baptists, are "contending for the faith."

Are you suprised at these things? Read the 9th verse, 18th chapt. of Gen. Lay your hands on every boy and girl you can, and do what you can to have them educated.

C. C. SUMMERVILLE.
Dist. Missionary, Rocky Mt.

FROM THE WESTERN DISTRICT.

DEAR BRETHREN: The work of co-operation has lost no place with our people, but instead, is still increasing in interest and prominence. We see a clearer sky for the work at this writing than in mid summer of last year. Brethren everywhere feel that they have unsurpassed advantages to improve their knowledge of the Bible, and that preaching is made much easier by attending the Institute. Our great need in Western North Carolina is a sufficent State Mission fund. More than fifty out stations in this section have preaching only a few months in the year, because of inability to support a minister. We hope our able pastors and large churches will take due notice of this, and lay aside on the first day of the week a sufficient sum till this work is fully on foot.

Many calls are made to our Gen. Missionary and the board for relief, but answers have been given. The money is not in hand. Let every church and Sunday school in Western North Carolina heed these calls, by sending a collection to our Treasurer, Dr. A. W. Pegues at Raleigh, N. C., and see if God will not supply every vacant and destitute field in this district. We hope to see every Association in the State organized into union meetings to meet every 5th Saturday and Sunday to raise money for this purpose.

The following are contributions by churches, Sundy schools and individuals to our convention work, and the names of persons taking the BAPTIST QUARTERLY and the *Christian Banner*, our National Baptist paper.

Institutes, Churches and Sunday schools of 1st quarter, 1897.

Institutes.—Shelby, $11.73; Wadesboro, $27.05; Concord, (Snow Storm) $1.10; Reidsville, $5; Winston, $15 25. Total Institute collections, $60.13.

Churches.—Ebenezer, Kings Mountain, Nov 2, $3.17; Alison Grove, Concord, Nov. 9, $3; 1st Baptist, Wadesboro, Nov. 15. $2.05; Phillipi, Lane's Church, $1.55; Flint Ridge, Marshville, Nov. 22, $1.69. Total for Nov. $11.46.

December.—1st Baptist, Reidsville, $3; Baptist Church, Wentworth, $1.80; Mt. Zion, Winston, $2 65. Total $6 45.

Jan. '97.—Baptist Church, High Point, $4.60; Baptist Sunday School, High Point, $1; Oak Grove Church, Sage Garden, 55 cents; Oak Grove Sunday School, Sage Garden, 66 cents; Mt. Pleasant, Winston, $2.15; Rising Ebenezer, Winston, $1.50; Liberty Zion, Trinity, $3.05; Liberty Zion Sunday School, Trinity, $1.10. Total $16.61.

Roll of honor, November, at Shelby.

Rev. J. C. Moore, 25; Rev. S. McCurry, 25; Rev. B. Bridgers, 25; Mr. Eli Roberts, 25; Rev. A. Johnson, 25; Joseph Oats, 25; Mrs. Rena Posten, 25; Mrs. M. A. Lutzs, 25; Martha Rippy, 25; Rev. W. C. Veal, 25; Jane Rippy, 25; R. W. Scott, 25.

Dec.—Phillip Wilson, 25; Clara Oats, 25; Castern Jemuson, 25; Moses Oats, 25; Rev. M. Beam, 25; Rev. W. A. Roberts, 25; Dr. J H. Cary, 25; Rev. T. J. Floyd, 25; Annie Jones, 25; Mary Kincade, 25; Mary Moore, 25; Susan Blanton, 25; Mittie McCurry, 25; Rev. S Shuford, 25.

Roll of honor at Wadesboro.

Rev. P. R. Lison, 25; Rev. A. D. Marshall, 25; Rev. R. Diggs, 25; Mrs. A. S. Loop, 25; Rev. S. M Wall, 25; Rev. D A. Lilmon, 25; Rev. Ratlipp, 25; Rev. A. Hammon, 25; Rev. J. F. Davis, 75; Mrs. E. Hall, 25; Rev. H D Tilman, 25; Rev. J. T. Ratlipp, 50; Rev. R. Tilman, 50; Dea. Weldon, Kendle, 25; Dea. Broadway, 25; Rev. B. J. Studervant, 25; Rev. J. A. Funderberk, 25; Rev. W. Y. Ingram, 25; Esther Sims, 25; Rev. P. G. Lowery, 25; Dea. A L. Leak, 25; Mariah Bennett, 25; Rev. A. C. McLendon, 25; Rev. P. D. Dunmas, 25; P. F. Maloy, 50; Mrs. S. Dunlap, 25; J. F. Bennett, 25; Mrs. E. Bancon, 25; Dea. S M. Marshal, 25; Rev. S. Dunlap, 25; Rev J. F. Bennett, 25; Rev. S. Bennett, 25; Miss E. P. Waugh, 25; Ellen Simons, 25; Dea. W. E. Kennel, 25; J. M. Bancom, 75; L. Bogans, 25; Rev. C. C. Horn, 25; Jessie Thomas, 25; Prof. S. S. Thomas, 25; Richard Hamons, 25; Julia McKoy, 25; Dea. D. Bennett, 25.

Roll of honor at Concord, Dec. 1, '96.

W. C. Colman, 25; Mrs. W. C. Colman, 25; Lula Jenkins, 25.

Roll of honor at Reidsville, Dec. 15, '96.

Mrs. C. C. Smmerville, 25; Mrs. A. Cartee, 25; Lucy Thompson, 25; Mary Martin, 25; G. E. Carter, 25; Mariah Martin, 25; Dr. J. A. Mundy, 25; Rev. F. N. Jones, 25; Annie McGeehe, 25; Mrs. J. C. Cruents, 25; M. L. Brenlfield, 25.

Roll of honor at Winston, Jan. 19. '97.

Rev. A. Hepler, 25; R. M. Mial, 25; Rev. G. W. Johnson, 75; E. E. Caldwell, 25; Rev. J. W. Jones, 25; Bo. P. Owen, $1.25; A. J. Brown, 30; W. M Cing, 25; Mrs. L. Lemmons, 25; Rev. G. W. Holland, 50; G. C. Edwards, 25; Rev. S. F. Conord, 25; Dr. H. A. Brown, 50; M. S. Toilver, 25; Dea. H. Alexander, 25; Addie Morris, $1; Rev. D. Johnson, 25; L. M Morton, 25; I. N. Pa'erson, 25; Robert Butler, 25; Henry Adams, 25; Prof. S. G. Atkins, 25.

Persons who subscribed to the QUARTERLY:

Rev. J. C. Hemphill, Franklin; Rev F. W. Wa'lace, Webster; Rev. J. F. Davis, Polkton; Samuel Stenard, G iflith; Margarett Chambers, Nimrod; Rev. H Palmer and D. J. Aery, Statesville; Rev. B. J. Studervant, Deep Creek; Rev. Robert Diggs, Pedee; J. W. Lowery, Rushing; Margarett Grady, Rushing; Rev. G. W. Brewer, Monroe; J. C. Lane, Franklin; Rev. P. D. Dremers, Wadesboro; P. Oxen, Winston; Addie Morris, and Mary L. Brown, Winston; Rev. G. W. Johnson and G. W. Holland, Winston; Rev. J. W. Jones, Winston; Dr. H. A. Brown, Winston; Rev. Hepler, Salem; Dr. J W. Jones, Winston; Rev. A. Wilburn, High Point; Rev. I. Little, Marshville; Rev. J. R. Nelson, Asheville; Rev. W. T. Minter, 250 Bomount. St. Asheville.

We rejoice to see our brethren and sisters take such commendable part in the success of our Convention work. This is what our good fathers prayed for, and the younger brethren rejoice to see. We are uniting in Western North Carolina for a great battle and victory to Baptist principles and Bible truth. Our young people are being stirred as never before by the educating influence of the New Era Institutes to work and make sacrifice for the successful accomplishment of our work.

We are very anxious to collect history of the work and progress, and of the lives of our aged fathers in the Baptist ministry and would thank any of the pastors to send in sketches of the work and labors of our old fathers. I feel that it is due their faithful and most worthy service that we younger pastors and minsters may collect all we can of their labors and lives and publish the same in our QUARTERLY from time to time.

P. F. MALOY,
Dist. Missionary.

CENTRAL DISTRICT.

Contributions from Central District Baptist church, Mebane. $1.40, Rev. J. H. Dunston, pastor.

Mrs. Moriah McAdan, 50 cents; Joseph Williams, 25; Albert Hester, 25; Mrs. Sarah Williams and others, 40 cents.

Institute at Savannah church, Cumberland county. Rev. W. H. Anders, pastor. Total contribution, $13.20.

Wm. McDonal, Beard, 50 cents; D. D. McDonald, Gray's Creek, 25; David Gilmore, Gray's Creek, 25; H. C. Edwards, Cedar Creek, 50; Mary Williams, Wade's Station, 50; A. G. McDonald, Gray's Creek, 35; Simpson Brown, Flat Springs, 25; Allen Johnson, Alderman's 50; B. J. Meloin, Gray's Creek, 25; Henry Hair, Gray's Creek, 19; E. R. J. Avant, Gray's Creek, 50; Foster Whitted, Gray's Creek, 50; James McNeil, Gray's Creek, 25; G. W. Johnson, Cedar Creek, 50; A. D. Meloin, Sherwood, 50.

Institute at Selma. Rev. E. B. Blake pastor.

Selma.—Miss Julia O'Neal, 25; N. E. Egerton, 50; John Graham, 65; William Lockhart, 25; Madison Blake, 25; Rev. A. A. Jones, —; Neison Smith, 50; Miss Lugenie Richardson 25; Miss J. H. Richardson, 25; Lugenie Langston, 25; Daisy Powers, 25; Mrs. Bettie Chavis, 25; Mrs. Eliza Richardson, 50; Laura Atkinson, 25; George O'Neal, 50; Bettie Eason, 25; Polly Langston, 25; Simon Price, 25; Celesia Blake, 50; Amanda Deems, 30; Rachel Smith, 25; Samantha Baker, 25; Elizabeth Jones, 50; Zilphia Alford, 30; Eddie Moore, 25; Eliza Atkins, 30; Jno. Lassiter, 25; Green Manly Lee, 25; Jennetha Alford, 30; Adeline Vine, 25, Sarah Mial, 25; Roberta Bunn, 25; Bertie Eason, 50; Celia Moore, 25; Rev. J. J. Jones, Clayton, 50. Collections, $7.65.

Lumberton Institute.—Lumberton—J. N. Booth, $1.00; Rev. A. H. Thompson, 1.00; Rev. J. D. Harrell, 25c; Rev. E. M. Thompson, 50; C. C. Singletary, 25; Rev. T. P. Norris, 50; Pierce Powell, 25; W. C. Pope, 25; Esther Moore, 50; Ed Smith, 25; Malcom McNeal, 25; Roxanna Thompson, 25; Jno. C. Grady, 50; William Cobb, 25; M. C. Moore, 25; Richard McNeal, 25; S. S. Stephens, 50; Lizzie Jenkins, 25; Rev. L. Melvin, 25; Mary Rowland, 25; J. C.

Inman, 50; Jennie Kelly, 25; E. B. McClellor Rowland, 25; Prof. D. P. Allen, 25; James Walker Hubb, 60; S. S. Stephens, 25; Rev. M. H. Hubb, 25; Rev. O. L. Stringfield, Raleigh, 1 00; Rev. George Williams, Register 50; Rev. D. J. Moore, Rosindale, 25; D. Brown, Cerogorda, 25; E. W. Thompson, Grady, 25; Thomas Davis, Ceregordo, 25; Pen Bonds, Grady, 50; Rev W. M. Jones, Maxton, 1 05; G. G Lasong, Grady, 25. Collections, $8 81.

Rockingham Institute.—Rockingham—Providence Baptist church, Rev. D. M. Jackson, pastor, $20 05.

Amanda Harris, 1 54; William Davis, 25; Florence A. Woodward, 25; Rev. W. H. Woodward, 50; Rev. W. C. Pope, 50; Rev. C. Campbell, 25; Samuel Ross, 25; Marilla McDonald, 25; Cattie J. Cooper, 25; Rev. R. Edward, 25; Mrs. A. J. Henderson, 25. Collections, 10 91; Miss Nora Campbell, 25; Nora Watkins, 25; Phebe Balding, 25; Rev. J. J. Hines, Hasty, 50; A. Elerby, Dockery's Store, 30; Caroline Dobbins' Hamlet, 25; Miss S. M. Dobbins, Hamlet, 50; Solomon Wall, Hamlet, 25; Hannah Simons, Hamlet, 25; Rev. S. M. Wall, Pedee, 25; Rev. A. Covington Dockery's Store, 50.

Laurinburg church reported by Rev. C. B. Harris, 75 cents.

Baptist church of Maxton, Rev. S. W. Dockery pastor, $2 00; Dr. W. R. Mapp, 25; R. B. Moorman, 25; church, 1 50.

Baptist church, Laurinburg, 2 00.
Baptist church, Nashville, Rev. J. J. Hines, pastor, 1 51; D. W. Monroe, MacNair, 25; Julia Monroe, MacNair, 25; James McLean, McNair, 25.

Spring Branch, Fontocal, Richmond county, 15c.

A. B. VINCENT,
Dis't. Missionary.

INSTITUTE WORK.

Our last quarter which closed with the month of January was telling in the New Era Institute work. Our first meeting was held with the two Baptist churches of Windsor, N. C. Although the success of the meeting depended largely on the pastors in and about Windsor, the meeting was a marked success. There were present twenty-three ministers and thirty-four deacons.

Rev. R. D. Cross, pastor of the white Baptist cnrch and Rev. L. M. Curtis, of Aulander, assisted the missionaries as teachers.

Rev. Cross, though comparatively young in the ministry, did himself and the work great credit on every occasion. Rev. Curtis had already commended himself to the brethren in the Tarboro meeting but the earnestness he manifested at Windsor brought him in touch with our brethren as never before. Said he, "So long as our colored brethren appreciate our help in the work so long will we help them." Brethren, let this "hint to the wise" be sufficient and with your means, with your influence and with your presence from time to time let our white brethren know you do appreciate their great help.

This meeting was the beginning of the work of Rev. C. C. Summerville as District Missionary. If any doubted the ability of our new District Missionary before this, when he closed his course of lectures every doubt was removed for he acquitted himself as a man.

Our next meeting was held with the First Baptist church of Washington, N. C.

Nowhere has a kindlier interest been manifested than was manifested by Rev. J. O. Alderman, of the white Baptist church. Not only did Bro. Alderman act his part nobly as a lecturer but said he, "Put me down for as much in your contributions as any other man gives."

This remark awakened a deeper interest throughout the vast audience and the result was realized in the fruitful gathering.

Prof. M. W. D. Norman reached us later on the meeting but not too late to act his part. And it may be said of him he was at his best. It would surprise us if after such a lecture the people of Washington were not awakened to the work of Christian education. It would be but repeating to speak of the work of Rev. Somerville in every meeting since the one at Windsor.

The next meeting we attended was at Wadesboro. We might justly style this as the Spiritual Institute for in no other meeting before or since have we realized such "an outpouring of the spirit." Some one may say it was because the Gen. Missionary was not there to extinguish the fire. Be that as it may when he reached the church it was at once evident that a work of no small proportions was going on among the people.

Sitting there swayed by the eloquence of Dr. Shepard "one could hear a pin drop." Two men only had done this great work and these men seemed to have vied with each other in quantity and quality and in setting forth the great truths contained in the lectures.

If the worth of a meeting could be realized in dollars and cents we would be safe in saying the one meeting at Wadesboro was worth the year's expenditures.

Rev. Maloy and the people of Wadesboro deserve great credit for such a meeting.

Our next meeting was at Savanah Baptist church. This church is about sixteen long "round-about" miles from Fayettville, in Rev. A. B. Vincent's district. It seemed too far for any of our white brethren to follow us, and too far for the Gen. Missionary again soon. So the entire course of thirteen lectures must be given by the missionaries.

This was the time and the place when and where Prof. Vincent could not modestly say, "let some one else take that lecture" but must act his part in these and never before did we know how proficiently he could act his part as a lecturer.

As in the Wadesboro meeting the part of the Gen. Missionary in the Selma meeting was but small. The meeting was conducted by Prof. Vincent but in no meeting were abler men secured as lecturers. Rev. J. H. Scott, of Shaw University; Rev. W. R. Cullom, of Wake Forest; Rev. J. J. Worlds, of Raleigh, and Rev. John E. White, of Raleigh. A simple mention of these names is sufficient to know the character of the meeting.

It seems to revolutionize that entire section and awaken in the people an endeavor for better living.

The first meeting for the third course of lectures under the plan of co-operation, was held at the solicitation of our white as well as colored brethren at Aulander.

Rev. L. M. Curtis, who assisted at Windsor; Rev. C. S. Brown, our ex-Gen. Missionary; Rev. J. B. Newton, and Rev. C. C. Somerville, were the lecturers.

All the brethren acquitted themselves creditably. We have never heard Rev. Brown do so well. The pastors took hold as never before. One brother said as a result of the impression made on him "money time and influence so far as he could see were on co-operation's altar" to be used at the direction of the missionaries."

Lumberton, already famous for good meetings, was our next place for an institute. The people showed their hopes for something good for their preparations were so ample, and expectations so far reaching until the rain which began the 2nd day, though it did not cease night or day until the close, did not stop the multitudes gathering from every direction and in every conceivable style of conveyance. Some whose patent had reached the patent office in Washington and some whose patent had never before reached Lumberton.

The pastors, Rev. S. W. Dockery, of the colored church, and Rev. J. M. Booth, of the white church, stuck to the meeting like men full of interest.

The simplicity of Rev. Booth's lectures always pleases our brethren. Rev. W. M. Jones, of Maxton, whom no one doubts as a scholar never spoke with such power to the brethren as he did at Lumberton.

It was expected that Rev. Jno. E. White, our efficient Corresponding Secretary would speak on the subject for which he is famed among our brethren, "Christian Education," but detained in Raleigh. He sent us Rev. O. S. Stringfield, soliciting agent for the Baptist Female College.

To look at Rev. Stringfield will give you one impression, to hear him will give the other. His power over his audience is wonderful. At one moment they may be filled with laughter, at the next they may be hushed in death-like stillness touched with his sublimnity.

The bad weather was against us at Winston, but many of the brethren in spite of the storm met us from time to time. Rev. Witherspoon, of Greensboro, and P. S. Lewis, of Salisbury, were there as they have been in several of our meetings to lecture.

The services of these two Baptist leaders are incalculable.

Dr. H. A. Brown, Rev. S. F. Conrad, of the white churches, Rev. G. W. Johnson, of the colored church, of Winston, and Rev. P. F. Maloy, were lecturers.

All the brethren seemed to be at their best, and when the meeting closed we felt truly we had a feast from beginning to the end. Our next meeting in Rev. Maloy's district was at High Point.

We had already heard so much of Rev. Kesler and Dr. Carrick we expected much from them and we did not fall short of our expectation.

Dr. Richardson and Rev. Maloy moved our brethren on the subject of mission work among the white brethren and colored brethren as we have rarely seen them moved on that subject.

Turning back to the Central District our next meeting was at Rockingham and there we had with us again Rev. J. H. Scott, of Shaw University and Rev. J. G Blalock, of the white church.

Every one who hears Prof. Scott feels proud of him as the head of the theological department of Shaw University. Rev. Blalock, though a young man, always impresses his audience with his thorough preparation and his earnestness.

Taking up our last meeting at Elizabeth City it concludes the institute work up to date.

Dr. Blackwell took the same course of lectures as last year, Biblical theology.

All who hear Dr. Blackwell feel that they have had something rare. Prof. Norman on preaching and church history was again at what we felt was his best or what gave us perfect satisfaction. Prof. Moore on Christian education the same as last year, gave a lecture full of thought.

To commend ministers and brethren who have been faithful in the work would make a long list for truly we can say from the mountains of North Carolina to the sea shore the brethren in the ministry and the laity are alive to the great work of the New Era Institutes and now in every district we are urged to hold meetings, for many of the brethren say and feel "we have never had anything like it." We feel especially proud of the eminent services of each of our District Missionaries of the warm welcome given us by our pastors, ministers, deacons and the brethren generally, especially are we proud of the spirit which characterizes our white brethren in their labors to do us good.

THEOLNGICAL TRAINING AT SHAW UNIVERSITY.

At no time since the organization of this school has the necessity for theological education been forgotten. Able men have given lectures in this department, and many students have gone forth to do successful service in this and other States. The work already done h is laid the foundation for a much wider work in the future. The students of Shaw who have gone forth —preachers, teachers, lawyers and physicians, have set a much higher standard for ministerial service, as a consequence the demand for better

TRAINED MEN

for the University is imperative. What would satisfy the churches five years ago will not avail now, men of better training and better scholarship are needed. Not only are such men needed, but they are imperatively demanded As the churches advance in wealth and culture so must the ministry advance. This improvement will always be prompted by the energetic and conservated pastor.

LIKE PASTOR, LIKE PEOPLE.

Our churches will not advance beyond their leaders, yet the spirit of the age is surely pointing to advance along all lines. This is no less true in the ministry than in national things. If our churches are not to fall behind in the rush of progress then our young men and women must see to it that they have the best training. Every church should have a student at Shaw, and at least every Association should have a student for the ministry. Would it not be well for each Association, at their next meeting to arrange for at least one student of theology to be here for next year? This would make a beginning and only a beginning of what this school would do for the State.

WHO SHOULD COME TO SHAW.

All young men who believe themselves called of God to preach the gospel, should take at least three years study in the Theological Department of Shaw University, this will enable them to get a fair mastery of the Bible and of the English language. They will thus be able to give to their people fresh and helpful sermons and to lead them into a much wider usefulness.

There is another class who can be helpful, we mean pastors who have already begun work but who feel that they should have a better education. These will be welcomed, though they cannot remain for more than two or three months.

SUBJECTS TAUGHT.

The work done in this department includes careful study of the Old Testament and New Testament outlines. This course is designed to acquaint the student with the main historical material of the Bible. This year the classes have covered the outlines of the Old Testament and the life of Christ. Next year they will take up the study of the apostolic church as shown in the Acts and Epistles. In addition to the above they have had lectures in church history, missions and constant instruction in church policy and pastoral duties as the subjects present themselves in the study of the life of Christ. As the students progress in their work instruction will be given more at length in Church History, Interpretation, Pastoral Theology and Organization of the Church. The management of the Prayer Meeting, the organization and conduct of Young Peoples' Societies and of Sunday-schools. In a word it is prepared to give help to enable the young pastor to take up his work with good prospect of success.

Those who come to Shaw University may be assured of a most cordial welcome.

SOME OBSERVATIONS ON THE LITERARY STATUS OF SHAW UNIVERSITY.

Three mistakes Shaw University has never made—she has never *focussed, narrowed* and *limited* in her culture, never sacrificed the larger side, on the contrary, she has constantly believed that her students are human beings with instincts, feelings, mental perceptions, infinite relations, with souls, all making a unit with character that must have free play at every stage or a defectively trained man must be the result. She has known that the "THREE R'S" contribute but a meager amount to any man's education. In a word, she has steadfastly maintained that it is important for the black man not to lose sight of the infinitely great while studying the infinitely small.

Another thing, Shaw does not make the mistake of trimming her sails to suit every breeze that blows, however favorable some of these seems, but prefers rather to stand still, anchored on truth, if need be for a time.

And thirdly; Shaw does not and

will not arrogate to herself too much importance, but chooses rather to speak through the lives and acts of those sent out.

Therefore, it can be said with reason, that the true answer to Shaw University is her men and women scattered throughout the nine states and two territories of America, in Africa and on several islands of adjacent seas. These men and women, without bluster and noise, but silently, with perseverence, presence of trained minds, deep sense of responsibility, and with devotion to duty are easy leaders wherever found, as farmers, teachers, heads of high schools, academies or departments of colleges and universities, whether as preachers, doctors, druggists, missionaries, lawyers, whatever they may be doing, they are doing their work without fear or grace of any man but the Great Spirit. They are doing it better than the average of any race engaged in the same work under equal conditions.

Any institution founded as this one upon such broad truth cannot but advance with the advancing times.

Thus at Shaw, since there has been no time lost in flirting with the *bedazzling popular craze*, that God made one man for the deepest and broadest culture along all lines, and the other for the plow, axe and hammer, all have been united on the one idea of training the fitted leaders, and to train these in the same way that leaders have always been trained, viz: by studying past civilizations in the languages of those civilizations, and endeavoring to be exact along all lines, fundamentals first, and then everything else that is within the reach of the human mind.

At Shaw therefore, a visitor may expect to see men and women too, in college pursuits in the forenoon determining a parabolical curve, locating a light house, given just three angles, studying laws of electricity and of reflex action, sympathizing with a betrayed and burning Troy, communing with Horace, feeling with Andromache, criticising American and English authors, debating and doing everything ever done anywhere, and in some cases doing very acceptable work, while in the afternoons these same men and women are at their work benches, some in the blacksmith shop, some painting, women working, sewing, while some men are assiduously playing ball, throwing hammer, playing tennis, riding first grade wheels and doing just the things in every way which aid in their full development of mind and body. And best of all, out of nearly four hundred students in all departments, all but five are active Christians working on the grounds with the Y. M. C. A. and other Christian organizations, for their own and for the salvation of the fellows who may do useful service at several mission points in the city including the jail every Sunday, street work for God and several Sunday-schools in needy parts.

Such pursuits, such systematic, broad training along all lines with perfect freedom and no limitations except those on the individual and separate souls of students must surely be the true training for the black boy and girl as for the blue. With the highest ideals constantly before the undergraduate, coming in close range of the best thought and of the leaders of thought by the happy location of Shaw here at North Carolina's capital, and being kept in touch with the spirit of this rushing, progressive electric age, it is no wonder that they are beginning to plan more wisely for longer, steadier, exacter training. Students are pursuing a liberal education here with no desire for titles or degrees except they come as a matter of course by merit and mean the same to them as any other race. They seem to know full well that high-sounding, empty names have already puffed up and made many appear so ridiculous, that now it is much better not to have any name but plain John Smith, the *doer*. It means much when a race of people begin so early to seek what is real useful and essential, when they begin to be able to prefer the real to the seeming. And so with a well arranged curriculum as will soon be with the kind of trained instructors as Shaw has always, for the most part, had with God at the helm as ever, under such leadership as Shaw has been peculiarly blessed, and with students willing and desirous of taking plenty of time, if by so doing, no training is denied them which they are capable of having. With such an outfit as this Shaw University will grow and perfect herself until all the world will call her blessed.

N. C. BRUCE.

WATERS NORMAL INSTITUTE.

This prosperous institute, now ten years old, is regarded throughout the State not only as the most successful enterprise of the kind fostered by the colored Baptist, but excelling many other institutions created and existing under more favorable circumstances. The wonderful progress which has so signally marked the development of this work is due largely to the indefatigible exertions of its founder, Rev. C. S. Brown. The founder is well and favorably known throughout the State, and honored and loved by all Baptists. He commands and holds the esteem and confidence of the people among whom he labors as but few men are able to do. He has year after year collected hundreds and even thousands of dollars out of the people of eastern Carolina for this work, and has by persistent effort founded a school now estimated to be worth nearly twelve thousand dollars. The school has been wisely located in the "black belt" of the State, in easy reach of the people, whose educational advantages have heretofore been meager. It deserves success, and success has been achieved.

Three buildings have been erected for the accommodation of students. The first is a two-story structure, containing a chapel and recitation rooms. The second is a dormitory for young men, where ample provision is made to entertain thirty. The last is a handsome edifice, known as "Reynold's Hall," and is admired by all who see it for its design, beauty and completeness. It is remarkable to consider how loyally the people in the immediate section have stood by this work, they have responded most liberally to every appeal made to maintain and extend the school.

Notwithstanding the cry of "hard times," the present year has so far brought to this school increased success, and its trustees are congratulating themselves over the favorable outlook.

Nearly two hundred students have been enrolled and a large increase has been made in the boarding department. Four teachers are constantly employed to give instructions, supplemented by five student teachers. The instructors sustain a favorable place among the educators of the State for ability and experience.

In addition to other multiplied duties, the President teaches four hours each day. Miss Cora B. Person, well known throughout the State as a professional teacher and a lady of rare culture and refinement, is employed as lady principal, and renders valuable service in the school room.

Mrs. Amaza J. Brown gives instruction in history, elocution and literature, and has been pronounced by competent judges as "excellent."

The fourth teacher is Mr. J. B. Catus, a gentleman of broad experience in the work, having followed teaching since leaving Hampton, about twenty years ago. With the facilities as heretofore described, and with a faculty competent, cultured, experienced, Waters Institute easily ranks as the leading institution for the education of colored youth east of Raleigh.

Already scores of young men and women educated there have gone out into life and are making a record which the founders of the school may justly be proud of.

It must however be remembered that a school must live by the charity of the people. It has behind it no endowment or permanent income, but must obtain "daily bread" by faith in Providence and confidence in the people. It stands out as a proud monument of race pride and indicates what might be done by unselfish concentration of our mites. To fully appreciate what is being done through this school, and how it is enshrined in the affections of the people, it is necessary for one to visit the place. It is a work to be proud of, and should have the united encouragement of the Baptists of the State.

So remarkable has been the success of the work that the American Baptist Home Mission Society, though burdened with an annual deficit, contributes towards paying the salaries of teachers, nearly twelve hundred dollars a year.

It is confidently believed that, when our brethren learn the real merits of the school they will cheerfully reach forth liberal hands to make Waters Institute what it should be, the chief educational center in eastern North Carolina.

SHILOH INSTITUTE.

WARRENTON, N. C.

This school was organized May 1st, 1885, and known as Warrenton High School.

The property containing two buildings and eight acres of land. Was purchased some years previous by the Shiloh Baptist Association.

Eight brethren within the bounds of said Association constituted a Board of Trustees under whose supervision and direction the school has been conducted.

By the arrangement of a number of the citizens of Warrenton known as the Warrenton Educational Association J. A. Whitted was secured as the principal, Mrs. Florence Ward as assistant. The school constantly grew in number and influence until some years later it was incorporated as Shiloh Institute.

Though the 12 years of i's history a number of efficient men and women have been employed from time to time as teachers, Misses C. B. Person, Nannie E. Hawkins. Messrs. J. P. Williams, B. Thornton and for the two years the State Normal School was attached to it, Prof. H. H Falkner and Dr. J. A Brockett.

Great has been the influence and usefulness of Shiloh Institute.

More than a hundred teachers and preachers have gone forth as light-bearers in different parts of North Carolina and other States.

J. A. Whitted having resigned the principalship in 1895 Rev. M. E. Hall of Littleton, N. C. was elected as his successor.

With Rev. Hall at the head and the Board of Trustees whose experience is somewhat extended, much is hoped for and expected of Shiloh Institute.

ROANOKE INSTITUTE.

ELIZABETH, CITY, N. C.

This Institute is the last organized among the Baptist schools of North Carolina and yet by far not the least.

The school is not yet a year old being organized last fall.

The property was purchased by the Association whose name it bears and a set of strong men constitute the Board of Trustees. Prof. M. W. D. Norman, who for several years was Prof. of theology in Shaw University, is the principal. The choice convinces us of the wisdom of the Board.

A son of old Roanoke when called to serve his people he left a position which any one might feel proud of to assume the new duties.

Prof. A. S. Dunston, whom no one shares more of the confidence of his brethren, together with the three females constitute the faculty.

At a leap the school has surpassed most of the other schools of the city in numbers and bids fair to rival any school in the East.

The trustees are preparing to erect a commodious building upon the site. Notices are coming in from every direction of students expecting to enter in the ensuing year.

The people in the surrounding churches are fast becoming alive to the work and we think the day is not far distant when the Roanoke Institute will take its place beside the leading institutions of the State.

DEAR BRETHREN :—I am preparing a list of the superintendents of Baptist Sunday-schools. I hope to get every one in the State on this list. I can meet the schools better and do them more good if I can prepare this list. I sincerely hope every Moderator of Associations who have not sent me a minute, will do so as early as possible.

Dear pastors, please send me the names of every Sunday-school superintendent under your charge at once. I want to try and do your people good, help me in this effort. Let the whole State of Baptist move this year as one man.

Please attend to this at once brethren. Yours in the work,

JOSEPH PERRY.

NEUSE RIVER INSTITUTE.

WELDON, N. C.

This Institute was established in the fall of 1889.

The property was purchased by the Neuse River Baptist Association. It is controlled by a Board of Trustees and Executive Board appointed from year to year by said Association.

The school has been under the management of Prof. A. P. Robinson.

It is the intention of the Board to erect such buildings and secure such teachers as will enable them to make the school the equal of any school of similar grade in the State.

With such men as the Association has at the head, we have every reason to hope the day is not far distant when Roanoke Institue will do the work contemplated.

The school opened the spring session with twenty-eight pupils and now has a regular attendance of seventy-nine.

Tuition, $1, 75 cents and 50 cents.

Board can be had in the town of Weldon at reasonable rates.

No pains will be spaired to have the school opened next fall with far better equipments, and a good faculty. It is hoped the friends will avail themselves of the superior advantages the school offers.

NEW ERA INSTITUTE—THIRD SESSION.

The New Era Institute has proved a great success. It is no longer an experiment. Hundreds of pastors and others are enthusiastic over it, declaring that it is one of the greatest blessings that has ever come to the colored Baptists of this State. They look forward with eager interest to the third meeting, the general programme of which is given in this leaflet. We hope to see every pastor and many others who were not at the previous Institute. Brethren, you cannot afford to miss this rare opportunity.

There will be twelve lectures at each Institute (unless special circumstances prevent), and seventy-two lectures for the entire 3 years' course. The subjects will include Biblical Theology, Church History, The Ministry, Christian Education, Missions, The Church and its Work, and other practical matters. It will be a kind of theological school brought nigh to the people. The best of available talent, both white and colored, will be secured for lecturers.

Everybody is invited. Every minister should attend every Institute. It will be of great value to him. It is proposed to publish a "Roll of Honor" of ministers who pursue the entire course of lectures. We look to the pastors to lead their people by word and by example in the new movement that promises so much for our cause in this State. Come, pastors, and bring with you as many of your people as you can.

Each lecture will be followed by a discussion, for about thirty minutes, when members of the conference may ask questions and present their views on the subject.

The following is the outline of lectures for the second Institute:

BIBLICAL THEOLOGY—FOUR LECTURES.

Redemption. Coming of a Redeemer. Significance of His name.

His testimony concerning Himself and His mission. His Divinity.

2. *Redemption.* Christ as the Light of the World; His teachings; miracles; life. Our example.

3. *Redemption.* The death of Christ; voluntary; his words concerning the purpose of his death. Teachings of the New Testament; the blood of Christ; life for life.

4. *Redemption.* His Resurrection; Ascension; intercession at the right hand of God.

CHURCH HISTORY—TWO LECTURES.

1. *Christianity in Europe from 500, to 1517.* The Roman Catholic Church supreme. Church and State. Worship of Images. Purgatory. Indulgences. Transubstantiation. Monasticism. Celibacy of the clergy. Capital punishment for heresy. General character of the middle or "dark ages."

2. *The Great Reformation.* Reformers before this. The Waldenses, and Albigenses: Wycliffe, Huss. *Luther:* a monk; visit to Rome and conversion; his theses; excitement; at Diet of Worms; his translation of the Bible; hymns; rapid spread of the new doctrines. Estimate of Luther's character and work.

THE GOSPEL MINISTRY—ONE LECTURE.

1. *Preparation of Sermons.* Importance of careful preparation. Prayer. Meditation. Bible study. How to study the Bible. Every sermon should have a plan and object. Criticism of plans of sermons.

CHRISTIAN MISSIONS—TWO LECTURES.

1. *Foreign Mission Work of Colored Baptists.* When begun. Total contributions. Number of missionaries. Fields of labor. Results. Obligations for the evangelization of Africa. Great opportunity.

2. *Foreign Mission work of the Northern and Southern white Baptists.* Their organizations. Fields occupied. Missionaries. Annual results. Prospects.

CHRISTIAN EDUCATION—ONE LECTURE.

1. *The growing demand for educated men and women among the colored people.* As american citizens, to know what they should do. As ministers of intelligent congregations. As teachers in the Sunday-school and public schools; educated young women needed here. As editors, physicians, professors in higher schools, etc.

THE CHURCH—TWO LECTURES.

1. *Reception of Members by the Church.* The general custom. Evils of hasty action. Relation of their Christian experience or conversion. What of visions? What are the Scriptural requirements for church membership?

Church Discipline. Scriptural authority for it. Necessity both for the offender's good and the honor of the church. Spirit in which it should be administered. The proper steps to take. How personal differences should be adjusted.

REV. J. A. WHITTED,
Raleigh, N. C.
General Missionary.

INSTITUTE OF SAVANAH CHURCH. CUMBERLAND COUNTY. DEC. 16-18.

This meeting conducted entirely by the District and General missionaries Vincent and Whitted was considered by those who attended intensly instructive and interesting through the whole three days. Indeed it has become very evident that some of our very best meetings are those held far out in the country from railroads. Rev. W. H. Andrews and his good people loyally stood by the missionaries and the meeting from beginning to close. Mr. B. J. Melvin and others personally and keenly felt the responsibility of making the occasion a success. Revs. N. B. Dunham, G. R. Richardson, H. C. McDonald, T. M. Council and others here as before in other meetings made considerable sacrifice to make the meeting a success Rev. W. H. Andrews and his people are to be congratulated for the good results secured. Let us have more like it.

A. B. VINCENT.

ROCKINGHAM INSTITUTE. FEB. 2-4.

In interest, devotion and good results, we would place the Rockingham Institute held with Rev. D. M. Jackson's church not a whit behind that of other meetings. Sickness for the first time caused the District Missionary to be behind a few hours in opening the meeting, however the faithfulness of the General Missionary showed itself by opening the exercies promptly. In company with Rev. J. H. Scott, the gentlemanly and profound theologian of Shaw University we reached Rockingham in time for the evening services. Rev. Scott was present and at once reached the hearts of his audience, and during his whole stay held the audience spell-bound. He reached the climax in his lectures the last night when he gave one of the most practical thoughtful, yet simple, addresses on Christian education yet delivered. The brethren of the State can but feel profoundly grateful for the wisdom of Brother Scott's selection and the fact that he has cast his lot among North Carolina Baptists.

The University is to be congratulated on the securing of his services for the work contemplated. Rev. J. G. Blalock and Rev. W. H. Fulford, of Rockingham, put in their usual excellent services which did so much to help the work last year. The District Missionary delivered one talk on missions and Rev. J. A. Whitted ably and acceptably carried out the remainder of the programme even to details. The church at this point, though weak, gives promise of a tower of strength for the future. Rev. Jackson and Rev. W. H. Woodwrad who are always engaged in some noble enterprise to promote the Baptist cause stood heroically by the meeting during the three days. Rev. Woodward used his paper, the Pedee Union, to interest the people in the work. Possibly at no place have the sisters of the church done more for the meetings than at Rockingham. Some of the sisters contributed more than the brethren. We close the first quarter of the second year in gratefulness to God and deep appreciation to all friends who have assisted.

Fraternally,
A. B. VINCENT.

Rev. G. W. Moore, of Fayetteville, succeeds Rev. C. C. Somerville at Reidsville, and Rev. H. H. Hines succeeds Rev. Moore.

AT LUMBERTON AGAIN.

The third series of lectures for the Central District were commenced in Sandy Grove church, Lumberton, Jan. 12, 1897.

We were able to get some idea of the growth and deepening interest which has been in progress during one year, for just one year ago the work in this district began at Lumberton. It would have rejoiced the hearts of our friends who have sacrificed so much for "co-operation" to have witnessed the great change which has come to this section in only one year. Although the weather grew very inclement and muddy in travel, yet crowds could be seen during the various sessions pulling their way promptly to every service, sometimes going for miles to and fro, in order to get everything said. The liberality too in giving to support the work notwithstanding the hard times was another indication of the deep and spiritual growth of truth in the hearts of the people. Christian growth unmistakably evidences itself in self-denials. It is indeed a bad sign to see individuals and churches grow narrow and closer in giving to support God's work. Possibly in no meeting has there been a more willing disposition to contribute. Pastor S. W. Dockery who has recently taken charge has indeed a promising field of labor. Deacon W. C. Pope and Lumber River Association are building up a school here which they hope to make a fitting or preparatory work to Shaw University. Some of these good people are so enthusiastic over the school that they are disposed to call it "Shaw University." This we told them could not be, then they said it must be a department or preparatory work to Shaw which we heartily endorsed. This intense desire which has absorbed these people for something nobler and better is an encouraging omen indeed of what co-operation will do wherever it is given a trial.

Able and instructive lectures were delivered by Revs. J. N. Booth of Lumberton, W. M. Jones, of Maxton, and O. L. Stringfield, of Raleigh, who in his eloquent speech on education, said Shaw University was one of the best schools in the world.

Rev. D. J. Moore preached acceptably the first night, and Rev. J. A. Whitted, as usual, did very excellent work through the whole meeting.

Thanks are due Rev. Booth for his interest during the Institute, to say the least, Bro. Booth has shown himself not only one of the best teachers, but one of the broadest and most liberal white Baptist ministers in North Carolina.

Rev. S. W. Dockery, as usual, did his best for the Institute. His people deserve credit for their devotion to the cause and deep interest in the work.

A. B. VINCENT.

SELMA INSTITUTE.

The New Era Institute at Selma the last week of December '96 was eminently successful.

Rev. E. B. Blake, the pastor left no stone unturned, although he had but little time to get his church and people ready.

The District Missionary was ably assisted by Rev. J. H. Scott and

Prof. W. R. Cullom of the Bible Departments of Shaw University and Wake Forest College. Rev. J. J. Worlds and Rev. Jno. E. White, Prof. J. W. Byrd of Smithfield also assisted and Gen. Missionary J. A. Whitted. The town of Selma was stirred for a higher and better life. The following are some of the many expressions made by those who attended the Institute.

"I wish we had the meeting every month," "I have not been hungry this week, I could not eat I was so full."

"I feel that I am going to live closer to God than ever before. Have never seen such a meeting."

"I was so thankful to see white and colored brethren in the pulpit together—and working together."

"Thank God for sending white and colored brethren to help us."

"If I could just keep up with these meetings I would be exactly fixed."

"I could not stay home and work. I was so afraid I would miss something."

"I only came to stay one day. Have been trying to go home but could not." This was said the last day.

"Yesterday morning I just felt like I was set free."

"Was so restless I could not be satisfied until I struck the path to the church."

"Lord help these people to keep coming down here."

Many other similar statements could be given. These expressions were made on the last day by the older mothers and fathers who went so full that the cup of joy ran over during the praise service. These expressions may give some hints as to the results of New Era Institutes in North Carolina.

We would mention the hospitality of Dr. Vick and Mr. N. E. Egerton, prominent white citizens of the Methodist church here, who so kindly and royally entertained Rev. Scott and Prof. Cullom.

Credit is due all the citizens, white and colored, Methodists and Baptists for assistance.

A. B. VINCENT.

INSTITUTES YET TO BE HELD.

THIRD COURSE LECTURES.

Rocky Mount,	March,	9	11
Clayton,	"	16	18
Charlotte,	"	23	25
Newberne,	" 30,	Apr.	1
Raleigh,	April	6	8
Monroe,	"	13	15
Wilmington,	"	20	22
Seaboard,	"	27	29
Gastonia,	May,	4	6
Edenton,	"	11	13
Graham,	"	18	20
Rutherfordton,	"	25	27
Clinton,	June,	1	3
Red Springs,	"	8	10
Williamsboro,	"	15	17

It was announced recently that Dr. I. T. Tichenor, the efficient Correspondent Secretary of the Home Mission Board of the Southern Baptist Convention was lying very ill. Dr. Tichenor has done a great work among his own brethren, and he has been a great friend to mission work among the colored people. If pleasing to God's will, we trust he may yet be spared to the great work of which he is the leader.

WHARTON NORMAL AND INDUSTRIAL SCHOOL.

CHARLOTTE, N. C., Feb. 4, 1894.

DEAR BRO. WHITTED:—Referring to your asking information concerning our school work, in reply would say that our school is in a very prosperous condition at the present time under the management of Mr. Robert W. Brown of Winston, N. C., and Mr. W. T. Christian, of the same place as assistant teacher and instructor of vocal and instrumental music. The average attendance is about 75. The enrollment being 96.

The Wharton Normal and Industrial School was organized in January of 1894, and opened in the lecture room of the First Baptist church, Charlotte, N. C., with 12 scholars. The school was conducted throughout the session by Mrs. M. T. Pope, under the auspices of the above named church.

The school was again opened the following session, Rev. C. H. Williamson was made principal, with Miss Alice Hughes of Henderson, assistant and music teacher. The school closed at the end of this, having been a very successful term, having had enrolled during the session 105 students. The Board decided that the lecture room was not suitable to accommodate the increasing numbers and erected with the help of friends a school building. Without money we began the erection of a building. Dr. H. M. Wharton, the great evangelist of Baltimore, hearing of our urgent need of a school of this nature in Western North Carolina, came at once to our rescue, giving us a helping hand. In recognition of which the Board voted that the school should be known as the Wharton Normal and Industrial School. The school is located in Charlotte, which is the centre of a large colored population, and the seat of many industries, remarkable for its business enterprise and progressiveness, and is healthy and inviting as a place of residence. The First Baptist church of Charlotte has ample grounds near its house of worship of which it gave a lot for the erection of a school building.

Prof. Brown succeeds Rev. C. H. Williamson as principal.

HOW MAINTAINED.

The school is maintained by the tuition of the scholars by voluntary contribution, and through the sacrificing efforts of the Board and teachers who have had but little to draw upon.

ITS NEEDS.

The school is greatly in need of funds at this time. If there be a friend to the work anywhere, who may read this sketch, and is interested in the educational work among our people please aid us a little.

ITS OBJECT.

The object of the Board is to improve the mental and moral condition of our people by instructing them in letters and work.

Yours,
A. SHEPARD.

Rev. L. T. Christmas, of the Central Baptist church, of Wilmington, has been installed as pastor of the Baptist church of Charleston, W. Va. North Carolina gives him up with reluctance, but we bid him God speed in his new charge.

ADDIE MORRIS SCHOOL.

Winston, N. C., Feb. 18, 1897.
Bro. Whitted,

Dear Sir:—Your letter received and contents noted, and will say in reply that I have 79 girls and 25 boys now enrolled in my school, total 104 scholars. My school was organized Oct. 1st, 1887. I have never had any assistant only when Miss Turner was here.

I worked up North five years and supported the school myself, and the last five years I have been working under the Home Mission Society of Chicago, a salary of $20 per month. $10 has been donated $50 by the Rowan Association, which met here last August, and $5 by the Womens' Convention that met at Salisbury.

Out of the $20 salary my other expenses are taken out, I furnish my own coal, wood and things that I use in my school and of course I do without a lot of things myself in order to meet my other expenses. I have only done this by economy learned while up North.

We have five afternoon sessions for Bible studies and industry. The children are progressing nicely. We also have Sunday school for the children. It has been organized four years, and it is quite a success. We have seven teachers for our Missionary Sunday School. Our average attendance is from 95 to 100.

Respectfully,
ADDIE C. MORRIS.
Cor. 6th and Chestnut Sts., Winston, N. C.

For the present session—the Charlotte Normal School has enrolled one hundred and fifteen students.

The daily average attendance being about seventy or seventy-five. The school is taught in the lecture room of the Ebenezer Baptist church and is composed of two departments, viz: Primary and Normal. The students of the primary department are those commonly taught in primary studies. The Normal Department—the same. School is in good condition—progressing successfully. This is a preparatory school for Shaw University.

C. L. DAVIS,
Principal.

CEDAR GROVE ACADEMY.

Roxboro, N. C.

Organized 1881. This school as yet has only one building and one acre of land near the corporate limits of Roxboro, on the road leading to Oxford, N. C.

Rev. C. L. Ragland was the first principal and served about four years. Afterward Rev. A. R. Satterfield assumed charge and conducted it in connection with the public school. Rev. R. H. Harris was his successor and is now at the head of the work.

Probably no county in the State stood in greater need of such an institution and comparatively none has done greater good.

This school has supplied teachers for almost the entire county and section. The location is healthy and good, and the school is crowded from time to time. It is hoped that the Board of Trustees may soon be able to erect buildings adequate to the needs of the school and it may accomplish a still greater good.

GARYSBURG HIGH SCHOOL.

ORGANIZED 1877 BY DR. R. I. WALDEN AND FRIENDS.

Board of Trustees:—Rev. N. F. F. Roberts, D. D., Oberlin, N. C.; Deacon W. Coats, Seaboard, N. C.; Rev. S. G. Newsome, Margarettsville, N. C.; Robert L. Perry, Louisburg, N. C.; Deacon Philip Garris, Garysburg, N. C.; L. B. Walden, Garysburg, N. C.; W. H. Haithcocks, Seaboard, N. C.

Faculty:—Rev. R. I. Walden, D. D., President; Robt. L. Perry, Teacher Mathematics; Alice Hughes, Preceptress in Music and Normal Teacher; Cora E. Walden, Teacher Preparatory Department; Mrs. R. I. Walden, Matron; J. W. Blacknall, State Teacher.

Location.—This school is beautifully located east of Garysburg, in fifteen minutes walk of the post office. This is the most healthy location in this district, good drainage, using water medicinal, non malarial. The health of this school for the past fourteen sessions justified the above statement. The instructions imparted to students of this school have afforded ample satisfaction in the past, but our facilites for the future are far superior to that of the past, having made more room for female lodging, and all the principal teachers are well equipped for the work. Furthermore this school was incorporated by the last Legislature of North Carolina. Also by the influence of Congressman Cheatham, the Public Library of the Second Congressional District has been placed at the school for the benefit of the students and patrons, these books are accessible to all free of charge. We have enlarged the girl's building and we can accommodate a much larger number than we have in the past, we are also making general improvements so that the coming session may be the grandest and most beneficial to any previous session.

This school has now enrolled eigthy-two pupils.

Seventy-five young men and women have been sent out as teachers in the public schools and high schools of North Carolina and Virginia.

Some of our leading ministers of Eastern North Carolina have been largely prepared under the instruction of Dr. Walden.

Twenty have gone out as graduates of the school and are quite meritorious in their labors. The school is supported at a great sacrifice to the teachers and friends, and especially to the president, Dr. Walden, who very often uses the money from his churches to carry on the school work.

Dr. Walden not only attends regularly upon the class room work but is forced to preach at two or more of our prominent churches for the maintenance of himself and largely the school. It is our pleasure to say of him that he ranks easily among our best preachers in North Carolina and we commend the work to the favorable consideration of friends North and South as fully worthy of your contributions and to parents and guardians as worthy of your patronage.

EDITOR BAPTIST QUARTERLY.—

Please allow me space in your valuable columns to say a few words concerning our pastor, Rev. J. W. Wood.

We feel that he deserves much credit for what he has done and is doing, as a young minister. Under his leadership we are succeeding wonderfully well. He is a Christian gentleman, and a preacher, in every sense of the word as pastor. Before he took charge of our church fifteen dollars was a large collection for us to raise in one day, but since he has been with us we have raised as much as $150 at one collection. He also raised at Gaston church, of which he is also pastor, $150 at one collection.

We are also glad to say that our new church is nearly completed, and will be one of the finest churches in Northampton county.

We can only say bless God for such a man as Rev. J. W. Wood.

Yours Respectfully,
COOL SPRING BAPTIST CHURCH.
Jan. 15, 1897.

WILMINGTON, N. C.,
Feb. 5, 1897.

MR. J. A. WHITTED, Raleigh, N. C.—*Dear Sir:*—Your letter came duly to hand some time ago, owing to illness of myself is why I have not written before now, and for which I hope you will pardon my long delay. In reply to yours of the 11th ult: The membership of the First Baptist church of Wilmington, N. C., corner of 5th and Campbell streets is two hundred, and was represented at the Baptist State Convention by Rev. Joseph Spells, pastor of said church, and donated one dollar.

We are struggling and trying to complete our church, and there is some indebtedness hanging over us and it will take one thousand dollars more to complete it. We ask the sympathy of all.

Respectfully Yours,
REV. JOSEPH SPELL, *Pastor.*
H. C. WILLIAMS, *Clerk.*

We are informed that there is one N. S. Scott claiming to be a representative of our Convention or of the Southern Convention. Brethren, beware of men who come to you thus. We have six regularly appointed missionaries, Revs. J. Perry and McRansom, representing the Sunday-school work; and Revs. P. F. Maloy, A. B. Vincent, C. C. Somerville and J. A. Whitted representing the church work. If others are appointed we will announce their appointment.

Col. Charles Banes, of Phila., a a friend of Shaw University, is now numbered with the many friends of Shaw who have died in the past few years, and we can only look to a kind Providence to raise up other friends for our struggling University.

※

Rev. A. R. Satterfield, Moderator of East Cedar Grove Association is in the city, and we fear he contemplates leaving the State. Rev. Satterfield, though comparatively young, has done and is doing a great work in his section both as teacher and preacher.

It would be well if our people could know the worth of men before they leave them.

NOTICE.

The next State Teachers' Association will convene at Shaw University, Raleigh, June 15-20. An unusual programme will be arranged embodying such practical school room work under specialists as will help every teacher in the State. The most eminent educators and experts, white and colored, will assist from time to time during the week's meeting and it is to be hoped that fully 500 teachers will attend. President Alderman, of the State University, and Dr. McIver, of the Normal and Industrial school for white girls at Greensboro. President Meserve and Dr. Roberts of Shaw University, Profs. S. G. Atkins, of Normal school, Winston; Dr. E. E. Smith, State Normal, Fayetteville, and other prominent educators will be secured so that any who comes will feast to a variety of treats during the whole week.

Very respectfully,
A. B. VINCENT.
Pres. State Teachers' Association.

BREWERVILLE, LIBERIA,
WEST C. AFRICA,
Jan. 31, 1896.

REV. J. A. FULLER, Oxford, N. C.—Dear Friend and Brother:

On the first Sunday in August last I opened a protracted meeting at Zion Grove, Brewerville, which resulted in the conversion of sixteen precious souls, twelve of which I baptized on the first Sunday in September and administered the Lord's Supper to a well filled house.

The most of the new members are natives and need to be taught "to observe all things whatsoever I have commanded you," otherwise we may expect them to return to their old country habits of idolatry.

Since my return to Liberia I have baptized and given the right hand of fellowship to 31 persons. Our Sunday-school is in a flourishing condition, with an average of fifty.

I suppose you know I am no longer connected with Ricks Institute, but that I am now at Brewerville endeavoring to found my school work in connection with my church.

By the last mail I received a copy of *The National Baptist Magazine,* from which I learned that the Baptist Foreign Mission Convention, under whose auspices I was returned to my former work here, has gone into the National Baptist Convention.

From March 20th, 1893 at which time I was commissioned in the city of Richmond, Va., with a salary of $500 00 per annum, up to last June, at which time I was forced to resign my post at Ricks Institute, for reasons given the Board. I had served under the auspices of the B F. R. Convention two years and three months, against which the Corresponding Secretary, Mrs. L. A. Coles, has remitted to me only $375 00, leaving a ballance now due me of $750 00. Who is now responsible for my pay, since the amalgamation? Have the kindness to let me hear from you at your earliest convenience. I trust this may find you and family well as it leaves us all. Mrs. Hayes sends love to Sister Fuller. Kindly remember me to all.

I am yours, most truly,
J. O. HAYES.

RALEIGH, N. C., Feb. 20, 197.
To the Baptists in N. C. Greeting,

DEAR BRETHREN AND SISTERS: I have been asked to write you concerning the Missionary Training School and its work.

This school is located in Raleigh, and is a department of Shaw University. It is under the auspices of the Womens' Baptist Home Mission Society, with headquarters in Chicago, and the American Baptist Home Mission Society, with headquarters in New York City.

The W. R. H. M. S. has been doing work among the colored people for 20 years. This has been done mostly by white women missionaries from the North, all of whom have had a special course of training to prepare them for that work in our Missionary Training School in Chicago. This work from the first has been greatly blessed of God.

It has been a work for the homes of the people, a work for the mothers and fathers, the young people and children, and many a pastor has been more perfectly instructed in the way of righteousness from the word of God by these Missionaries.

Last year this society of Christian women in the North supported 25 missionaries among the colored people, besides sustaining three Missionary Training Schools for the training of colored women.

This was done at the expense of over $14,000. Of these missionaries 18 were colored women who have been trained either in these schools or by missionaries on the field.

We want every Baptist in North Carolina to bcome acquainted with the work we are trying to do in these Training Schools.

In our school in Raleigh there are three divisions of labor. The close room work, household duties and field work. In our close room we have six periods of recitations daily, besides the morning and evening worship and Bible lesson.

A variety of subjects are taught—such as Bible Normal, Old Testament and New Testament studies, missionary studies, physiology, temperance, social purity, and nursing. The training teachers, Misses Miller and Hamilton are assisted by several pastors and others of Raleigh, such as Dr. Carter, Rev. Spillman, Rev. White and Mr. Broughton. Also several from the medical faculty of the University have given us lectures adapted to the needs of those who will have often to care for the sick and teach other people have had to do.

The training given our girls in household duties is no small part of their work. The care of the home, washing, ironing, cooking, sewing, etc., and the art of making home neat, pleasant and cheerful—this, all women should know and this is not only given in theory but daily practice. It is not how much do you know about these things but how well can you do them. It is of utmost importance that a missionary both knows how to do them and how to teach other people to do them.

Last but not least in our field work in which training is given under the close supervision of the training teachers. This work consists of two Sunday schools, one industrial school, three womens' meetings, and two children's meetings each week, besides house to house visiting in the homes of the people. All of these meetings are conducted in turn by the pupils a month at a time. As it is in household duties so in field work, the question is not how much do you know about it but how well can you do it.

This training school is open to three classes of students, those who desire to prepare themselves for missionary work among their people in the South, those who wish to go to Africa, and those who desire to take the course in order that they may be better fitted for work in their own homes and churches.

The course extends through two years and some may need to remain longer. We desire the most thorough education possible on the part of those who come. The best possible opportunities should be used by those who seek to enter missionary service. The expense of the school is $6 per month and this provides for board, a furnished protect and lighted room and the privilege of washing. All students who are able are expected to pay this amount in full, a limited number of those who may not be able to meet their entire expenses may be helped in part under conditions if application is made early in the year. It is best that all applications for admission to the school be made before the first of May. We would be glad to correspond with any consecrated Christian woman who desires to fit herself for more efficient service for God. We do not take any one under 21 years of age. A good christian character, and fitness for the work are necessary as well as sufficient education to be able to understand the branches taught.

Pastors speak a word of encouragement to such among your people and tell them of the school and help them to come to it. Some one encouraged and helped you, pass the help along.

Read 1st Tim. 2:15.

Yours for service,
EMMA L. MILLIR.

WILKESBORO, N.C., Oct. 21, '96.
To the Baptist State Convention, greeting:

DEAR BRETHREN:—I am proud to know that the representatives of the colored Baptist churches of N. Carolina are now assembled in convention.

I hoped all along to be able to meet with you, but Providence has willed otherwise.

However, I pen a few lines which I hope the Convention will take the time to consider.

I labor in the mountain section of our State, and am doing in a feeble way, what I can to enlighten our people.

The work in this section is truly a missionary work, and seemingly out of the knowledge of the leaders of the denomination. The missionaries who are sent never find their way into these isolated places where dwells the great majority of the colored Baptists. Coming west from Salisbury, very few Baptists are to be found in the towns. We have a great many pious, but incompetent leaders, who would like to do something for the cause if they could succeed without the co-operation of the more intelligent leaders. Within a radius of thirty miles of this place can be counted 1,500 Baptists that are practically out of the fight, because their leaders, though good meaning men, do not favor human progress.

Some brethren who know me, and who are kind enough to come among us some times, (very seldom), but do not stay long enough to learn the nature of the case, discount me because I do not succeed with these people as they do with theirs.

They do not understand the situation. Their being strange makes them admired, should they tarry for the grain to mature, long ere harvest time, they would meet the frozen face.

There are three things absolutely necessary to bring the Baptists of Western North Carolina to the front, viz: First; ministers who are paid to travel and work must continue to reach farther and farther into the rural districts, appreciating whatever talent they can find, encouraging the same when used in the right direction.

Second—More of the intelligent ministers must accept permanent work with us. A visit once or twice a year does very little lasting good. We need men that can stay and bear the brunt. It will be a sacrifice only for a while. It will take a hero to do this, yes, the worthy man who labors here and bears the vituperation and abuse heaped upon him by false leaders, and bears also the privation and want caused by their mischievous ingenuity together with the ignorance of the people —that man is a hero, and instead of being ostracised by the more favored of his brethren he should be encouraged in every way possible.

Third—We must be educated, other denominations around us, appreciating this fact are establishing local schools and academies; we must do the same. It is a mistake for us to presume that the masses of the Baptists of rural western N. Carolina will send their boys and girls to Shaw or any similar institution until there is an educational awakening among them through minor schools at home. Under this conviction a few such schools are being established by concentrating the force of a few individual Baptists here and there, as the Yadkin and Davie Academy at Yadkinville, and the Yadkin Academy at Wilkesboro. We have the habit of calling such schools "little" and "insignificant," other denominations hail them as a good omen; for instance, the Presbyterians opened a school near here last fall, it ran eight months, enrolling 19 students, representing two counties. The leader rallied to their support, and now they have money to push their work.

The Baptists opened school here last fall, ran seven months, and enrolled seventy-one students, representing six counties. No recognition yet by our leaders. School has opened again, and from present indications we will enroll from 150 to 200 students.

We have purchased twelve and a half acres of land and are making efforts to erect a suitable building to teach in. What we have done has been done in less time than a a year, but as yet we have no reason to say that our efforts meet the approval of the (our) denomination out of this immediate section.

By the help of God and good

men we hope to succeed, nevertheless.

Should the Convention remember us in its appropriations, we will feel glad and thankful.

Wishing the Convention every possible degree of success, I am
Fraternally,
R. B. WATTS,
Principal of Yadkin Valley Academy.

Wilkesboro, N. C., Box 24.

P. S.—I was appointed to represent the Yadkin and Davie Association in the Convention, but the Treasurer failed to send me the funds, will try to have it sent to the Secretary of the Convention.

HICKORY GROVE ACADEMY.

WARRENTON, N. C.

This school was organized Nov. 1893. The school is under the direction of the following named brethren: Rev. G. W. Perry, of Raleigh; T. S. Stokes, of Wakefield; T. B. Ellis, of Wakefield; Richard High, of Wakefield; H. R. Goodson, Eagle Rock; Lumnel Shamble, of Wakefield; Willis High, of Wakefield; I. Saiah Hall, of Eagle Rock; Geo. W. Sledd, of Rosenburg.

Rev. D. S. Salter, at one time pastor of the First Baptist church of Raleigh, is the principal, and Miss Eugenia Hill, of Raleigh, assistant.

There are now enrolled eighty-five pupils and the school bids fair to become a power in Shaw University and other similar Institutions.

NEUSE RIVER ASSOCIATION.

No. of churches,	72
Total amount raised,	$212.61
Ordained ministers,	60
Licenciates,	59
Total membership of the Association,	16,000

Rev. W. R. Mason, President.
Rev. W. H. Shaw, Vice-Pres.
A. R. Robinson, Secretary.
Rev. S. G. Newsom, Cor. Sec'y.
Dr. R. J. Walden, Statistical Secretary.
Rev. J. W. Wood, Auditor.
Philip Garris, Treasurer.

CO-OPERATION CONTRIBUTION.

The folloing churches contributed:

1st African Baptist Goldsboro,	$ 2 50
Warrenton	9 00
Hillsboro	7 30
Fayetteville	7 20
Haywood	5 65
Luisburg	2 15
Piney Woods Chapel	10 00
Rockingham	1 00
Poplar Springs	1 00
Laurinburg	90
South Winston	4 50
St. Paul, Tarboro	5 00

CONTRIBUTIONS FROM CHURCHES.

Gray's Creek, Rev. H. C. McDonald, $7 08.

Hilly Branch, Rev. A. H. Thompson, $1 62.

Lumber River Association, Moderator, A. H. Thompson, $10 00.

Baptist church Hubb, Rev. J. A. Spaulding, $3 55; Rev. B. Williams, 50 cents; James Walker, 50 cents.

First church, Littleton, Rev. L. J. Alexander $2 00.

Miss Cora Pair, Shotwell, 40c.
White Rock church, Durham, Rev. A. P. Eaton, $1 25.
Pleasant Grove church, Rev. H. C. McDonald, $1 75.
Northeast Chapel, Rev. J. H. Dunston, 56; Miss Liddia Jones, 25 cents; Miss China Kittrells, 25 cts;
Baptist church, Mebane, Rev. J. H. Dunston $1 40.
Baptist church of Selma, $1 10.
Baptist church, Hamlet, $2 25.
Baptist church, Maxton, $2 00.
The following gave 25 cents: Dr. W. R. Mapp and R. B. Morman.
Nashville Baptist church, Rev. J. J. Hines, $1 51.
Mt. Moriah church, $2 00.
Respectfully,
A. B. VINCENT,
Missionary.

A CALL TO DUTY.

DEAR BRO. WHITTED:—As I understand that the forthcoming QUARTERLY is to be devoted largely to our educational interests in the State, I beg you to allow me to a few suggestions and propositions to our brethren, which, if endorsed, will greatly strengthen our educational work, as well as encourage our friends who, for the past thirty years, have contributed so liberally towards the maintainence of mission schools among us.

To be direct in my references, let me briefly invite you to consider the obligations resting upon us to take hold of Shaw University as we have never done before. Brethren, have we done our duty towards Shaw University, our great school, the pride of the State, maintained solely through the philanthropy of Northern Baptists? It requires no prophet to see that that the day is not distant when the colored Baptist will be called upon to support in part, if not wholly, that institution. A demand of this kind would not be unreasonable, when we consider how rapidly the colored Baptists are growing in intelligence and wealth.

Hundreds of young men and women have gone out from Shaw who could easily spare a contribution annually to aid in supporting the institution, many of them educated for a pittance, command good positions, receive good salaries, live in good houses, and are sufficiently able to do something for their *alma mater*. And again, to their shame, it must be said that many whose circumstances are equally as good as I have stated, do nothing comparatively to advance denominational interests in the State. They have honor and position, but real charity seems to be an unknown quality in their lives. We must be educated to give—to help the race and race enterprises. The obligation to help Shaw is too obvious to admit of contradiction. The fact too is clear that we have failed even to manifest becoming gratitude, all have failed, students, graduates, preachers, churches, unions, Sunday-school Conventions and Associations. But is it too late to improve?

Now for my proposition:

First—Let the colored Baptists of North Carolina support Dr. N. F. Robberts as a professor and Vice-President of Shaw University.

Second—Let us obligate ourselves to pay into the Treasury of the American Baptist Home Mission Society Annually not less than eight hundred dollars to be used in paying Dr. Roberts' salary. We are proud of Dr. Roberts, proud of his record as a Prof. in the school. and proud of his connection with our work in the State. There has not gone from the institution a single student who does not respect and honor Dr. Roberts, and no man stands higher in the esteem of the colored Baptists of the State than he. His name connected with a movement of this kind would be an inspiration in all our meetings to persons disposed to give. Shall we not begin such a movement at once? I suggest further that those who endorse these suggestions write to Rev. J. A. Whitted, Raleigh, N. C., pledging what they will give in this direction. I stand ready to be one of eight to help raise eight hundred dollars this year. Will not the whole army who have gone out into life's battle field from Shaw join in one great procession and rally to the support of that great institution? Yours for the promotion of Baptist interests in the State.

C. S. BROWN.

CONTRIBUTIONS.

EASTERN DISTRICT.
C. C. SOMERVILLE, November, December and January.

Windsor, $26 05, Zion Hill, Plymouth, 1 00; St. Paul, 1 50; Spring Garden, 1 15; Spring Garden, 22 00; Jones' Church, 1 00; New Hope, 3 16; Winton Chapel, 5 00; Harrell's Chapel, 4 00; Aulanda, 25 00; Pleasant Plain, 8 03; Ahoski, 5 03; Jordan's Grove, 25 cents; Mt. Moriah, 8 00; Second Baptist, Murfreesboro, 2 04; First Baptist, Rich Square, 58 cents; Kelford, 1 35; Greenville, 4 40; Union, of Eastern Association, 2 05;

WINDSOR, N. C.

H. Hyman 25 cents, M. T. Smallwood 25 cents, Samuel Dews 25 cents, Rev. J. A. Paulk, Elizabeth City, 1 00, Pender Lee, 25 cents; M. S. Sutton, 25 cents; David M. Cherry, 25 cents; Peter Pritchard, 25 cents; Hester A. Pierce, 25 cents; Rev. W. H. Leath, Windsor, 1 25; Ann Hoggard, 35 cts; Luke Pierce, 39 cents; Tom Brown, Windsor, 50 cents; Andrew Slaughter, 25 cents; L. H. Haughton, 25 cents; Julia Carter, 25 cents; Washington Allen, 25 cents; Lewis Barnes, 25 cents; West Barnes, 50 cents; Rev. B. H. Gray, Windsor, 50 cents; H. C. Cherry, 25 cents; Granville R. Cherry, 25 cents cents; Susan Radford, 25 cents; Milly Webb, 25 cents; C. M. Cartwright, Edenton, 1 00; G. E. Freeman, Powellsville, 80; J. J. Thompson, 25 cents; G. W, Bolden, Murry Hill, 50 cents.

CO-OPERATION CONTRIBUTIONS AND MISSIONS IN NORTH CAROLINA.

Tarboro —Joshua Bunn, 25 cents; Mrs. Francit Griffin, 25 cents; J. L. Faithful, 25 cents; Mrs. Rebecca Edgerton, 25 cents; Jno. Fuller, 50 cents.

Durham.—Ellen Burnet, 25 cents; Daniel Bobbitt, 25 cents; R. D Carlton 25 cents; Mrs. Pattie Webb, 25 cents.

Wise, N. C —Rev. L J. Alexander, 25 cts.

Rockingham—A. Everet, 25 cents; F. T. Town, 50 cents.

Winston—Miss Addie C. Morris $1 00.

Winton, N. C —Rev C S Brown, 50 cts; Walter Myrick, 25 cents; Jack Vain, 50 cts. Levi Brown, 50 cents; G. L. Vame, 50 cents; King Outlaw 50 cents, Mrs. Elizabeth Reynolds, 50 cents; Mrs Saphrona Moore, 50 cents; Herbert Clark, 50 cents

Powellsville, N. C —Mrs. Matilda Cowen, 50 cents; Granville Freeman, 25 cents; Henrietta Ward, 25 cents; Miss Fannie Cherry, 25 cents; A D. Morris, 50 cents; W. E Bennett, 25 cents; Norfleet Askew, 25 cents; Miss O Livermore, 25 cents; Morgan Mitchell, 25 cents.

Rosemeade, N. C —Miss R. A. Simons, 50 cents.

Laurinburg, N. C —Rev. C. B Harris, 25 cents.

Rockingham—Rev. T. M. Jones. 50 cents; W. H. Diggs, 15 cents; Martin Taylor, 50c.

Hillsboro— Rev Alvis Whitted, 50 cents; Frank C. Dixon, 50 cents; Mrs Emeline Graues, 25 cents; Daniel Lattie, 25 cents; Rev. M. T. Hawkins, 25 cents; John Young, 50 cents; Anthony Neal, 25 cents

Jackson Mitchell, 25 cents; Turner Barnes, 25 cents; Mrs Ellen Williams, 75 cents; Mrs. Lizzie Roulhac, 37 cents; L. Roulhac, 25 cents; Isaac Barnes, 25 cents; Newbern Sessoms, 25 cents; Benj. Reynolds, 25 cents; G. W. Brown, 25 cents; G. W. Stewart, 25 cents; Pacsar Smallwood, 25 cents; Solomon Pugh, 25 cents; W. Peele, 25 cents; Sarah C. Holly 25 cents; G. W Gray, 25cts;

LIST OF CONTRIBUTORS.

Rev. J O. Alderman $1 19, Gabriel Williams, 25; Rev. C C. Lawson, 50 cents; Mrs. Hannah Williams, President W H. M. S., 25 cents; Katie Parker, 25 cents; Deacon B

J Bridgers, 50 cents; Sallie B anch, 50 cts.; Silvia Oten, 25 cents; Rev P. S Satchell, 25 Caroline Latham, 25 cents; Mrs W. A. B idges, 50 cent ; W. A. Bridges, 50 cents; Eliza Pitts. 25 cents; Rev. A. Foreman, 25 cents; Rev. J J Franklin, 50 cents; Ma tha Perry, 50 cents; Emma Peaton, 25 cents; Sarah Winfield. Vice-President of W H. M S , 25 cents; Lucy Satchel!, 25 cents; Rev. W. H Pender, 25 cents; Mrs. Vinos Cotton, 50 cents; Mrs Clarinda Foxhall, 25 cents; W. H Pitts, 25 cents; Jane Langley, 25 cts; Mary Branch, 25 cents; Clara Grimes, 25c; Mollie Latham, 50 cents; Eliza Pitts. 25 cts; E. L Langley, 50 cents; R. P Mann, $1 20; Mrs. Loney Mitchell, 25 cents.

Murfreesboro—Albert Southall, 25 cents; J. W. Jenkins, 25 cents; J. W. H. Pool. 25 cents

Kelford—J H. Biggs. 25 cents; W. R. Simmons, 25 cents

Winton, N. C.—Thomas Jerrigan, 50 cts; Moses Vann, 50 cents; John Wilson, 75 cts; Walter M rick, 50 cents; Willy Jones, 25 cents; P. J. Vann. 25 cents; Jackson Vann, 25 cents

Greenville, N C.—J H Britt, 50 cents; S. M. Fleming, 25 cents; Mrs Jennie Elks. 50 cents; J. W Eaton, 50 cents; Catherine Knot, 25 cents; M H, Henryhorn, 25 cents; Francis House, 25 cents; Mary Davis, 50 cts.

Wi ton, N C —James Reynolds, 25 cts ; James M. Walden, 50 cents; Edward G. Turner, 218, W. Dolphin St., Baltimore, Md., 50 ce ts; A. W. Jones, 25 cents; Peter F. Hair, 25 cents; Frank Morriss 25 cents; King Outlaw, 25 cents; A. T. Beverly, 25 cents; Jackson Vann, 25 cents.

Harrellsville.—Daniel Sharp, 25 cents; H. E. Sessom, 25 cents; Jackson Askew, 25 cts; Thomas Sharp, 50 cents; Rev. W. P. Sharp, 50 cents; Dorah Askew, 25 cents; C E. Askew, 25 cents.

Aulander.— '. A. Lewter, 50 cts; John I. Ross, 25 cents; N. H Revell, 50 cents; Peter i wter, 90 cents; Julia Ransom, 25 cents; Junius Oliver, 25 cents; E. L Rawls, 50 cts; Goodman Early, 25 cents; Jackson Jones, 25 cent; Stephen Early, 25 cents; J W. Jackson. 50 cents; A J Lee, 25 cents; Silas Mitchell, 50 cents; Budd Ruffin, 50 cents; W. H Lewter, 25 cents; Katie Harmon, 25 cents; Agnes Higgs, 25 cents; Minnie Wilson, 25 cents; Rebecca Bryant, 25 cents; G. E. Freeman, 25 cents; John R. Rawls, 50 cents; Charles Sessom, 25 cents; G W. Anderson, 25 cents; Isaac Jordan, 25 cents; Rebecca Bryant, 50 cents.

Aluskie, N C —Rev R B. Tilley, 50 cts; Kader Askew, 50 cents; C. C. Summervi le, 25 cents; Frank Peele, 25 cents.

Powellsville.—D S. Sessoms, 50 cents; John Vaughan, 25 cents; J. J. Mitchell, 50 cents; Martin Taylor, 25 cents.

Murfreesboro—Henry Vaughan, 50 cents; William Reid, 25 cents.
Como—John Riddick, 50; Cornelia Dudley. 25 cents.
St. John's, Hertford County.—Thomas Early, 25 cents; Jacob Daniel, 50 cents.
Harrellsville—Thomas Parker, 50 cents; H Hardy, 25 cents; Levi Brown, 25 cents.

REV. C. C. SOMERVILLE.

On the 16th day of March 1859, near the little town of Ridgeway, N. C., in the county of Warren, the subject of this brief sketch, the Rev. Clinton Clay Somerville, was born of humble parents, Richard and Mary, who were owned as slaves by Dr. Henry Plummer. The foundation of his early training was laid in the public schools of Warrenton, and from the first young Somerville manifested great eagerness to learn and advanced rapidly in his b oks.

In th year 1878 he was led to accept faith in Christ, and was baptized into the fellowship of the First Baptist church of Warrenton.

Desiring to extend his education, he entered the State Normal School at Salisbury in 1881, and graduated at the head of his class in 1885, having won the Peabody medal for proficiency in scholarship.

While yet a student in school, he was licensed to preach the gospel by his church, and was almost immediately called to the pastorate of St. John's Baptist Church, of Gold Hill, N. C. In his new and sacred calling he rapidly advanced, displaying earnestness, devotion and power; and the following year he was regularly ordained to the gospel ministry by the Rowan Association, fifty-four churches representing.

In 1891 he was chosen moderator, in which position he served for two years, in the same years he was elected Recording Secretary of the Baptist State Convention and filled the office with credit and ability until chosen to the work of missionary,

Subsequently he was called to the pastorate of the church at Statesville, which he served with great acceptance for three years, during which time he built a splendid house of worship. While serving that people a stragetic point for the Baptists—he was invited to assume charge of the work at Reidsville, which appeared to be a more important point. Here he has labored with ability and skill for more than five years, and forced himself to the front as one of the strongest, ablest and most aggressive leaders in the Baptist church in the State. As a preacher, Rev. Somerville is able, earnest and eloquent, and is generally recognized among his brethren as one of their best pulpit orators. He entertains an audience with his dashing oratory, splendid periods and charming climaxes as few speakers are able to do. As an educator, his career has been noteworthy. He has stood examinations in eleven counties for teachers' certificates, and has held nothing less than a first grade certificate but twice. He served one year as principal of the graded school in Salisbury, and held the same position in Reidsville four years.

In 1886 he married Miss addie L. Brown, sister of the distinguished President of Waters Institute, Rev. C. S. Brown, from which union there have sprung one son and four graceful daughters.

Rev. Somerville has also achieved distinction as a writer. In 1886 he published a booklet entitled "My Brothers" which had quite a wide sale. As associate editor of the "Baptist Headlight," he wrote for two years under the name "Vigil," which articles were widely read and very favorably commented on throughout the State.

In October last he was chosen to serve as District Missionary, under the plan of co-operation, and is now on the field doing a work highly creditable to the denomination. To say the least, he is pre-eminently qualified to do the work peculiar to the position. He is intellectual, strong, courageous, he is earnest, active, enterprising, he is indeed the man for the place, and if given the cordial support of the brethren he will accomplish a work in eastern North Carolina of which the denomination through out the State will justly feel proud.

Girl's Training School and Baptist Institue.

FRANKLINTON, N. C.
Founded by Rev. T. O. Fuller 1891, and incorporated by the General Assembly of North Carolina in 1895.

FACULTY.—Misses Augusta C. Curtis, principal; Laura M. Curtis, Laura B. Falkner, Rev. T. O. Fuller, A. M.

The above Institution is located on a beautiful site in the already famous school town of Franklinton, N. C.

This little town near the city of Raleigh is not only famous for its multiplicity of schools, but churches as well, which places its many students under wholesome religious influences.

Not only affording its pupils an opportunity to pursue the studies usually taught in schools of similar grade, but cooking, sewing, laundry work and housekeeping.

Special attention also is given to the study of the Bible and the development of Christian character.

Upward of one hundred and sixty pupils were enrolled in '95 and '96. Under the general direction of Rev. Fuller and the lady principal, the school has made wonderful development and improvement.

A beautiful edifice has been erected at considerable sacrifice. Other suitable buildings are in contemplation, and with the great competition as only Franklinton can give such an institution, if in so short a time all the others are outnumbered, what may we expect with onward movement of such a school?

God bless the faithful efforts of the few who are doing this wonderful work.

☛ All persons whose yearly supscription closes with this issue will kindly renew their subscription by enclosing amount of 50 cents to the Managing Editor, J. A. Whitted, Box 145, Raleigh, N. C.

BAPTIST STATE CONVENTION
Baptist ✣ Book ✣ Store.

SUPPLIES OF ALL KINDS.

Send all orders for Sunday School

**Quarterlies, Papers,
Roll Books, Lesson Cards,
Bible Lesson Pictures,
Reward Cards, Banners,**

And anything you want, to the Baptist Book Store.

Sunday School Libraries,

Books for Prizes, etc., at all prices, and selected with great care. We have all kinds and descriptions of

**Hymn and Song Books,
Bibles and Testaments**

For Superintendents, Teachers, Scholars and Ministers.

We Want Your Orders, and Guarantee Satisfaction as to Quality and Price.

When sending orders for Quarterlies, state what series is wanted, and write name and post-office address in full.

Sunday Schools do not lose anything in ordering from this Store, as we fill their orders at

Publisher's Prices.

But the orders do help to carry on the work of State Missions.

Correspondence solicited. Information and samples furnished upon application. Address

BAPTIST BOOK STORE,

BOX 164. RALEIGH, N. C.

SOUTHERN RAILWAY.

Condensed Schedule.

IN EFFECT, JUNE 14th, 1896.

TRAIN LEAVE RALEIGH DAILY.

"Norfolk and Chattanooga Limited."

3:40 P. M. DAILY—Solid vestibuled train with sleeper from Raleigh to Chattanooga via., Salisbury, Morganton, Asheville, Hot Springs and Knoxville.

Connects at Durham for Oxford, Clarksville and Keysville, except Sunday. At Greensboro with the Washington and Southwestern Vestibuled (Limited), train for all points North, and with main line train No. 12 for Danville, Richmond and intermediate local stations; also has connection for Winston-Salem and with main line train No. 35, "United States Fast Mail" for Charlotte, Spartanburg, Greenville, Atlanta and all points South; also Columbia Augusta, Charleston, Savannah, Jacksonville and all points in Florida, Sleeping Car for Atlanta, Jacksonville and at Charlotte with Sleeping Car for Augusta.

"Chattanooga and Norfolk Limited."

11:45 A. M. DAILY—Solid train, consisting Pullman Sleeping Cars and coaches from Chattanooga to Raleigh, arriving Norfalk 5:00 p. m. in time to connect with the Old Dominion Merchants' and Miners', Norfolk and Washington and Baltimore, Chesapeake and Richmond S. S. Co's for all points North and East.

Connects at Selma for Fayetteville and intermediate stations on the Wilson and Fayetteville Short Cut, daily; daily except Sunday for Newbern and Morehead City; daily for Goldsboro, and Wilmington and intermediate stations on the Wilmington and Weldon Railroad.

Express Train.

8:53 A. M. DAILY—Connects at Durham for Oxford, Keysville, Richmond; at Greensboro for Washington and all points north.

Express Train.

3:00 P. M. DAILY—For Goldsboro and intermediate stations.

Local.

2:30 A. M. DAILY—Connects at Greensboro for all points North and South and Winston-Salem and points on the Northwestern North Carolina Railroad; at Salsbury, for all points in Western North Carolina, Knoxville, Tenn., Cincinnati and western points; at Charlotte, for Spartanburg, Greenville, Athens, Atlanta and all points south.

TRAINS ARRIVE AT RALEIGH, N. C.:

Express Train.

3:00 P. M. DAILY—From Atlanta, Charlotte, Greensboro and all points South.

Local.

7:20 A. M. DAILY—From Greensboro and all points North and South. Sleeping Car from Greensboro to Raleigh.

Norfolk and Chattanooga Limited.

3:40 P. M. DAILY—From all points east, Norfolk, Tarboro, Wilson and water lines.

From Goldsboro, Wilmington, Fayetteville and all points in Eastern Carolina.

Chattanooga and Norfolk Limited.

11:30 A. M. DAILY—From New York, Washington, Lynchburg, Danville and Greensboro, Chattanooga, Knoxville, Hot Springs and Asheville.

Local.

9:30 P. M. Daily except Sunday—From Goldsboro and all points East.

Express Train.

8:53 A. M. DAILY—From Goldsboro and intermediate stations.

For tickets, routes, and rates or other information, call on or write to

THAD. C. STURGIS,
Ticket Agent, Raleigh, N. C.
W. H. GREEN,
General Superintendent.
W. A. TURK,
General Passenger Agent,
Washington, D. C.
J. M. CULP, Traffic Manager.

Rambler

BICYCLES, $80

Crescents Mens, $50
Ladies, to $75

The Finest Line of Bicycles on Earth.

THOS. H. BRIGGS & SONS,
RALEIGH, N. C.

SOLE AGENTS FOR

THE GREAT
White
Enamel
Line of

There is only
One
Best
and these are
the Best.

The Capital Printing Company,
Raleigh, N. C.

MOST RELIABLE JOB PRINTING OFFICE IN NORTH CAROLINA!

Do more printing for the Colored people than any other House in the State.

LOOK!   **LOOK!**   **LOOK!**

For $1.00 Cash!

WE WILL SEND POST-PAID.

- 100 Nice Letter Heads.
- 100 Envelopes to match,
- 1 Lead Pencil,
- 1 Pen Holder,
- 6 Pen Points,
- 3 Blotters,

with the name of your Association, your Churches in charge, and your name as Pastor, and Post office address all nicely printed on the paper and envelopes. All of the above for only $1.00.

 **EVERY** PASTOR ought to use Printed Paper and Envelopes.
CHURCH CLERK ought to use Printed Paper and Envelopes.
SUNDAY SCHOOL Superintendent and Clerk ought to use Printed Paper and Envelopes.

```
PUNCH CARDS—by mail post-paid per 100  $ .75
GIFT ENVELOPES     "         "      "  100   .75
CHURCH             "         "      "  100   .50
                   "         "   by express, " 1,000  1.25
```

All of these are specially printed for your church.

Mr. Guy V. Barnes, the President of the Company has a personal acquaintance with most of the leading Colored Baptists of the State, and refers you to such men as Revs. Brown, Whitted, Roberts, Pegues, Vincent, and many others, who will testify as to the quality of work, reasonable charges and faithful performance of any work entrusted to their charge.

Send us your Minutes to print.

CAPITAL PRINTING C., ... RALEIGH, N. C.

—MARCH, 1897.—

The Baptist Quarterly.

Edited by Board of Managers Baptist E. and M. Convention,
J. A. WHITTED, Managing Editor.
Box 145, Raleigh, N. C.

CONTENTS:

	PAGE
SOME OF THE PIONEERS OF THE WORK AMONG THE BAPTISTS OF NORTH CAROLINA	1
A MODEL CHURCH	3
FROM THE WESTERN DISTRICT	5
CENTRAL DISTRICT	7
INSTITUTE WORK	8
THEOLOGICAL TRAINING AT SHAW UNIVERSITY	11
SOME OBSERVATIONS ON THE LITERARY STATUS OF SHAW UNIVERSITY	12
INSTITUTES	14
SCHOOLS	22
COMMUNICATIONS	26
A CALL TO DUTY	31
CONTRIBUTIONS	30 and 32

Baptist
Educational and Missionary Convention
of North Carolina.

Next Session will be Held in Charlotte, N. C.,
October 21, 1897.

Officers 1896-97.

Rev. N. F. ROBERTS, D. D., President, Raleigh.
Rev. C. S. BROWN, Secretary, Winton.
J. A. WHITTED, Cor. Secretary and General Missionary, Raleigh.
A. W. PEGUES, Ph. D., Treasurer, Raleigh.
Rev. G. W. MOORE, Auditor, Fayetteville.

Missionaries.

J. A. WHITTED, General, Raleigh.
Rev. P. F. MALOY, Western District, Greensboro.
Rev. A. B. VINCENT, Central District, Raleigh.
Rev. C. C. SUMMERVILLE, Eastern District, Rocky Mount.

☞ All communications concerning State Work, New Era Institutes, Co-operation, and the Baptist Quarterly, should be directed to the Corresponding Secretary and General Misssonary at Raleigh.

REV. C. C. SOMERVILLE.

Baptist Quarterly.

SOME OF THE PIONEERS OF THE WORK AMONG THE BAPTISTS OF N. C.

Rev. H. Cowen, of Salisbury, is the oldest Baptist minister in the State, and has done a great work in laying the foundation for Baptist principles and establishing Baptist churches in western North Carolina. He is now in his 85th year, but manifests more direct interest in the general advancement of our State work than many of our young active pastors. He attends the State Convention and his own Association every year; has organized churches all the way from Charlotte to Durham, and from Reidsville across the State to Wadesboro, N. C. His whole life seems fraught with burning zeal and unfailing love for the Master's cause.

***

Rev. G. W. Holland, of Winston, N. C., has planted Baptist churches from Greensboro to Wilksboro, and from the Virginia line to the Yadkin river above Salisbury. He came to Winston from Danville when there was not a single place of worship in the town, for it was only a town then; he began holding prayer meeting and preaching about the place and continued till now. We now have five Baptist churches in that city, all of which are branch churches from the first Baptist church of which he is still pastor, and which is by far the largest and strongest congregation in the city. Mt Zion church, of which Rev. G.W. Johnson is pastor, is a most popular and thriving daughter. Rev. Johnson being a man of quick thought, far sight and well educated, would not rest till his congregation is regarded among the best in the State. Rev. Holland laid hands on Rev. Johnson and consecrated him to that work, and he regards him as his most successful son in the gospel. He also owns a large farm.

***

REV. THOMAS PARKER.

The subject of this sketch, Rev. Thomas Parker, of Warsaw, N. C., has just passed his three score years and six, professing faith in Christ in 1862, he was baptized by Dr. Young and united himself with the white Baptist church, of Wilmington, N. C.

He realized a call to the ministry in 1868, and since it may be said of him, though often at the peril of his life he has preached the word successfully and "with no uncertain sound."

One thousand and one hundred and sixty persons have been plunged in the "watery grave" by his hands, and in spite of his years, if he could he would plunge as many more.

No, one who has ever known Rev. Parker doubts his loyalty to the Baptist cause.

Like every leader should be, his "sheep hear his voice" and to have his approval in any measure among his people, means the approval of the entire flock.

REV. A. WILBURN, OF TRINITY COLLEGE, N. C.

Rev. Wilburn was born in 1840, he became a member of the Baptist church in 1870, and was ordained a deacon of his church the same day. He was licensed in 1870 and ordained to the gospel ministry in 1872; he was then associated in the ministry with our reverend Father, Rev. Harry Cowan. For twenty-one years he has served the High Point church, Simon's Grove, New Hope, two years, at Lexington; Thomasville, twelve years; Liberty Grove, fourteen years.

Probably no minister of the State has preached more funerals, and many of them persons outside the Baptist church. Rev. Wilburn has baptized one thousand persons, he was Moderator of the High Point Association one year, and Treasurer of the Rowan Association four years, which position he now holds.

What Rev. Wilburn has done for the cause in western North Carolina will be known only when the deeds of mortals are fully revealed. Long may he be spared to the Master's cause.

* * *

REV. ZION H. BERRY, OF ELIZABETH CITY, N. C.

He was born in Camden county, April 24, 1830, united with the Baptist church in 1848. He felt his call to the gospel ministry in the year of 1860, and was ordained in 1866. He has held charges over the following churches: Corinth, Philadelphia, New Sawyer's Creek, Olive Branch, Union, New Chapel, Hertford, Pool's Grove, Galatia, Corner Stone, Harrell's Creek, Roanoke Island, New Shiloh.

As one of the results or the labors of Rev. Berry, 4,953 persons have been baptized. Rev. Berry has been Moderator of the Roanoke Baptist Missionary Association and holds a very prominent place in the councils of his brethren in eastern North Carolina. He deserves great credit for his push in every effort to lift up his church and his race. He, though passed his three score by six years, is full of energy and as active in the work as if twenty-five.

* * *

REV. GEORGE W. PERRY, OF RALEIGH, N. C.

The subject of this sketch was born in Franklin county, near Louisburg, in 1833, united with the white Baptist church, of Louisburg, N C., in 1853; ordained to the gospel ministry and held pastoral charge over the following churches:

Assistant pastor, Louisburg, St. Matthews, Rolesville, Wakefield, Macedonia, First Baptist church of Raleigh, for some months after the death of Rev. Wm. A. Greene.

Upward of five hundred persons have been baptized by Rev. Perry in his different pastorates, being the first student of Shaw University, he was afterward chosen to be a trustee.

As a missionary, Rev. Perry has done efficient work in North Carolina. He was the first Treasurer for the proposed Orphan Asylum nine years and did much in shaping the history of that institution of which we are all so justly proud.

* * *

REV. CHAS. E. HODGES, LAND OF PROMISE, VA.

Rev. Hodges was born in Princess Ann county, Va., on May 7th, 1819, he was baptized May 4th, 1743, and ordained to the gospel ministry Apr. 1st, 1861. During the years of his ministry he organized the following churches: Union Chapel and Galilee, in Pasquotank county; Readie Grove and Pool's Grove, in Perquimans county; Willow Grove, St. Matthew, Mt. Tabor, St. Pauls, Pleasant Valley, in Norfolk county, Va.; Oak Grove and Piney Grove, in Princess Ann county, Va.; Anders Grove, Chowan county; Chesnut Grove, Halifax county; Pastolich, Brooklyn, N. Y.; Christian Home, Currituck county and others.

Twenty-six brethren, some now holding important churches, have been ordained to the ministry by Rev. Hodges. At one time he was the honored pastor of the First Baptist church of Brooklyn, N. Y. He has held many prominent churches in North Carolina and Virginia. Sixteen hundred and seventy-three persons have been baptized by him.

Several times he has been elected to the important position of Moderator of the Roanoke Baptist Association, which position he now holds. He is greatly loved and respected by his brethren.

A MODEL CHURCH.

According to the almost endless varieties of churches that meet one's gaze in every section of the country, from the antique Dutch chapel with its pigeon hole windows, scarcely large enough for a private residence to the modern handsome church edifice with its large gothic windows and chancel, offering evry opportunity to scientific acaustics, and well nigh perfect ventilation, it would be hard to describe a church that would be suited to so many tastes. All churches should be constructed primarily with a view to comfort for all seasons, so that there must be a groundless objection for the disinterested and careless class who are sometimes found in our churches; besides, the entire architecture ought to display taste and beauty in its mechanism, however simple the design, for that individual must be unusually coarse and vulgar who does not desire beauty even in a church.

While much can be said about a "model church" and with profit, much more can be said about the pastor, officers and members of such a church, for after all a congregation of Christ's baptized disciples constitute the real basis of a New Testament church.

The two first classes alluded to should be progressive, and spiritual. These two qualities go together, for wherever there is a lack of one the other seriously suffers. The non-progressive pastor is a positive hindrance to his church. He may not intentionally keep the ox from the hay, but virtually he is playing the same trick. Lest he should become top-heavy for want of ballast, he should abound in the grace of spirituality. "Like priest like prophet" a dead preacher will have a dead congregation—a thing very different from a "model church."

Church officers ought to be intelligent business men of broad and liberal views and of marked piety; for if they are wanting in these graces they will soon become so narrow and contracted that they will be mere sycophants, whose only office is to serve some selfish end, and not the good of the church and the glory of God.

Indifference in the selection of deacons, or over-anxiety to make a "board" has been the means of writing "Ichabod" over an otherwise prosperous and contented church. The members of the church ought to be plainly taught the grace of "Christian liberty" and given to know that as great a falsehood can be told by willfully refusing to pay your salary as can be told about anything else. Every member of the church should strive to cultivate a fraternal feeling and courtesy in speech to each other, and at all times should be solicitous of the comfort of the visitors and the welfare of the pastor. In all the departments of the church work all parties ought to be cordially in touch with each other—"my brother co-laborers together with God."

Of the interests fostered by a model church, we shall speak first of the Sunday school. Where no Sunday school exists, and where the pastor and deacons are averse to such an agency, you need not be surprised to pass that way in a few years, and musing on the ruins of broken windows, a dilapidated building, a moss-grown walk, you read out in the reflection from every fluttering leaf and solitary songster who may chance to pass that way that preaching used to be held there. The children must be gathered and taught. Whenever practicable a young people's society should be organized and the fires kept burning. A well organized Woman's Home Mission Society, managed and officered by Christian women, who are imbued with the spirit of missions, is an indispensibility. It can do the work for the relief of the poor, the spread of the gospel, Baptist retrenchment, that is not possible for any other seperate agency to perform.

A church that is not alive to missions generally fails of its high calling. The demand for home and foreign missions is as constant as the throbbing of the pulse—"the poor ye have always" is a call to missions as imperative now as when the Saviour spoke it; yet many of our churches neglect the subject until the missionary comes. Africa must not be forgotten. We must provide something for the enlightenmen of the 300,000,000 souls in a comparatively hopeless night. A "model church" has not done its duty unless it provides for its superannuated and disabled members. Unless Christianity comes to the rescue of these unfortunate ones, the church need not be surprised that in proportion as it declines societies will flourish.

The church should be alert to its educational interest. It *does* make a difference where our children are educated, and by whom taught. Sainted Dr. H. M. Tupper, though dead, yet speaketh through the teachers and preachers all over North Carolina who as Baptists, are "contending for the faith."

Are you suprised at these things? Read the 9th verse, 18th chapt. of Gen. Lay your hands on every boy and girl you can, and do what you can to have them educated.

C. C. SUMMERVILLE.
Dist. Missionary, Rocky Mt.

FROM THE WESTERN DISTRICT.

Dear Brethren: The work of co-operation has lost no place with our people, but instead, is still increasing in interest and prominence. We see a clearer sky for the work at this writing than in mid summer of last year. Brethren everywhere feel that they have unsurpassed advantages to improve their knowledge of the Bible, and that preaching is made much easier by attending the Institute. Our great need in Western North Carolina is a sufficent State Mission fund. More than fifty out stations in this section have preaching only a few months in the year, because of inability to support a minister. We hope our able pastors and large churches will take due notice of this, and lay aside on the first day of the week a sufficient sum till this work is fully on foot.

Many calls are made to our Gen. Missionary and the board for relief, but answers have been given. The money is not in hand. Let every church and Sunday school in Western North Carolina heed these calls, by sending a collection to our Treasurer, Dr. A. W. Pegues at Raleigh, N. C., and see if God will not supply every vacant and destitute field in this district. We hope to see every Association in the State organized into union meetings to meet every 5th Saturday and Sunday to raise money for this purpose.

The following are contribu ions by churches, Sundy schools and individuals to our convention work, and the names of persons taking the Baptist Quarterly and the *Christian Banner*, our National Baptist paper.

Institutes, Churches and Sunday schools of 1st quarter, 1897.

Institutes.—Shelby, $11.73; Wadesboro, $27.05; Concord, (Snow Storm) $1.10; Reidsville, $5; Winston, $15.25. Total Institute collections, $60.13.

Churches.—Ebenezer, Kings Mountain, Nov 2, $3.17; Alison Grove, Concord, Nov. 9, $3; 1st Baptist, Wadesboro, Nov. 15, $2.05; Phillipi, Lane's Church, $1.55; Flint Ridge, Marshville, Nov. 22, $1.69. Total for Nov. $11.46.

December.—1st Baptist, Reidsville, $3; Baptist Church, Wentworth, $1.80; Mt. Zion, Winston, $2.65. Total $6.45.

Jan. '97.—Baptist Church, High Point, $4.60; Baptist Sunday School, High Point, $1; Oak Grove Church, Sage Garden, 55 cents; Oak Grove Sunday School, Sage Garden, 66 cents; Mt. Pleasant, Winston, $2.15; Rising Ebenezer, Winston, $1.50; Liberty Zion, Trinity, $3.05; Liberty Zion Sunday School, Trinity, $1.10. Total $16.61.

Roll of honor, November, at Shelby.

Rev. J. C. Moore, 25; Rev. S. McCurry, 25; Rev. B. Bridgers, 25; Mr. Eli Roberts, 25; Rev. A. Johnson, 25; Joseph Oats, 25; Mrs. Rena Posten, 25; Mrs. M. A. Lutzs, 25; Martha Rippy, 25; Rev. W. C. Veal, 25; Jane Rippy, 25; R. W. Scott, 25.

Dec.—Phillip Wilson, 25; Clara Oats, 25; Eastern Jemuson, 25; Moses Oats, 25; Rev. M. Beam, 25; Rev. W. A. Roberts, 25; Dr. J H. Cary, 25; Rev. T. J. Floyd, 25; Annie Jones, 25; Mary Kincade, 25; Mary Moore, 25; Susan Blanton, 25; Mittie McCurry, 25; Rev. S Shuford, 25.

Roll of honor at Wadesboro.

Rev. P. R. Lison, 25; Rev. A. D. Marshall, 25; Rev. R. Diggs, 25; Mrs. A. S. Loop, 25; Rev. S. M Wall, 25; Rev. D A. Lilmon, 25; Rev. Ratlipp, 25; Rev. A. Hammon, 25; Rev. J. F. Davis, 75; Mrs. E. Hall, 25; Rev. H D Tilman, 25; Rev. J. T. Ratlipp, 50; Rev. R. Tilman, 50; Dea. Weldon, Kendle, 25; Dea. Broadway, 25; Rev. B. J. Studervant, 25; Rev. J. A. Fnnderberk, 25; Rev. W. Y. Ingram, 25; Esther Sims, 25; Rev. P. G. Lowery, 25; Dea. A L. Leak, 25; Mariah Bennett, 25; Rev. A. C. McLendon, 25; Rev. P. D. Dunmas, 25; P. F. Maloy, 50; Mrs. S. Dunlap, 25; J. F. Bennett, 25; Mrs. E. Bancon, 25; Dea. S M. Marshal, 25; Rev. S. Dunlap, 25; Rev J. R. Bennett, 25; Rev. S. Bennett, 25; Miss E. P. Waugh, 25; Ellen Simons, 25; Dea. W. E. Kennel, 25; J. M. Bancom, 75; L. Bogans, 25; Rev. C. C. Horn, 25; Jessie Thomas, 25; Prof S. S. Thomas, 25; Richard Hamons, 25; Julia McKoy, 25; Dea. D. Bennett, 25.

Roll of honor at Concord, Dec. 1, '96.

W. C. Colman, 25; Mrs. W. C. Colman, 25; Lula Jenkins, 25.

Roll of honor at Reidsville, Dec. 15, '96.

Mrs. C. C. Smmerville, 25; Mrs. A. Cartee, 25; Lucy Thompson, 2::; Mary Martin, 25; G. E. Carter, 25; Mariah Martin, 25; Dr. J. A. Mundy, 25; Rev. F. N. Jones, 25; Annie McGeehe, 25; Mrs. J. C. Cruents, 25; M. L. Brenfield, 25.

Roll of honor at Winston, Jan. 19. '97.

Rev. A. Hepler, 25; R. M. Mial, 25; Rev. G. W. Johnson, 75; E. E. Caldwell, 25; Rev. J. W. Jones, 25; Bo. P. Owen, $1.25; A. J. Brown, 30; W. M Cing, 25; Mrs. L. Lemmons, 25; Rev. G. W. Holland, 50; G. C. Edwards, 25; Rev. S. F. Conord, 25; Dr. H. A. Brown, 50; M. S. Toilver, 25; Dea. H. Alexander, 25; Addie Morris, $1; Rev. D. Johnson, 25; L. M Morton, 25; I. N. Pa'erson, 25; Robert Butler, 25; Henry Adams, 25; Prof. S. G. Atkins, 25.

Persons who subscribed to the QUARTERLY:

Rev. J. C. Hemphill, Franklin; Rev F. W. Wa lace, Webster; Rev. J. F. Davis, Polkton; Samuel Stenard, G iffith; Margarett Chambers, Nimrod; Rev. H Palmer and D. J. Aery, Statesville; Rev. B. J. Studervant, Deep Creek; Rev. Robert Diggs, Pedee; J. W. Lowery, Rushing; Margarett Grady, Rushing; Rev. G. W. Brewer, Monroe; J. C. Lane, Franklin; Rev. P. D. Dremers, Wadesboro; P. Oxen, Winston; Addie Morris, and Mary L. Brown, Winston; Rev. G. W. Johnson and G. W. Holland, Winston; Rev. J. W. Jones, Winston; Dr. H. A. Brown, Winston; Rev. Hepler, Salem; Dr. J W. Jones, Winston; Rev. A. Wilburn, High Point; Rev. I. Little, Marshville; Rev. J. R. Nelson, Asheville; Rev. W. T. Minter, 250 Bomount, St. Asheville.

We rejoice to see our brethren and sisters take such commendable part in the success of our Convention work. This is what our good fathers prayed for, and the younger brethren rejoice to see. We are uniting in Western North Carolina for a great battle and victory to Baptist principles and Bible truth. Our young people are being stirred as never before by the educating influence of the New Era Institutes to work and make sacrifice for the successful accomplishment of our work.

We are very anxious to collect history of the work and progress, and of the lives of our aged fathers in the Baptist ministry and would thank any of the pastors to send in sketches of the work and labors of our old fathers. I feel that it is due their faithful and most worthy service that we younger pastors and minsters may collect all we can of their labors and lives and publish the same in our QUARTERLY from time to time.

P. F. MALOY,
Dist. Missionary.

CENTRAL DISTRICT.

Contributions from Central District Baptist church, Mebane, $1.40, Rev. J. H. Dunston, pastor.

Mrs. Moriah McAdan, 50 cents; Joseph Williams, 25; Albert Hester, 25; Mrs. Sarah Williams and others, 40 cents.

Institute at Savannah church, Cumberland county. Rev. W. H. Anders, pastor. Total contribution, $13.20.

Wm. McDonal, Beard, 50 cents; D. D. McDonald, Gray's Creek, 25; David Gilmore, Gray's Creek, 25; H. C. Edwards, Cedar Creek, 50; Mary Williams, Wade's Station, 50; A. G. McDonald, Gray's Creek, 35; Simpson Brown, Flat Springs, 25; Allen Johnson, Alderman's 50; B. J. Meloin, Gray's Creek, 25; Henry Hair, Gray's Creek, 19; E. R. J. Avant, Gray's Creek, 50; Foster Whitted, Gray's Creek, 50; James McNeil, Gray's Creek, 25; G. W. Johnson, Cedar Creek. 50; A. D. Meloin, Sherwood, 50.

Institute at Selma, Rev. E. B. Blake pastor.

Selma.—Miss Julia O'Neal, 25; N. E. Egerton, 50; John Graham, 65; William Lockhart, 25; Madison Blake, 25; Rev. A. A. Jones, —; Neison Smith, 50; Miss Lugenie Richardson 25; Miss J. H. Richardson, 25; Lugenie Langston, 25; Daisy Powers, 25; Mrs. Bettie Chavis, 25; Mrs. Eliza Richardson, 50; Laura Atkinson, 25; George O'Neal, 50; Bettie Eason, 25; Polly Langston, 25; Simon Price, 25; Celesia Blake, 50; Amanda Deems, 30; Rachel Smith, 25; Samantha Baker, 25; Elizabeth Jones, 50; Zilphia Alford, 30; Eddie Moore, 25; Eliza Atkins, 30; Jno. Lassiter, 25; Green Manly Lee, 25; Jennetha Alford, 30; Adeline Vine, 25, Sarah Mial, 25; Roberta Bunn, 25; Bertie Eason, 50; Celia Moore, 25; Rev. J. J. Jones, Clayton, 50. Collections, $7.65.

Lumberton Institute.—Lumberton—J. N. Booth, $1.00; Rev. A. H. Thompson, 1.00; Rev. J. D. Harrell, 25c; Rev. E. M. Thompson, 50; C. C. Singletary, 25; Rev. T. P. Norris, 50; Pierce Powell, 25; W. C. Pope, 25; Esther Moore, 50; Ed Smith, 25; Malcom McNeal, 25; Roxanna Thompson, 25; Jno. C. Grady, 50; William Cobb, 25; M. C. Moore, 25; Richard McNeal, 25; S. S. Stephens, 50; Lizzie Jenkins, 25; Rev. L. Melvin, 25; Mary Rowland, 25; J. C.

Inman, 50; Jennie Kelly, 25; E. B. McClellor Rowland, 25; Prof. D. P. Allen, 25; James Walker Hubb, 60; S. S. Stephens, 25; Rev. M. H. Hubb, 25; Rev. O L. Stringfield, Raleigh, 1 00; Rev. George Williams, Register 50; Rev. D. J. Moore, Rosindale, 25; D. Brown, Cerogorda, 25; E. W. Thompson, Grady, 25; Thomas Davis, Ceregordo, 25; Pen Bonds, Grady, 50; Rev W. M. Jones, Maxton, 1 05; G. G Lasong, Grady, 25. Collections, $8 81.

Rockingham Institute.—Rockingham—Providence Baptist church, Rev. D. M. Jackson, pastor, $20 05.

Amanda Harris, 1 54; William Davis, 25; Florence A. Woodward, 25; Rev. W. H. Woodward, 50; Rev. W. C. Pope, 50; Rev. C. Campbell, 25; Samuel Ross, 25; Marilla McDonald, 25; Cattie J. Cooper, 25; Rev. R. Edward, 25; Mrs. A. J. Henderson, 25. Collections, 10 91; Miss Nora Campbell, 25; Nora Watkins, 25; Phebe Balding, 25; Rev. J. J. Hines, Hasty, 50; A. Elerby, Dockery's S ore, 30; Caroline Dobbins' Hamlet, 25; Miss S. M. Dobbins, Ham'et, 50; Solomon Wall, Hamlet, 25; Hannah Simons, Hamlet, 25; Rev. S. M. Wall, Pedee, 25; Rev. A. Covington Dockery's Store, 50.

Laurinburg church reported by Rev. C. B. Harris, 75 cents.

Bap'ist church of Maxton, Rev. S. W. Dockery pastor, $2 00; Dr. W. R. Mapp, 25; R. B. Moorman, 25; church, 1 50.

Baptist church, Laurinburg, 2 00.

Baptist church, Nashville, Rev. J. J. Hines, pastor, 1 51; D. W. Monroe, MacNair, 25; Julia Monroe, MacNair, 25; James McLean, McNair, 25.

Spring Branch, Fontocal, Richmond county, 15c.

A. B. VINCENT,
Dis't. Missionary.

INSTITUTE WORK.

Our last quarter which closed with the month of Jannary was telling in the New Era Institute work. Our first meeting was held with the two Baptist churches of Windsor, N. C. Although the success of the meeting depended largely on the pastors in and about Windsor, the meeting was a marked success. There were present twenty-three ministers and thirty-four deacons.

Rev. R. D. Cross, pastor of the white Baptist curch and Rev. L. M. Curtis, of Anlander, assisted the missionaries as teachers.

Rev. Cross, though comparatively young in the ministry, did himself and the work great credit on every occasion. Rev. Curtis had already commended himself to the brethren in the Tarboro meeting but the earnestness he manifested at Windsor brought him in touch with our brethren as never before. Said he, "So long as our colored brethren appreciate our help in the work so long will we help them." Brethren, let this "hint to the wise" be sufficient and with your means, with your influence and with your presence from time to time let our white brethren know you do appreciate their great help.

This meeting was the beginning of the work of Rev. C. C. Summerville as District Missionary. If any doubted the ability of our new District Missionary before this, when he closed his course of lectures every doubt was removed for he acquitted himself as a man.

Our next meeting was held with the First Baptist church of Washington, N. C.

Nowhere has a kindlier interest been manifested than was manifested by Rev. J. O. Alderman, of the white Baptist church. Not only did Bro. Alderman act his part nobly as a lecturer but said he, "Put me down for as much in your contributions as any other man gives."

This remark awakened a deeper interest throughout the vast audience and the result was realized in the fruitful gathering.

Prof. M. W. D. Norman reached us later on the meeting but not too late to act his part. And it may be said of him he was at his best. It would surprise us if after such a lecture the people of Washington were not awakened to the work of Christian education. It would be but repeating to speak of the work of Rev. Somerville in every meeting since the one at Windsor.

The next meeting we attended was at Wadesboro. We might justly style this as the Spiritual Institute for in no other meeting before or since have we realized such "an outpouring of the spirit." Some one may say it was because the Gen. Missionary was not there to extinguish the fire. Be that as it may when he reached the church it was at once evident that a work of no small proportions was going on among the people.

Sitting there swayed by the eloquence of Dr. Shepard "one could hear a pin drop." Two men only had done this great work and these men seemed to have vied with each other in quantity and quality and in setting forth the great truths contained in the lectures.

If the worth of a meeting could be realized in dollars and cents we would be safe in saying the one meeting at Wadesboro was worth the year's expenditures.

Rev. Maloy and the people of Wadesboro deserve great credit for such a meeting.

Our next meeting was at Savanah Baptist church. This church is about sixteen long "round-about" miles from Fayettville, in Rev. A. B. Vincent's district. It seemed too far for any of our white brethren to follow us, and too far for the Gen. Missionary again soon. So the entire course of thirteen lectures must be given by the missionaries.

This was the time and the place when and where Prof. Vincent could not modestly say, "let some one else take that lecture" but must act his part in these and never before did we know how proficiently he could act his part as a lecturer.

As in the Wadesboro meeting the part of the Gen. Missionary in the Selma meeting was but small. The meeting was conducted by Prof. Vincent but in no meeting were abler men secured as lecturers. Rev. J. H. Scott, of Shaw University; Rev. W. R. Cullom, of Wake Forest; Rev. J. J. Worlds, of Raleigh, and Rev. John E. White, of Raleigh. A simple mention of these names is sufficient to know the character of the meeting.

It seems to revolutionize that entire section and awaken in the people an endeavor for better living.

The first meeting for the third course of lectures under the plan of co-operation, was held at the solicitation of our white as well as colored brethren at Aulander.

Rev. L. M. Curtis, who assisted at Windsor; Rev. C. S. Brown, our ex-Gen. Missionary; Rev. J. B. Newton, and Rev. C. C. Somerville, were the lecturers.

All the brethren acquitted themselves creditably. We have never heard Rev. Brown do so well. The pastors took hold as never before. One brother said as a result of the impression made on him "money time and influence so far as he could see were on co-operation's altar" to be used at the direction of the missionaries."

Lumberton, already famous for good meetings, was our next place for an institute. The people showed their hopes for something good for their preparations were so ample, and expectations so far reaching until the rain which began the 2nd day, though it did not cease night or day until the close, did not stop the multitudes gathering from every direction and in every conceivable style of conveyance. Some whose patent had reached the patent office in Washington and some whose patent had never before reached Lumberton.

The pastors, Rev. S. W. Dockery, of the colored church, and Rev. J. M. Booth, of the white church. stuck to the meeting like men full of interest.

The simplicity of Rev. Booth's lectures always pleases our brethren. Rev. W. M. Jones, of Maxton, whom no one doubts as a scholar never spoke with such power to the brethren as he did at Lumberton.

It was expected that Rev. Jno. E. White, our efficient Corresponding Secretary would speak on the subject for which he is famed among our brethren, "Christian Education," but detained in Raleigh. He sent us Rev. O. S. Stringfield, soliciting agent for the Baptist Female College.

To look at Rev. Stringfield will give you one impression, to hear him will give the other. His power over his audience is wonderful. At one moment they may be filled with laughter, at the next they may be hushed in death-like stillness touched with his sublimnity.

The bad weather was against us at Winston, but many of the brethren in spite of the storm met us from time to time. Rev. Witherspoon, of Greensboro, and P. S. Lewis, of Salisbury, were there as they have been in several of our meetings to lecture.

The services of these two Baptist leaders are incalculable.

Dr. H. A. Brown, Rev. S. F. Conrad, of the white churches, Rev. G. W. Johnson, of the colored church, of Winston, and Rev. P. F. Maloy, were lecturers.

All the brethren seemed to be at their best, and when the meeting closed we felt truly we had a feast from beginning to the end. Our next meeting in Rev. Maloy's district was at High Point.

We had already heard so much of Rev. Kesler and Dr. Carrick we expected much from them and we did not fall short of our expectation.

Dr. Richardson and Rev. Maloy moved our brethren on the subject of mission work among the white brethren and colored brethren as we have rarely seen them moved on that subject.

Turning back to the Central District our next meeting was at Rockingham and there we had with us again Rev. J. H. Scott, of Shaw University and Rev. J. G Blalock, of the white church.

Every one who hears Prof. Scott feels proud of him as the head of the theological department of Shaw University. Rev. Blalock, though a young man, always impresses his audience with his thorough preparation and his earnestness.

Taking up our last meeting at Elizabeth City it concludes the institute work up to date.

Dr. Blackwell took the same course of lectures as last year, Biblical theology.

All who hear Dr. Blackwell feel that they have had something rare. Prof. Norman on preaching and church history was again at what we felt was his best or what gave us perfect satisfaction. Prof. Moore on Christian education the same as last year, gave a lecture full of thought.

To commend ministers and brethren who have been faithful in the work would make a long list for truly we can say from the mountains of North Carolina to the sea shore the brethren in the ministry and the laity are alive to the great work of the New Era Institutes and now in every district we are urged to hold meetings, for many of the brethren say and feel "we have never had anything like it." We feel especially proud of the eminent services of each of our District Missionaries of the warm welcome given us by our pastors, ministers, deacons and the brethren generally, especially are we proud of the spirit which characterizes our white brethren in their labors to do us good.

THEOLNGICAL TRAINING AT SHAW UNIVERSITY.

At no time since the organization of this school has the necessity for theological education been forgotten. Able men have given lectures in this department, and many students have gone forth to do successful service in this and other States. The work already done has laid the foundation for a much wider work in the future. The students of Shaw who have gone forth —preachers, teachers, lawyers and physicians, have set a much higher standard for ministerial service, as a consequence the demand for better

TRAINED MEN

for the University is imperative. What would satisfy the churches five years ago will not avail now, men of better training and better scholarship are needed. Not only are such men needed, but they are imperatively demanded As the churches advance in wealth and culture so must the ministry advance. This improvement will always be prompted by the energetic and conservated pastor.

LIKE PASTOR, LIKE PEOPLE.

Our churches will not advance beyond their leaders, yet the spirit of the age is surely pointing to advance along all lines. This is no less true in the ministry than in national things. If our churches are not to fall behind in the rush of progress then our young men and women must see to it that they have the best training. Every church should have a student at Shaw, and at least every Association should have a student for the ministry. Would it not be well for each Association, at their next meeting to arrange for at least one student of theology to be here for next year? This would make a beginning and only a beginning of what this school would do for the State.

WHO SHOULD COME TO SHAW.

All young men who believe themselves called of God to preach the gospel, should take at least three years study in the Theological Department of Shaw University, this will enable them to get a fair mastery of the Bible and of the English language. They will thus be able to give to their people fresh and helpful sermons and to lead them into a much wider usefulness.

There is another class who can be helpful, we mean pastors who have already begun work but who feel that they should have a better education. These will be welcomed, though they cannot remain for more than two or three months.

SUBJECTS TAUGHT.

The work done in this department includes careful study of the Old Testament and New Testament outlines. This course is designed to acquaint the student with the main historical material of the Bible. This year the classes have covered the outlines of the Old Testament and the life of Christ. Next year they will take up the study of the apostolic church as shown in the Acts and Epistles. In addition to the above they have had lectures in church history, missions and constant instruction in church policy and pastoral duties as the subjects present themselves in the study of the life of Christ. As the students progress in their work instruction will be given more at length in Church History, Interpretation, Pastoral Theology and Organization of the Church. The management of the Prayer Meeting, the organization and conduct of Young Peoples' Societies and of Sunday-schools. In a word it is prepared to give help to enable the young pastor to take up his work with good prospect of success.

Those who come to Shaw University may be assured of a most cordial welcome.

SOME OBSERVATIONS ON THE LITERARY STATUS OF SHAW UNIVERSITY.

Three mistakes Shaw University has never made—she has never *focussed, narrowed* and *limited* in her culture, never sacrificed the larger side, on the contrary, she has constantly believed that her students are human beings with instincts, feelings, mental perceptions, infinite relations, with souls, all making a unit with character that must have free play at every stage or a defectively trained man must be the result. She has known that the "THREE R'S" contribute but a meager amount to any man's education. In a word, she has steadfastly maintained that it is important for the black man not to lose sight of the infinitely great while studying the infinitely small.

Another thing, Shaw does not make the mistake of trimming her sails to suit every breeze that blows, however favorable some of these seems, but prefers rather to stand still, anchored on truth, if need be for a time.

And thirdly; Shaw does not and

will not arrogate to herself too much importance, but chooses rather to speak through the lives and acts of those sent out.

Therefore, it can be said with reason, that the true answer to Shaw University is her men and women scattered throughout the nine states and two territories of America, in Africa and on several islands of adjacent seas. These men and women, without bluster and noise, but silently, with perseverence, presence of trained minds, deep sense of responsibility, and with devotion to duty are easy leaders wherever found, as farmers, teachers, heads of high schools, academies or departments of colleges and universities, whether as preachers, doctors, druggists, missionaries, lawyers, whatever they may be doing, they are doing their work without fear or grace of any man but the Great Spirit. They are doing it better than the average of any race engaged in the same work under equal conditions.

Any institution founded as this one upon such broad truth cannot but advance with the advancing times.

Thus at Shaw, since there has been no time lost in flirting with the *bedazzling popular craze*, that God made one man for the deepest and broadest culture along all lines, and the other for the plow, axe and hammer, all have been united on the one idea of training the fitted leaders, and to train these in the same way that leaders have always been trained, viz: by studying past civilizations in the languages of those civilizations, and endeavoring to be exact along all lines, fundamentals first, and then everything else that is within the reach of the human mind.

At Shaw therefore, a visitor may expect to see men and women too, in college pursuits in the forenoon determining a parabolical curve, locating a light house, given just three angles, studying laws of electricity and of reflex action, sympathizing with a betrayed and burning Troy, communing with Horace, feeling with Andromiche, criticising American and English authors, debating and doing everything ever done anywhere, and in some cases doing very acceptable work, while in the afternoons these same men and women are at their work benches, some in the blacksmith shop, some painting, women working, sewing, while some men are assiduously playing ball, throwing hammer, playing tennis, riding first grade wheels and doing just the things in every way which aid in their full development of mind and body. And best of all, out of nearly four hundred students in all departments, all but five are active Christians working on the grounds with the Y. M. C. A. and other Christian organizations, for their own and for the salvation of the fellows who may do useful service at several mission points in the city including the jail every Sunday, street work for God and several Sunday-schools in needy parts.

Such pursuits, such systematic, broad training along all lines with perfect freedom and no limitations except those on the individual and separate souls of students must surely be the true training for the black boy and girl as for the blue. With the highest ideals constantly before the undergraduate, coming in close range of the best thought and of the leaders of thought by the happy location of Shaw here at North Carolina's capital, and being kept in touch with the spirit of this rushing, progressive electric age, it is no wonder that they are beginning to plan more wisely for longer, steadier, exacter training. Students are pursuing a liberal education here with no desire for titles or degrees except they come as a matter of course by merit and mean the same to them as any other race. They seem to know full well that high-sounding, empty names have already puffed up and made many appear so ridiculous, that now it is much better not to have any name but plain John Smith, the *doer*. It means much when a race of people begin so early to seek what is real useful and essential, when they begin to be able to prefer the real to the seeming. And so with a well arranged curriculum as will soon be with the kind of trained instructors as Shaw has always, for the most part, had with God at the helm as ever, under such leadership as Shaw has been peculiarly blessed, and with students willing and desirous of taking plenty of time, if by so doing, no training is denied them which they are capable of having. With such an outfit as this Shaw University will grow and perfect herself until all the world will call her blessed.

N. C. BRUCE.

WATERS NORMAL INSTITUTE.

This prosperous institute, now ten years old, is regarded throughout the State not only as the most successful enterprise of the kind fostered by the colored Baptist, but excelling many other institutions created and existing under more favorable circumstances. The wonderful progress which has so signally marked the development of this work is due largely to the indefatigible exertions of its founder, Rev. C. S. Brown. The founder is well and favorably known throughout the State, and honored and loved by all Baptists. He commands and holds the esteem and confidence of the people among whom he labors as but few men are able to do He has year after year collected hundreds and even thousands of dollars out of the people of eastern Carolina for this work, and has by persistent effort founded a school now estimated to be worth nearly twelve thousand dollars. The school has been wisely located in the "black belt" of the State, in easy reach of the people, whose educational advantages have heretofore been meager. It deserves success, and success has been achieved.

Three buildings have been erected for the accommodation of students. The first is a two-story structure, containing a chapel and recitation rooms. The second is a dormitory for young men, where ample provision is made to entertain thirty. The last is a handsome edifice, known as "Reynold's Hall," and is admired by all who see it for its design, beauty and completeness. It is remarkable to consider how loyally the people in the immediate section have stood by this work, they have responded most liberally to every appeal made to maintain and extend the school.

Notwithstanding the cry of "hard times," the present year has so far brought to this school increased success, and its trustees are congratulating themselves over the favorable outlook.

Nearly two hundred students have been enrolled and a large increase has been made in the boarding department. Four teachers are constantly employed to give instructions, supplemented by five student teachers. The instructors sustain a favorable place among the educators of the State for ability and experience.

In addition to other multiplied duties, the President teaches four hours each day. Miss Cora B. Person, well known throughout the State as a professional teacher and a lady of rare culture and refinement, is employed as lady principal, and renders valuable service in the school room.

Mrs. Amaza J. Brown gives instruction in history, elocution and literature, and has been pronounced by competent judges as "excellent."

The fourth teacher is Mr. J. B. Catus, a gentleman of broad experience in the work, having followed teaching since leaving Hampton, about twenty years ago. With the facilities as heretofore described, and with a faculty competent, cultured, experienced, Waters Institute easily ranks as the leading institution for the education of colored youth east of Raleigh.

Already scores of young men and women educated there have gone out into life and are making a record which the founders of the school may justly be proud of.

It must however be remembered that a school must live by the charity of the people. It has behind it no endowment or permanent income, but must obtain "daily bread" by faith in Providence and confidence in the people. It stands out as a proud monument of race pride and indicates what might be done by unselfish concentration of our mites. To fully appreciate what is being done through this school, and how it is enshrined in the affections of the people, it is necessary for one to visit the place. It is a work to be proud of, and should have the united encouragement of the Baptists of the State.

So remarkable has been the success of the work that the American Baptist Home Mission Society, though burdened with an annual deficit, contributes towards paying the salaries of teachers, nearly twelve hundred dollars a year.

It is confidently believed that, when our brethren learn the real merits of the school they will cheerfully reach forth liberal hands to make Waters Institute what it should be, the chief educational center in eastern North Carolina.

SHILOH INSTITUTE.

WARRENTON, N. C.

This school was organized May 1st, 1885, and known as Warrenton High School.

The property containing two buildings and eight acres of land. Was purchased some years previous by the Shiloh Baptist Association.

Eight brethen within the bounds of said Association constituted a Board of Trustees under whose supervision and direction the school has been conducted.

By the arrangement of a number of the citizens of Warrenton known as the Warrenton Educational Association J A. Whitted was secured as the principal, Mrs. Florence Ward as assistant. The school constantly grew in number and influence until some years later it was incorporated as Shiloh Institute.

Though the 12 years of i's history a number of efficient men and women have been employed from time to time as teachers, Misses C. B. Person, Nannie E. Hawkins Messrs. J. P. Williams, B. Thornton and for the two years the State Normal School was attached to it, Prof. H. H. Falkner and Dr. J. A. Brockett.

Great has been the influence and usefulness of Shiloh Institute.

More than a hundred teachers and preachers have gone forth as light-bearers in different parts of North Carolina and other States.

J. A. Whitted having resigned the principalship in 1895 Rev. M. E. Hall of Littleton, N. C. was elected as his successor.

With Rev. Hall at the head and the Board of Trustees whose experience is somewhat extended, much is hoped for and expected of Shiloh Institute.

ROANOKE INSTITUTE.

ELIZABETH, CITY, N. C.

This Institute is the last organized among the Baptist schools of North Carolina and yet by far not the least.

The school is not yet a year old being organized last fall.

The property was purchased by the Association whose name it bears and a set of strong men constitute the Board of Trustees. Prof. M. W. D. Norman, who for several years was Prof. of theology in Shaw University, is the principal. The choice convinces us of the wisdom of the Board.

A son of old Roanoke when called to serve his people he left a position which any one might feel proud of to assume the new duties.

Prof. A. S. Dunston, whom no one shares more of the confidence of his brethren, together with the three females constitute the faculty.

At a leap the school has surpassed most of the other schools of the city in numbers and bids fair to rival any school in the East.

The trustees are preparing to erect a commodious building upon the site. Notices are coming in from every direction of students expecting to enter in the ensuing year.

The people in the surrounding churches are fast becoming alive to the work and we think the day is not far distant when the Roanoke Institute will take its place beside the leading institutions of the State.

DEAR BRETHREN :—I am preparing a list of the superintendents of Baptist Sunday-schools. I hope to get every one in the State on this list. I can meet the schools better and do them more good if I can prepare this list. I sincerely hope every Moderator of Associations who have not sent me a minute, will do so as early as possible.

Dear pastors, please send me the names of every Sunday-school superintendent under your charge at once. I want to try and do your people good, help me in this effort. Let the whole State of Baptist move this year as one man.

Please attend to this at once brethren. Yours in the work,
JOSEPH PERRY.

NEUSE RIVER INSTITUTE.

WELDON, N. C.

This Institute was established in the fall of 1889.

The property was purchased by the Neuse River Baptist Association. It is controlled by a Board of Trustees and Executive Board appointed from year to year by said Association.

The school has been under the management of Prof. A. P. Robinson.

It is the intention of the Board to erect such buildings and secure such teachers as will enable them to make the school the equal of any school of similar grade in the State.

With such men as the Association has at the head, we have every reason to hope the day is not far distant when Roanoke Institue will do the work contemplated.

The school opened the spring session with twenty-eight pupils and now has a regular attendance of seventy-nine.

Tuition, $1, 75 cents and 50 cents.

Board can be had in the town of Weldon at reasonable rates.

No pains will be spaired to have the school opened next fall with far better equipments, and a good faculty. It is hoped the friends will avail themselves of the superior advantages the school offers.

NEW ERA INSTITUTE—THIRD SESSION.

The New Era Institute has proved a great success. It is no longer an experiment. Hundreds of pastors and others are enthusiastic over it, declaring that it is one of the greatest blessings that has ever come to the colored Baptists of this State. They look forward with eager interest to the third meeting, the general programme of which is given in this leaflet. We hope to see every pastor and many others who were not at the previous Institute. Brethren, you cannot afford to miss this rare opportunity.

There will be twelve lectures at each Institute (unless special circumstances prevent), and seventy-two lectures for the entire 3 years' course. The subjects will include Biblical Theology, Church History, The Ministry, Christian Education, Missions, The Church and its Work, and other practical matters. It will be a kind of theological school brought nigh to the people. The best of available talent, both white and colored, will be secured for lecturers.

Everybody is invited. Every minister should attend every Institute. It will be of great value to him. It is proposed to publish a "Roll of Honor" of ministers who pursue the entire course of lectures. We look to the pastors to lead their people by word and by example in the new movement that promises so much for our cause in this State. Come, pastors, and bring with you as many of your people as you can.

Each lecture will be followed by a discussion, for about thirty minutes, when members of the conference may ask questions and present their views on the subject.

The following is the outline of lectures for the second Institute:

BIBLICAL THEOLOGY—FOUR LECTURES.

Redemption. Coming of a Redeemer. Significance of His name.

His testimony concerning Himself and His mission. His Divinity.

2. *Redemption.* Christ as the Light of the World; His teachings; miracles; life. Our example.

3. *Redemption.* The death of Christ; voluntary; his words concerning the purpose of his death. Teachings of the New Testament; the blood of Christ; life for life.

4. *Redemption.* His Resurrection; Ascension; intercession at the right hand of God.

CHURCH HISTORY—TWO LECTURES.

1. *Christianity in Europe from 500, to 1517.* The Roman Catholic Church supreme. Church and State. Worship of Images. Purgatory. Indulgences. Transubstantiation. Monasticism. Celibacy of the clergy. Capital punishment for heresy. General character of the middle or "dark ages."

2. *The Great Reformation.* Reformers before this. The Waldenses, and Albigenses: Wycliffe, Huss. *Luther:* a monk; visit to Rome and conversion: his theses; excitement; at Diet of Worms: his translation of the Bible; hymns; rapid spread of the new doctrines. Estimate of Luther's character and work.

THE GOSPEL MINISTRY—ONE LECTURE.

1. *Preparation of Sermons.* Importance of careful preparation. Prayer. Meditation. Bible study. How to study the Bible. Every sermon should have a plan and object. Criticism of plans of sermons.

CHRISTIAN MISSIONS—TWO LECTURES.

1. *Foreign Mission Work of Colored Baptists.* When begun. Total contributions. Number of missionaries. Fields of labor. Results. Obligations for the evangelization of Africa. Great opportunity.

2. *Foreign Mission work of the Northern and Southern white Baptists.* Their organizations. Fields occupied. Missionaries. Annual results. Prospects.

CHRISTIAN EDUCATION—ONE LECTURE.

1. *The growing demand for educated men and women among the colored people.* As american citizens, to know what they should do. As ministers of intelligent congregations. As teachers in the Sunday-school and public schools; educated young women needed here. As editors, physicians, professors in higher schools, etc.

THE CHURCH—TWO LECTURES.

1. *Reception of Members by the Church.* The general custom. Evils of hasty action. Relation of their Caristian experience or conversion. What of visions? What are the Scriptural requirements for church membership?

Church Discipline. Scriptural authority for it. Necessity both for the offender's good and the honor of the church. Spirit in which it should be administered. The proper steps to take. How personal differences should be adjusted.

REV. J. A. WHITTED,
Raleigh, N. C.
General Missionary.

INSTITUTE OF SAVANAH CHURCH, CUMBERLAND COUNTY, DEC. 16-18.

This meeting conducted entirely by the District and General missionaries Vincent and Whitted was considered by those who attended intensly instructive and interesting through the whole three days. Indeed it has become very evident that some of our very best meetings are those held far out in the country from railroads. Rev. W. H. Andrews and his good people loyally stood by the missionaries and the meeting from beginning to close. Mr. B. J. Melvin and others personally and keenly felt the responsibility of making the occasion a success. Revs. N. B. Dunham, G. R. Richardson, H. C. McDonald, T. M. Council and others here as before in other meetings made considerable sacrifice to make the meeting a success. Rev. W. H. Andrews and his people are to be congratulated for the good results secured. Let us have more like it.

A. B. VINCENT.

ROCKINGHAM INSTITUTE. FEB. 2-4.

In interest, devotion and good results, we would place the Rockingham Institute held with Rev. D. M. Jackson's church not a whit behind that of other meetings. Sickness for the first time caused the District Missionary to be behind a few hours in opening the meeting, however the faithfulness of the General Missionary showed itself by opening the exercises promptly. In company with Rev. J. H. Scott, the gentlemanly and profound theologian of Shaw University we reached Rockingham in time for the evening services. Rev. Scott was present and at once reached the hearts of his audience, and during his whole stay held the audience spell-bound. He reached the climax in his lectures the last night when he gave one of the most practical thoughtful, yet simple, addresses on Christian education yet delivered. The brethren of the State can but feel profoundly grateful for the wisdom of Brother Scott's selection and the fact that he has cast his lot among North Carolina Baptists.

The University is to be congratulated on the securing of his services for the work contemplated, Rev. J. G. Blalock and Rev. W. H. Fulford, of Rockingham, put in their usual excellent services which did so much to help the work last year. The District Missionary delivered one talk on missions and Rev. J. A. Whitted ably and acceptably carried out the remainder of the programme even to details. The church at this point, though weak, gives promise of a tower of strength for the future. Rev. Jackson and Rev. W. H. Woodwrad who are always engaged in some noble enterprise to promote the Baptist cause stood heroically by the meeting during the three days. Rev. Woodward used his paper, the Pedee Union, to interest the people in the work. Possibly at no place have the sisters of the church done more for the meetings than at Rockingham. Some of the sisters contributed more than the brethren. We close the first quarter of the second year in gratefulness to God and deep appreciation to all friends who have assisted.

Fraternally,
A. B. VINCENT.

Rev. G. W. Moore, of Fayetteville, succeeds Rev. C. C. Somerville at Reidsville, and Rev. H. H. Hines succeeds Rev. Moore.

AT LUMBERTON AGAIN.

The third series of lectures for the Central District were commenced in Sandy Grove church, Lumberton, Jan. 12, 1897.

We were able to get some idea of the growth and deepening interest which has been in progress during one year, for just one year ago the work in this district began at Lumberton. It would have rejoiced the hearts of our friends who have sacrificed so much for "co-operation" to have witnessed the great change which has come to this section in only one year. Although the weather grew very inclement and muddy in travel, yet crowds could be seen during the various sessions pulling their way promptly to every service, sometimes going for miles to and fro, in order to get everything said. The liberality too in giving to support the work notwithstanding the hard times was another indication of the deep and spiritual growth of truth in the hearts of the people. Christian growth unmistakably evidences itself in self-denials. It is indeed a bad sign to see individuals and churches grow narrow and closer in giving to support God's work. Possibly in no meeting has there been a more willing disposition to contribute. Pastor S. W. Dockery who has recently taken charge has indeed a promising field of labor. Deacon W. C. Pope and Lumber River Association are building up a school here which they hope to make a fitting or preparatory work to Shaw University. Some of these good people are so enthusiastic over the school that they are disposed to call it "Shaw University." This we told them could not be, then they said it must be a department or preparatory work to Shaw which we heartily endorsed. This intense desire which has absorbed these people for something nobler and better is an encouraging omen indeed of what co-operation will do wherever it is given a trial.

Able and instructive lectures were delivered by Revs. J. N. Booth of Lumberton, W. M. Jones, of Maxton, and O. L. Stringfield, of Raleigh, who in his eloquent speech on education, said Shaw University was one of the best schools in the world.

Rev. D. J. Moore preached acceptably the first night, and Rev. J. A. Whitted, as usual, did very excellent work through the whole meeting.

Thanks are due Rev. Booth for his interest during the Institute, to say the least, Bro. Booth has shown himself not only one of the best teachers, but one of the broadest and most liberal white Baptist ministers in North Carolina.

Rev. S. W. Dockery, as usual, did his best for the Institute. His people deserve credit for their devotion to the cause and deep interest in the work.

A. B. VINCENT.

SELMA INSTITUTE.

The New Era Institute at Selma the last week of December '96 was eminently successful.

Rev. E. B. Blake, the pastor left no stone unturned, although he had but little time to get his church and people ready.

The District Missionary was ably assisted by Rev. J. H. Scott and

Prof. W. R. Cullom of the Bible Departments of Shaw University and Wake Forest College. Rev. J. J. Worlds and Rev. Jno. E. White, Prof. J. W. Byrd of Smithfield also assisted and Gen. Missionary J. A. Whitted. The town of Selma was stirred for a higher and better life. The following are some of the many expressions made by those who attended the Institute.

"I wish we had the meeting every month," "I have not been hungry this week, I could not eat I was so full."

"I feel that I am going to live closer to God than ever before. Have never seen such a meeting."

"I was so thankful to see white and colored brethren in the pulpit together—and working together."

"Thank God for sending white and colored brethren to help us."

"If I could just keep up with these meetings I would be exactly fixed."

"I could not stay home and work. I was so afraid I would miss something."

"I only came to stay one day. Have been trying to go home but could not." This was said the last day.

"Yesterday morning I just felt like I was set free."

"Was so restless I could not be satisfied until I struck the path to the church."

"Lord help these people to keep coming down here."

Many other similar statements could be given. These expressions were made on the last day by the older mothers and fathers who went so full that the cup of joy ran over during the praise service. These expressions may give some hints as to the results of New Era Institutes in North Carolina.

We would mention the hospitality of Dr. Vick and Mr. N. E. Egerton, prominent white citizens of the Methodist church here, who so kindly and royally entertained Rev. Scott and Prof. Cullom.

Credit is due all the citizens, white and colored, Methodists and Baptists for assistance.

A. B. VINCENT.

INSTITUTES YET TO BE HELD.

THIRD COURSE LECTURES.

Rocky Mount,	March,	9	11
Clayton,	"	16	18
Charlotte,	"	23	25
Newberne,	" 30,	Apr.	1
Raleigh,	April	6	8
Monroe,	"	13	15
Wilmington,	"	20	22
Seaboard,	"	27	29
Gastonia,	May,	4	6
Edenton,	"	11	13
Graham,	"	18	20
Rutherfordton,	"	25	27
Clinton,	June,	1	3
Red Springs,	"	8	10
Williamsboro,	"	15	17

It was announced recently that Dr. I. T. Tichenor, the efficient Correspondent Secretary of the Home Mission Board of the Southern Baptist Convention was lying very ill. Dr. Tichenor has done a great work among his own brethren, and he has been a great friend to mission work among the colored people. If pleasing to God's will, we trust he may yet be spared to the great work of which he is the leader.

WHARTON NORMAL AND INDUSTRIAL SCHOOL.

CHARLOTTE, N. C., Feb. 4, 1894.

DEAR BRO. WHITTED:—Referring to your asking information concerning our school work, in reply would say that our school is in a very prosperous condition at the present time under the management of Mr. Robert W. Brown of Winston, N. C., and Mr. W. T. Christian, of the same place as assistant teacher and instructor of vocal and instrumental music. The average attendance is about 75. The enrollment being 96.

The Wharton Normal and Industrial School was organized in January of 1894, and opened in the lecture room of the First Baptist church, Charlotte, N. C., with 12 scholars. The school was conducted throughout the session by Mrs. M. T. Pope, under the auspices of the above named church.

The school was again opened the following session, Rev. C. H. Williamson was made principal, with Miss Alice Hughes of Henderson, assistant and music teacher.

The school closed at the end of this, having been a very successful term, having had enrolled during the session 105 students. The Board decided that the lecture room was not suitable to accommodate the increasing numbers and erected with the help of friends a school building. Without money we began the erection of a building. Dr. H. M. Wharton, the great evangelist of Baltimore, hearing of our urgent need of a school of this nature in Western North Carolina, came at once to our rescue, giving us a helping hand. In recognition of which the Board voted that the school should be known as the Wharton Normal and Industrial School. The school is located in Charlotte, which is the centre of a large colored population, and the seat of many industries, remarkable for its business enterprise and progressiveness, and is healthy and inviting as a place of residence. The First Baptist church of Charlotte has ample grounds near its house of worship of which it gave a lot for the erection of a school building.

Prof. Brown succeeds Rev. C. H. Williamson as principal.

HOW MAINTAINED.

The school is maintained by the tuition of the scholars by voluntary contribution, and through the sacrificing efforts of the Board and teachers who have had but little to draw upon.

ITS NEEDS.

The school is greatly in need of funds at this time. If there be a friend to the work anywhere, who may read this sketch, and is interested in the educational work among our people please aid us a little.

ITS OBJECT.

The object of the Board is to improve the mental and moral condition of our people by instructing them in letters and work.

Yours,
A. SHEPARD.

Rev. L. T. Christmas, of the Central Baptist church, of Wilmington, has been installed as pastor of the Baptist church of Charleston, W. Va. North Carolina gives him up with reluctance, but we bid him God speed in his new charge.

ADDIE MORRIS SCHOOL.

Winston, N. C., Feb. 18, 1897.
Bro. Whitted,

Dear Sir:—Your letter received and contents noted, and will say in reply that I have 79 girls and 25 boys now enrolled in my school, total 104 scholars. My school was organized Oct. 1st, 1887. I have never had any assistant only when Miss Turner was here.

I worked up North five years and supported the school myself, and the last five years I have been working under the Home Mission Society of Chicago, a salary of $20 per month. $10 has been donated $50 by the Rowan Association, which met here last August, and $5 by the Womens' Convention that met at Salisbury.

Out of the $20 salary my other expenses are taken out. I furnish my own coal, wood and things that I use in my school and of course I do without a lot of things myself in order to meet my other expenses. I have only done this by economy learned while up North.

We have five afternoon sessions for Bible studies and industry. The children are progressing nicely. We also have Sunday school for the children. It has been organized four years, and it is quite a success. We have seven teachers for our Missionary Sunday School. Our average attendance is from 95 to 100.

Respectfully,
ADDIE C. MORRIS.
Cor. 6th and Chestnut Sts., Winston, N. C

※

For the present session—the Charlotte Normal School has enrolled one hundred and fifteen students. The daily average attendance being about seventy or seventy-five. The school is taught in the lecture room of the Ebenezer Baptist church and is composed of two departments, viz: Primary and Normal. The students of the primary department are those commonly taught in primary studies. The Normal Department—the same. School is in good condition—progressing successfully. This is a preparatory school for Shaw University.

C. L. DAVIS,
Principal.

※

CEDAR GROVE ACADEMY.

Roxboro, N. C.

Organized 1881. This school as yet has only one building and one acre of land near the corporate limits of Roxboro, on the road leading to Oxford, N. C.

Rev. C. L. Ragland was the first principal and served about four years. Afterward Rev. A. R. Satterfield assumed charge and conducted it in connection with the public school. Rev. R. H. Harris was his successor and is now at the head of the work.

Probably no county in the State stood in greater need of such an institution and comparatively none has done greater good.

This school has supplied teachers for almost the entire county and section. The location is healthy and good, and the school is crowded from time to time. It is hoped that the Board of Trustees may soon be able to erect buildings adequate to the needs of the school and it may accomplish a still greater good.

GARYSBURG HIGH SCHOOL.

ORGANIZED 1877 BY DR. R. I. WALDEN AND FRIENDS.

Board of Trustees:—Rev. N. F. F. Roberts, D. D., Oberlin, N. C.; Deacon W. Coats, Seaboard, N. C.; Rev. S. G. Newsome, Margarettsville, N. C.; Robert L. Perry, Louisburg, N. C.; Deacon Philip Garris, Garysburg, N. C.; L. B. Walden, Garysburg, N. C.; W. H. Haithcocks, Seaboard, N. C.

Faculty:—Rev. R. I. Walden, D. D., President; Robt. L. Perry, Teacher Mathematics; Alice Hughes, Preceptress in Music and Normal Teacher; Cora E. Walden, Teacher Preparatory Department; Mrs. R. I. Walden, Matron; J. W. Blacknall, State Teacher.

Location.—This school is beautifully located east of Garysburg, in fifteen minutes walk of the post office. This is the most healthy location in this district, good drainage, using water medicinal, non malarial. The health of this school for the past fourteen sessions justified the above statement. The instructions imparted to students of this school have afforded ample satisfaction in the past, but our facilites for the future are far superior to that of the past, having made more room for female lodging, and all the principal teachers are well equipped for the work. Furthermore this school was incorporated by the last Legislature of North Carolina. Also by the influence of Congressman Cheatham, the Public Library of the Second Congressional District has been placed at the school for the benefit of the students and patrons, these books are accessible to all free of charge. We have enlarged the girl's building and we can accommodate a much larger number than we have in the past, we are also making general improvements so that the coming session may be the grandest and most beneficial to any previous session.

This school has now enrolled eigthy-two pupils.

Seventy-five young men and women have been sent out as teachers in the public schools and high schools of North Carolina and Virginia.

Some of our leading ministers of Eastern North Carolina have been largely prepared under the instruction of Dr. Walden.

Twenty have gone out as graduates of the school and are quite meritorious in their labors. The school is supported at a great sacrifice to the teachers and friends, and especially to the president, Dr. Walden, who very often uses the money from his churches to carry on the school work.

Dr. Walden not only attends regularly upon the class room work but is forced to preach at two or more of our prominent churches for the maintenance of himself and largely the school. It is our pleasure to say of him that he ranks easily among our best preachers in North Carolina and we commend the work to the favorable consideration of friends North and South as fully worthy of your contributions and to parents and guardians as worthy of your patronage.

EDITOR BAPTIST QUARTERLY.—Please allow me space in your valuable columns to say a few words concerning our pastor, Rev. J. W. Wood.

We feel that he deserves much credit for what he has done and is doing, as a young minister. Under his leadership we are succeeding wonderfully well. He is a Christian gentleman, and a preacher, in every sense of the word as pastor. Before he took charge of our church fifteen dollars was a large collection for us to raise in one day, but since he has been with us we have raised as much as $150 at one collection. He also raised at Gaston church, of which he is also pastor, $150 at one collection.

We are also glad to say that our new church is nearly completed, and will be one of the finest churches in Northampton county.

We can only say bless God for such a man as Rev. J. W. Wood.

Yours Respectfully,
COOL SPRING BAPTIST CHURCH.
Jan. 15, 1897.

WILMINGTON, N. C.,
Feb. 5, 1897.

MR. J. A. WHITTED, Raleigh, N. C.—*Dear Sir:*—Your letter came duly to hand some time ago, owing to illness of myself is why I have not written before now, and for which I hope you will pardon my long delay. In reply to yours of the 11th ult: The membership of the First Baptist church of Wilmington, N. C., corner of 5th and Campbell streets is two hundred, and was represented at the Baptist State Convention by Rev. Joseph Spells, pastor of said church, and donated one dollar.

We are struggling and trying to complete our church, and there is some indebtedness hanging over us and it will take one thousand dollars more to complete it. We ask the sympathy of all.

Respectfully Yours,
REV. JOSEPH SPELL., *Pastor.*
H. C. WILLIAMS, *Clerk.*

We are informed that there is one N. S. Scott claiming to be a representative of our Convention or of the Southern Convention. Brethren, beware of men who come to you thus. We have six regularly appointed missionaries, Revs. J. Perry and McRansom, representing the Sunday-school work; and Revs. P. F. Maloy, A. B. Vincent, C. C. Somerville and J. A. Whitted representing the church work. If others are appointed we will announce their appointment.

Col. Charles Banes, of Phila., a friend of Shaw University, is now numbered with the many friends of Shaw who have died in the past few years, and we can only look to a kind Providence to raise up other friends for our struggling University.

※

Rev. A. R. Satterfield, Moderator of East Cedar Grove Association is in the city, and we fear he contemplates leaving the State. Rev. Satterfield, though comparatively young, has done and is doing a great work in his section both as teacher and preacher.

It would be well if our people could know the worth of men before they leave them.

NOTICE.

The next State Teachers' Association will convene at Shaw University, Raleigh, June 15-20. An unusual programme will be arranged embodying such practical school room work under specialists as will help every teacher in the State. The most eminent educators and experts, white and colored, will assist from time to time during the week's meeting and it is to be hoped that fully 500 teachers will attend. President Alderman, of the State University, and Dr. McIver, of the Normal and Industrial school for white girls at Greensboro. President Meserve and Dr. Roberts of Shaw University. Profs. S. G. Atkins, of Normal school, Winston; Dr. E. E. Smith, State Normal, Fayetteville, and other prominent educators will be secured so that any who comes will feast to a variety of treats during the whole week.

Very respectfully,
A. B. VINCENT.
Pres. State Teachers' Association.

BREWERVILLE, LIBERIA,
WEST C. AFRICA,
Jan. 31, 1896.

REV. J. A. FULLER, Oxford, N. C.—Dear Friend and Brother:

On the first Sunday in August last I opened a protracted meeting at Zion Grove, Brewerville, which resulted in the conversion of sixteen precious souls, twelve of which I baptized on the first Sunday in September and administered the Lord's Supper to a well filled house.

The most of the new members are natives and need to be taught "to observe all things whatsoever I have commanded you," otherwise we may expect them to return to their old country habits of idolatry.

Since my return to Liberia I have baptized and given the right hand of fellowship to 31 persons. Our Sunday-school is in a flourishing condition, with an average of fifty.

I suppose you know I am no longer connected with Ricks Institute, but that I am now at Brewerville endeavoring to found my school work in connection with my church.

By the last mail I received a copy of *The National Baptist Magazine*, from which I learned that the Baptist Foreign Mission Convention, under whose auspices I was returned to my former work here, has gone into the National Baptist Convention.

From March 20th, 1893 at which time I was commissioned in the city of Richmond, Va., with a salary of $500 00 per annum, up to last June, at which time I was forced to resign my post at Ricks Institute, for reasons given the Board. I had served under the auspices of the B F. R. Convention two years and three months, against which the Corresponding Secretary, Mrs. L. A. Coles, has remitted to me only $375 00, leaving a ballance now due me of $750 00. Who is now responsible for my pay, since the amalgamation? Have the kindness to let me hear from you at your earliest convenience. I trust this may find you and family well as it leaves us all. Mrs. Hayes sends love to Sister Fuller. Kindly remember me to all.

I am yours, most truly,
J. O. HAYES.

Raleigh, N. C., Feb. 20, 197.
To the Baptists in N. C. Greeting,

Dear Brethren and Sisters: I have been asked to write you concerning the Missionary Training School and its work.

This school is located in Raleigh, and is a department of Shaw University. It is under the auspices of the Womens' Baptist Home Mission Society, with headquarters in Chicago, and the American Baptist Home Mission Society, with headquarters in New York City.

The W. R. H. M. S. has been doing work among the colored people for 20 years. This has been done mostly by white women missionaries from the North, all of whom have had a special course of training to prepare them for that work in our Missionary Training School in Chicago. This work from the first has been greatly blessed of God.

It has been a work for the homes of the people, a work for the mothers and fathers, the young people and children, and many a pastor has been more perfectly instructed in the way of righteousness from the word of God by these Missionaries.

Last year this society of Christian women in the North supported 25 missionaries among the colored people, besides sustaining three Missionary Training Schools for the training of colored women.

This was done at the expense of over $14,000. Of these missionaries 18 were colored women who have been trained either in these schools or by missionaries on the field.

We want every Baptist in North Carolina to bcome acquainted with the work we are trying to do in these Training Schools.

In our school in Raleigh there are three divisions of labor. The close room work, household duties and field work. In our close room we have six periods of recitations daily, besides the morning and evening worship and Bible lesson.

A variety of subjects are taught— such as Bible Normal, Old Testament and New Testament studies, missionary studies, physiology, temperance, social purity, and nursing. The training teachers, Misses Miller and Hamilton are assisted by several pastors and others of Raleigh, such as Dr. Carter, Rev. Spillman, Rev. White and Mr. Broughton. Also several from the medical faculty of the University have given us lectures adapted to the needs of those who will have often to care for the sick and teach other people have had to do.

The training given our girls in household duties is no small part of their work. The care of the home, washing, ironing, cooking, sewing, etc., and the art of making home neat, pleasant and cheerful—this, all women should know and this is not only given in theory but daily practice. It is not how much do you know about these things but how well can you do them. It is of utmost importance that a missionary both knows how to do them and how to teach other people to do them.

Last but not least in our field work in which training is given under the close supervision of the training teachers. This work consists of two Sunday schools, one industrial school, three womens' meetings, and two children's meetings each week, besides house to house visiting in the homes of the people. All of these meetings are conducted in turn by the pupils a month at a time. As it is in household duties so in field work, the question is not how much do you know about it but how well can you do it.

This training school is open to three classes of students, those who desire to prepare themselves for missionary work among their people in the South, those who wish to go to Africa, and those who desire to take the course in order that they may be better fitted for work in their own homes and churches.

The course extends through two years and some may need to remain longer. We desire the most thorough education possible on the part of those who come. The best possible opportunities should be used by those who seek to enter missionary service. The expense of the school is $6 per month and this provides for board, a furnished protect and lighted room and the privilege of washing. All students who are able are expected to pay this amount in full, a limited number of those who may not be able to meet their entire expenses may be helped in part under conditions if application is made early in the year. It is best that all applications for admission to the school be made before the first of May. We would be glad to correspond with any consecrated Christian woman who desires to fit herself for more efficient service for God. We do not take any one under 21 years of age. A good christian character, and fitness for the work are necessary as well as sufficient education to be able to understand the branches taught.

Pastors speak a word of encouragement to such among your people and tell them of the school and help them to come to it. Some one encouraged and helped you, pass the help along.

Read 1st Tim. 2:15.

Yours for service,
EMMA L. MILLER.

WILKESBORO, N. C., Oct. 21, '96.
To the Baptist State Convention, greeting:

DEAR BRETHREN:—I am proud to know that the representatives of the colored Baptist churches of N. Carolina are now assembled in convention.

I hoped all along to be able to meet with you, but Providence has willed otherwise.

However, I pen a few lines which I hope the Convention will take the time to consider.

I labor in the mountain section of our State, and am doing in a feeble way, what I can to enlighten our people.

The work in this section is truly a missionary work, and seemingly out of the knowledge of the leaders of the denomination. The missionaries who are sent never find their way into these isolated places where dwells the great majority of the colored Baptists. Coming west from Salisbury, very few Baptists are to be found in the towns. We have a great many pious, but incompetent leaders, who would like to do something for the cause if they could succeed without the co-operation of the more intelligent leaders. Within a radius of thirty miles of this place can be counted 1,500 Baptists that are practically out of the fight, because their leaders, though good meaning men, do not favor human progress.

Some brethren who know me, and who are kind enough to come among us some times, (very seldom), but do not stay long enough to learn the nature of the case, discount me because I do not succeed with these people as they do with theirs.

They do not understand the situation. Their being strange makes them admired, should they tarry for the grain to mature, long ere harvest time, they would meet the frozen face.

There are three things absolutely necessary to bring the Baptists of Western North Carolina to the front, viz: First; ministers who are paid to travel and work must continue to reach farther and farther into the rural districts, appreciating whatever talent they can find, encouraging the same when used in the right direction.

Second—More of the intelligent ministers must accept permanent work with us. A visit once or twice a year does very little lasting good. We need men that can stay and bear the brunt. It will be a sacrifice only for a while. It will take a hero to do this, yes, the worthy man who labors here and bears the vituperation and abuse heaped upon him by false leaders, and bears also the privation and want caused by their mischievous ingenuity together with the ignorance of the people —that man is a hero, and instead of being ostracised by the more favored of his brethren he should be encouraged in every way possible.

Third—We must be educated, other denominations around us, appreciating this fact are establishing local schools and academies; we must do the same. It is a mistake for us to presume that the masses of the Baptists of rural western N. Carolina will send their boys and girls to Shaw or any similar institution until there is an educational awakening among them through minor schools at home. Under this conviction a few such schools are being established by concentrating the force of a few individual Baptists here and there, as the Yadkin and Davie Academy at Yadkinville, and the Yadkin Academy at Wilkesboro. We have the habit of calling such schools "little" and "insignificant," other denominations hail them as a good omen; for instance, the Presbyterians opened a school near here last fall, it ran eight months, enrolling 19 students, representing two counties. The leader rallied to their support, and now they have money to push their work.

The Baptists opened school here last fall, ran seven months, and enrolled seventy-one students, representing six counties. No recognition yet by our leaders. School has opened again, and from present indications we will enroll from 150 to 200 students.

We have purchased twelve and a half acres of land and are making efforts to erect a suitable building to teach in. What we have done has been done in less time than a a year, but as yet we have no reason to say that our efforts meet the approval of the (our) denomination out of this immediate section.

By the help of God and good

men we hope to succeed, nevertheless.

Should the Convention remember us in its appropriations, we will feel glad and thankful.

Wishing the Convention every possible degree of success, I am

Fraternally,
R. B. WATTS,

Principal of Yadkin Valley Academy.

Wilkesboro, N. C., Box 24.

P. S.—I was appointed to represent the Yadkin and Davie Association in the Convention, but the Treasurer failed to send me the funds, will try to have it sent to the Secretary of the Convention.

HICKORY GROVE ACADEMY.

WARRENTON, N. C.

This school was organized Nov. 1893. The school is under the direction of the following named brethren: Rev. G. W. Perry, of Raleigh; T. S. Stokes, of Wakefield; T. B. Ellis, of Wakefield; Richard High, of Wakefield; H. R. Goodson, Eagle Rock; Lumuel Shamble, of Wakefield; Willis High, of Wakefield; I. Saiab Hall, of Eagle Rock; Geo. W. Sledd, of Rosenburg

Rev. D. S. Salter, at one time pastor of the First Baptist church of Raleigh, is the principal, and Miss Eugenia Hill, of Raleigh, assistant.

There are now enrolled eighty-five pupils and the school bids fair to become a power in Shaw University and other similar Institutions.

NEUSE RIVER ASSOCIATION.

No. of churches,	72
Total amount raised	$212.61
Ordained ministers	60
Licenciates	59
Total membership of the Association	16,000

Rev. W. R. Mason, President.
Rev. W. H. Shaw, Vice-Pres.
A. R. Robinson, Secretary.
Rev. S. G. Newsom, Cor. Sec'y.
Dr. R. J. Walden, Statistical Secretary.
Rev. J. W. Wood, Auditor.
Philip Garris, Treasurer.

CO-OPERATION CONTRIBUTION.

The folloing churches contributed:

1st African Baptist Goldsboro,	$2 50
Warrenton	9 00
Hillsboro	7 30
Fayetteville	7 20
Haywood	5 65
Luisburg	2 15
Piney Woods Chapel	10 00
Rockingham	1 00
Poplar Springs	1 00
Laurinburg	90
South Winston	4 50
St. Paul, Tarboro	5 00

CONTRIBUTIONS FROM CHURCHES.

Gray's Creek, Rev. H. C. McDonald, $7 08.

Hilly Branch, Rev. A. H. Thompson, $1 62.

Lumber River Association, Moderator, A. H. Thompson, $10 00.

Baptist church Hubb, Rev. J. A. Spaulding, $3 55; Rev. B. Williams, 50 cents; James Walker, 50 cents.

First church, Littleton, Rev. L. J. Alexander $2 00.

Miss Cora Pair, Shotwell, 40c.
White Rock church, Durham, Rev. A. P. Eaton, $1 25.
Pleasant Grove church, Rev. H. C. McDonald, $1 75.
Northeast Chapel, Rev. J. H. Dunston, 56; Miss Liddia Jones, 25 cents; Miss China Kittrells, 25 cts;
Baptist church, Mebane, Rev. J. H. Dunston $1 40.
Baptist church of Selma, $1 10.
Baptist church, Hamlet, $2 25.
Baptist church, Maxton, $2 00.
The following gave 25 cents: Dr. W. R. Mapp and R. B. Morman.
Nashville Baptist church, Rev. J. J. Hines, $1 51.
Mt. Moriah church, $2 00.
Respectfully,
A. B. VINCENT,
Missionary.

A CALL TO DUTY.

DEAR BRO. WHITTED:—As I understand that the forthcoming QUARTERLY is to be devoted largely to our educational interests in the State, I beg you to allow me to a few suggestions and propositions to our brethren, which, if endorsed, will greatly strengthen our educational work, as well as encourage our friends who, for the past thirty years, have contributed so liberally towards the maintainence of mission schools among us.

To be direct in my references, let me briefly invite you to consider the obligations resting upon us to take hold of Shaw University as we have never done before. Brethren, have we done our duty towards Shaw University, our great school, the pride of the State, maintained solely through the philanthropy of Northern Baptists? It requires no prophet to see that that the day is not distant when the colored Baptist will be called upon to support in part, if not wholly, that institution. A demand of this kind would not be unreasonable, when we consider how rapidly the colored Baptists are growing in intelligence and wealth.

Hundreds of young men and women have gone out from Shaw who could easily spare a contribution annually to aid in supporting the institution, many of them educated for a pittance, command good positions, receive good salaries, live in good houses, and are sufficiently able to do something for their *alma mater*. And again, to their shame, it must be said that many whose circumstances are equally as good as I have stated, do nothing comparatively to advance denominational interests in the State. They have honor and position, but real charity seems to be an unknown quality in their lives. We must be educated to give—to help the race and race enterprises. The obligation to help Shaw is too obvious to admit of contradiction. The fact too is clear that we have failed even to manifest becoming gratitude, all have failed, students, graduates, preachers, churches, unions, Sunday-school Conventions and Associations. But is it too late to improve?

Now for my proposition:

First—Let the colored Baptists of North Carolina support Dr. N. F. Robberts as a professor and Vice-President of Shaw University.

Second—Let us obligate ourselves to pay into the Treasury of the American Baptist Home Mission Society Annually not less than eight hundred dollars to be used in paying Dr. Roberts' salary. We are proud of Dr. Roberts, proud of his record as a Prof. in the school, and proud of his connection with our work in the State. There has not gone from the institution a single student who does not respect and honor Dr. Roberts, and no man stands higher in the esteem of the colored Baptists of the State than he. His name connected with a movement of this kind would be an inspiration in all our meetings to persons disposed to give. Shall we not begin such a movement at once? I suggest further that those who endorse these suggestions write to Rev. J. A. Whitted, Raleigh, N. C., pledging what they will give in this direction. I stand ready to be one of eight to help raise eight hundred dollars this year. Will not the whole army who have gone out into life's battle field from Shaw join in one great procession and rally to the support of that great institution? Yours for the promotion of Baptist interests in the State.

C. S. BROWN.

CONTRIBUTIONS.

EASTERN DISTRICT.
C. C. SOMERVILLE, November, December and January.

Windsor, $26 05; Zion Hill, Plymouth, 1 00; St. Paul, 1 50; Spring Garden, 1 15; Spring Garden, 22 00; Jones' Church, 1 00; New Hope, 3 16; Winton Chapel, 5 00; Harrell's Chapel, 4 00; Aulanda, 25 00; Pleasant Plain, 8 03; Ahoski, 5 03; Jordan's Grove, 25 cents; Mt. Moriah, 8 00; Second Baptist, Murfreesboro, 2 04; First Baptist, Rich Square, 58 cents; Kelford, 1 35; Greenville, 4 40; Union, of Eastern Association, 2 05;

WINDSOR, N. C.

H. Hyman 25 cents, M. T. Smallwood 25 cents, Samuel Dews 25 cents, Rev. J. A. Faulk, Elizabeth City, 1 00, Pender Lee, 25 cents; M. S. Sutton, 25 cents; David M. Cherry, 25 cents; Peter Pritchard, 25 cents; Hester A. Pierce, 25 cents; Rev. W. H. Leath, Windsor, 1 25; Ann Hoggard, 35 cts; Luke Pierce, 39 cents; Tom Brown, Windsor, 50 cents; Andrew Slaughter, 25 cents; L. H. Haughton, 25 cents; Julia Carter, 25 cents; Washington Allen, 25 cents; Lewis Barnes, 25 cents; West Barnes, 50 cents; Rev. B. H. Gray, Windsor, 50 cents; H. C. Cherry, 25 cents; Granville R. Cherry, 25 cents cents; Susan Radford, 25 cents; Milly Webb, 25 cents; C. M. Cartwright, Edenton, 1 00; G. E. Freeman, Powellsville, 80; J. J. Thompson, 25 cents; G. W. Bolden, Murry Hill, 50 cents.

CO-OPERATION CONTRIBUTIONS AND MISSIONS IN NORTH CAROLINA.

Tarboro.—Joshua Bunn, 25 cents; Mrs. Francit Griffin, 25 cents; J. L. Faithful, 25 cents; Mrs. Rebecca Edgerton, 25 cents; Jno. Fullee, 50 cents.
Durham.—Ellen Burnet, 25 cents; Daniel Bobbitt, 25 cents; R. D Carlton 25 cents; Mrs. Pattie Webb, 25 cents.
Wise, N. C —Rev. L J. Alexander, 25 cts.
Rockingham—A. Everet, 25 cents; F. T. Town, 50 cents.
Winston—Miss Addie C. Morris $1 00.
Winton, N. C.—Rev C S Brown, 50 cts; Walter Myrick, 25 cents Jack Vain, 50 cts. Levi Brown, 50 cents; G. L. Vame, 50 cents; King Outlaw 50 cents, Mrs. Elizabeth Reynolds, 50 cents; Mrs. Saphrona Moore, 50 cents; Herbert Clark, 50 cents.
Powellsville, N. C — Mrs. Matilda Cowen, 50 cents; Granville Freeman, 25 cents; Henrietta Ward, 25 cents; Miss Fannie Cherry, 25 cents; A D Morris, 50 cents; W. E Bennett, 25 cents; Norfleet Askew, 25 cents; Miss O Livermore, 25 cents; Morgan Mitchell, 25 cents.
Rosemeade, N. C —Miss R. A. Simons, 50 cents.
Laurinburg, N C —Rev C. B Harris, 25 cents.
Rockingham—Rev. T. M. Jones, 50 cents; W. H. Diggs, 15 cents; Martin Taylor, 50c.
Hillsboro—Rev Alvis Whitted, 50 cents; Frank U. Dixon, 50 cents; Mrs Emeline Graves, 25 cents; Daniel Lattie, 25 cents; Rev. M. T. Hawkins, 25 cents; John Young, 50 cents; Anthony Neal, 25 cents
Jackson Mitchell, 25 cents; Turner Barnes, 25 cents; Mrs Ellen Williams, 75 cents; Mrs. Lizzie Roulhac, 37 cents; L. Roulhac, 25 cents; Isaac Barnes, 25 cents; Newbern Sessoms, 25 cents; Benj. Reynolds, 25 cents; G. W. Brown, 25 cents; G. W. Stewart, 25 cents; Paesar Smallwood, 25 cents; Solomon Pugh, 25 cents; W. Peele, 25 cents; Sarah C. Holly 25 cents; G. W Gray, 25cts;

LIST OF CONTRIBUTORS.

Rev. J O. Alderman $1 19, Gabriel Williams, 25; Rev. C C. Lawson, 50 cents; Mrs. Hannah Williams, President W H. M. S., 25 cents; Katie Parker, 25 cents; Deacon B

J Bridgers, 50 cents; Sallie B anch, 50 cts.;
Silvia Oten, 25 cents; Rev P. S Satchell, 25
Caroline Latham, 25 cents; Mrs W. A.
B idges, 50 cent ; W. A. Bridges, 50 cents;
Eliza Pitts, 25 cents; Rev. A. Foreman, 25
cents; Rev. J J Franklin, 50 cents; Ma tha
Perry, 50 cents; Emma Peaton, 25 cents;
Sarah Winfield. Vice-President of W H. M
S. 25 cents; Lucy Satchell, 25 cents; Rev.
W. H Pender, 25 cents; Mrs. Vinos Cotton,
50 cents; Mrs Clarinda Foxhall, 25 cents;
W. H Pitts, 25 cents; Jane Laughey, 25 cts;
Mary Branch, 25 cents; Clara Grimes, 25c;
Mollie Latham, 50 cents; Eliza Pitts 25 cts;
E. L Langley, 50 cents; R. P Maun, $1 20;
Mrs. Loney Mitchell, 25 cents.

Murfreesboro Albert Southall, 25 cents;
J. W. Jenkins, 25 cents; J. W. H. Pool, 25
ce ts

Kelford—J H. Biggs. 25 cent ; W. R.
Simmons, 25 cents

Winton, N. C.—Thomas Jerrigan, 50 cts;
Moses Vann, 50 cents; John Wilson, 75 cts;
Walter Myri s, 50 cents; Willy Jones, 25
cents; P. J. Vann 25 cents; Jackson Vann,
25 cents

Greenville, N C.—J. H Britt, 50 cents; S.
M. Fleming, 25 cents; Mrs Jennie Elks, 50
cents; J. W Eaton, 50 cents; Catherine
R d, 25 cents; M H, Henryhorn, 25 cents;
F anci House, 25 cents; Mary Davis, 50 cts.

Wi ton, N C — James Reynolds, 25 cts ;
James M Walden. 5 cents; Edward G. Turner, 21¢, W Dolphin St., Baltimore, Md.,
50 ce ts; A. W. Jones, 25 cents; Peter F.
Hair, 25 cents; Frank Morriss 25 cents;
King Outlaw, 25 cents; A. T. Beverly, 25
cen s; Jackson Vann, 25 cents

Harrellsville.—Daniel Sharp, 25 cents; H.
F. Sessoms, 25 cents; Jackson Askew, 25 cts;
Tho mas Sharp, 50 cents; Rev. W. P. Sharp,
50 cents; Dorah Askew, 25 cents; C E. Askew, 25 cents.

Aulander A. A. Lewter, 50 cts; John I.
Ross, 25 cents; N. H Revell, 5 cents; Peter
wter, 50 cents; Julia Ransom, 25 cents;
Junius Oliver, 25 cents; E. L Rawls, 50 cts;
Goodman Early, 25 cents; Jackson Jones, 25
cents; Stephen Early, 25 cents; J W. Jackson, 20 cents; A J Lee, 25 cents; Si as
Mitchell, 50 cents; Budd Ruffin, 50 cents;
W. H Lewter, 25 cents; Katie Harmon, 25
cents; Agnes Higgs, 25 cents; Minnie Wilson, 25 cents; Rebecca Bryant, 25 cents; G.
E. Freeman, 25 cents; John R. Rawls, 50
cents; Charles Sessom, 25 cents; G W. Anderson, 25 cents; Isaac Jordan, 25 cents; Rebecca Bryant, 50 cents.

Ahoskie, N C —Rev R B. Tilley, 50 cts;
Kader Askew, 50 cents; C. C. Summervi le,
25 cents; Frank Peele, 25 cents.

Powellsville.—D S. Sessoms, 50 cents;
John Vaughan, 25 cents; J. J. Mitchell, 50
cents; Martin Taylor, 25 cents.

Murfreesboro—Henry Vaughan, 50 cents;
William Reid, 25 cents.
Como—John Riddick, 50; Cornelia Dud-
ley, 25 cents.
St. John's, Hertford County.—Thomas
Early, 25 cents; Jacob Daniel, 50 cents.
Harrellsville—Thomas Parker, 50 cents;
H Hardy, 25 cents; Levi Brown, 25 cents.

REV. C. C. SOMERVILLE.

On the 16th day of March 1859, near the little town of Ridgeway, N. C., in the county of Warren, the subject of this brief sketch, the Rev. Clinton Clay Somerville was born of humble parents, Richard and Mary, who were owned as slaves by Dr. Henry Plummer. The foundation of his early training was laid in the public schools of Warrenton, and from the first young Somerville manifested great eagerness to learn and advanced rapidly in his books.

In the year 1878 he was led to accept faith in Christ, and was baptized into the fellowship of the First Baptist church of Warrenton.

Desiring to extend his education, he entered the State Normal School at Salisbury in 1881, and graduated at the head of his class in 1885, having won the Peabody medal for proficiency in scholarship.

While yet a student in school, he was licensed to preach the gospel by his church, and was almost immediately called to the pastorate of St. John's Baptist Church, of Gold Hill, N. C. In his new and sacred calling he rapidly advanced, displaying earnestness, devotion and power; and the following year he was regularly ordained to the gospel ministry by the Rowan Association, fifty-four churches representing.

In 1891 he was chosen moderator, in which position he served for two years, in the same years he was elected Recording Secretary of the Baptist State Convention and filled the office with credit and ability until chosen to the work of missionary.

Subsequently he was called to the pastorate of the church at Statesville, which he served with great acceptance for three years, during which time he built a splendid house of worship. While serving that people a stragetic point for the Baptists—he was invited to assume charge of the work at Reidsville, which appeared to be a more important point. Here he has labored with ability and skill for more than five years, and forced himself to the front as one of the strongest, ablest and most aggressive leaders in the Baptist church in the State. As a preacher, Rev. Somerville is able, earnest and eloquent, and is generally recognized among his brethren as one of their best pulpit orators. He entertains an audience with his dashing oratory, splendid periods and charming climaxes as few speakers are able to do. As an educator, his career has been noteworthy. He has stood examinations in eleven counties for teachers' certificates, and has held nothing less than a first grade certificate but twice. He served one year as principal of the graded school in Salisbury, and held the same position in Reidsville four years.

In 1886 he married Miss addie L. Brown, sister of the distinguished President of Waters Institute, Rev. C. S. Brown, from which union there have sprung one son and four graceful daughters.

Rev. Somerville has also achieved distinction as a writer. In 1886 he published a booklet entitled "My Brothers" which had quite a wide sale. As associate editor of the "Baptist Headlight," he wrote for two years under the name "Vigil," which articles were widely read and very favorably commented on throughout the State.

In October last he was chosen to serve as District Missionary, under the plan of co-operation, and is now on the field doing a work highly creditable to the denomination. To say the least, he is pre-eminently qualified to do the work peculiar to the position. He is intellectual, strong, courageous, he is earnest, active, enterprising, he is indeed the man for the place, and if given the cordial support of the brethren he will accomplish a work in eastern North Carolina of which the denominatton through out the State will justly feel proud.

Girl's Training School and Baptist Institue.

FRANKLINTON, N. C.
Founded by Rev. T. O. Fuller 1891, and incorporated by the General Assembly of North Carolina in 1895.

FACULTY.—Misses Augusta C. Curtis, principal; Laura M. Curtis, Laura B. Falkner, Rev. T. O. Fuller, A. M.

The above Institution is located on a beautiful site in the already famous school town of Franklinton, N. C.

This little town near the city of Raleigh is not only famous for its multiplicity of schools, but churches as well, which places its many students under wholesome religious influences.

Not only affording its pupils an opportunity to pursue the studies usually taught in schools of similar grade, but cooking, sewing, laundry work and housekeeping.

Special attention also is given to the study of the Bible and the development of Christian character.

Upward of one hundred and sixty pupils were enrolled in '95 and '96. Under the general direction of Rev. Fuller and the lady principal, the school has made wonderful development and improvement.

A beautiful edifice has been erected at considerable sacrifice. Other suitable buildings are in contemplation, and with the great competition as only Franklinton can give such an institution, if in so short a time all the others are outnumbered, what may we expect with onward movement of such a school?

God bless the faithful efforts of the few who are doing this wonderful work.

☞ All persons whose yearly supscription closes with this issue will kindly renew their subscription by enclosing amount of 50 cents to the Managing Editor, J. A. Whitted, Box 145, Raleigh, N. C.

BAPTIST STATE CONVENTION
Baptist ✦ Book ✦ Store.

SUPPLIES OF ALL KINDS.

Send all orders for Sunday School

**Quarterlies, Papers,
Roll Books, Lesson Cards,
Bible Lesson Pictures,
Reward Cards, Banners,**

And anything you want, to the Baptist Book Store.

Sunday School Libraries,

Books for Prizes, etc., at all prices, and selected with great care. We have all kinds and descriptions of

Hymn and Song Books, Bibles and Testaments

For Superintendents, Teachers, Scholars and Ministers.

We Want Your Orders, and Guarantee Satisfaction as to Quality and Price.

When sending orders for Quarterlies, state what series is wanted, and write name and post-office address in full.

Sunday Schools do not lose anything in ordering from this Store, as we fill their orders at

Publisher's Prices.

But the orders do help to carry on the work of State Missions.

Correspondence solicited. Information and samples furnished upon application. Address

BAPTIST BOOK STORE,

BOX 164. RALEIGH, N. C.

SOUTHERN RAILWAY.

Condensed Schedule.

IN EFFECT, JUNE 14th, 1896.

TRAINS LEAVE RALEIGH DAILY.

"Norfolk and Chattanooga Limited."

3:40 P. M. DAILY—Solid vestibuled train with sleeper from Raleigh to Chattanooga via, Salisbury, Morganton, Asheville, Hot Springs and Knoxville.

Connects at Durham for Oxford, Clarksville and Keysville, except Sunday. At Greensboro with the Washington and Southwestern Vestibuled (Limited), train for all points North, and with main line train No. 12 for Danville, Richmond and intermediate local stations; also has connection for Winston-Salem and with main line train No. 35, "United States Fast Mail" for Charlotte, Spartanburg, Greenville, Atlanta and all points South; also Columbia, Augusta, Charleston, Savannah, Jacksonville and all points in Florida, Sleeping Car for Atlanta, Jacksonville and at Charlotte with Sleeping Car for Augusta.

"Chattanooga and Norfolk Limited."

11:45 A. M. DAILY—Solid train, consisting Pullman Sleeping Cars and coaches from Chattanooga to Raleigh, arriving Norfolk 5:30 p. m. in time to connect with the Old Dominion Merchants' and Miners,' Norfolk and Washington and Baltimore, Chesapeake and Richmond S. S. Co's for all points North and East.

Connects at Selma for Fayetteville and intermediate stations on the Wilson and Fayetteville Short Cut, daily; daily except Sunday for Newbern and Morehead City; daily for Goldsboro, and Wilmington and intermediate stations on the Wilmington and Weldon Railroad.

Express Train.

8:53 A. M. DAILY—Connects at Durham for Oxford, Keysville, Richmond; at Greensboro for Washington and all points north.

Express Train.

3:30 P. M. DAILY—For Goldsboro and intermediate stations.

Local.

2:30 A. M. DAILY—Connects at Greensboro for all points North and South and Winston-Salem and points on the Northwestern North Carolina Railroad; at Salisbury, for all points in Western North Carolina, Knoxville, Tenn., Cincinnati and western points; at Charlotte, for Spartanburg, Greenville, Athens, Atlanta and all points south.

TRAINS ARRIVE AT RALEIGH, N. C.:

Express Train.

3:30 P. M. DAILY—From Atlanta, Charlotte, Greensboro and all points South.

Local.

7:20 A. M. DAILY—From Greensboro and all points North and South. Sleeping Car from Greensboro to Raleigh.

Norfolk and Chattanooga Limited.

3:40 P. M. DAILY—From all points east, Norfolk, Tarboro, Wilson and water lines.

From Goldsboro, Wilmington, Fayetteville and all points in Eastern Carolina.

Chattanooga and Norfolk Limited.

11:40 A. M. DAILY—From New York, Washington, Lynchburg, Danville and Greensboro, Chattanooga, Knoxville, Hot Springs and Asheville.

Local.

9:30 P. M. Daily except Sunday—From Goldsboro and all points East.

Express Train.

8:53 A. M. DAILY—From Goldsboro and intermediate stations.

For tickets, routes, and rates or other information, call on or write to

THAD. C. STURGIS,
Ticket Agent, Raleigh, N. C.
W. H. GREEN,
General Superintendent.
W. A. TURK,
General Passenger Agent,
Washington, D. C.
J. M. CULP, Traffic Manager.

Rambler
Bicycles, $80

Crescents Mens, $50
Ladies, to $75

The Finest Line of Bicycles on Earth.

THOS. H. BRIGGS & SONS,
RALEIGH, N. C.

SOLE AGENTS FOR

THE GREAT
White
Enamel
Line of

There is only
One
Best
and these are
the Best.

MOST RELIABLE JOB PRINTING OFFICE IN NORTH CAROLINA!

Do more printing for the Colored people than any other House in the State.

LOOK! LOOK! LOOK!

For $1.00 Cash!

WE WILL SEND POST-PAID,

- 100 Nice Letter Heads,
- 100 Envelopes to match,
- 1 Lead Pencil,
- 1 Pen Holder,
- 6 Pen Points,
- 3 Blotters,

with the name of your Association, your Churches in charge, and your name as Pastor, and Post office address all nicely printed on the paper and envelopes. All of the above for only $1.00.

VERY PASTOR ought to use Printed Paper and Envelopes.
CHURCH CLERK ought to use Printed Paper and Envelopes.
SUNDAY SCHOOL Superintendent and Clerk ought to use Printed Paper and Envelopes.

PUNCH CARDS—by mail post-paid per 100 $ .75
GIFT ENVELOPES   "   "   " 100 .75
CHURCH   "   "   " 100 .50
                 "   " by express, " 1,000 1.25

All of these are specially printed for your church.

Mr. Guy V. Barnes, the President of the Company has a personal acquaintance with most of the leading Colored Baptists of the State, and refers you to such men as Revs. Brown, Whitted, Roberts, Pegues, Vincent, and many others, who will testify as to the quality of work, reasonable charges and faithful performance of any work entrusted to their charge.

Send us your Minutes to print.

CAPITAL PRINTING C., ... RALEIGH, N. C.

WAKE FOREST COLLEGE
LIBRARY

JULY, 1897.

The Baptist Quarterly.

Edited by Board of Managers Baptist E. and M. Convention.

J. A. WHITTED, Managing Editor,

Box 145, Raleigh, N. C.

CONTENTS:

	PAGE.
EDITORIALS	1
REPORT OF EASTERN DISTRICT	3
REPORT FROM CENTRAL DISTRICT.	5
INSTITUTES.	6
THE MISSION OF A NEW TESTAMENT CHURCH	9
WESTERN DISTRICT.	11
ASSOCIATIONS, TIME AND PLACE	12
PLACES AND TIME FOR FOURTH COURSE OF LECTURES, NEW ERA INSTITUTE WESTERN DISTRICT	13
NEW ERA INSTITUTE—FOURTH SESSION	14
PROGRAMME BAPTIST MISSIONARY AND EDUCATION OF NORTH CAROLINA	15
THE MODEL DEACON	17
SCHOOL OF MISSIONARY TRAINING—SHAW UNIVERSITY, 1897	19
SKETCHES OF BAPTIST HISTORY AND BIOGRAPHY	23
JOTTINGS FROM WESTERN NORTH CAROLINA	24
COMMUNICATIONS	25
WOMEN'S MEETING IN CONNECTION WITH NEW ERA INSTITUTE WORK,	27
SHAW DAY	28
LETTER FROM AFRICA	28
REV. JOHN E. WHITE	29
COMMUNICATION	30
CONSTITUTION OF BAPTIST STATE CONVENTION OF NORTH CAROLINA.	31

| AMERICAN BAPTIST PUBLICATION SOCIETY | Philadelphia Boston New York Chicago St. Louis Dallas Atlanta | "There is no reason why Baptists should go to any other publishing house for their Sunday-school literature when their own Society so well supplies the need."—*The Standard*. |

Ring Them In

BAPTIST PERIODICALS

The best GRADED, the best MADE, the best CIRCULATED, the CHEAPEST denominational literature in the world.

HERE ARE THE PRESENT PRICES

Note Carefully, and Compare with Prices of Other Houses

Club Prices of Five or More Copies to one Address for One Quarter

	Per Copy		Per Copy
Baptist Superintendent,	7 cts.	Our Little Ones (Weekly),	6¼ cts.
Baptist Teacher,	10 "	Reaper (Monthly),	2 "
Senior Quarterly,	4 "	Reaper (Semi-monthly),	4 "
Advanced Quarterly,	2 "	Our Boys and Girls,	8 "
Intermediate Quarterly,	2 "	A New Juvenile Weekly.	
Primary Quarterly,	2 "	Our Young People, in clubs of four or more (Weekly),	13 "
Picture Lessons,	3 "		
Bible Lessons,	1 "	Colporter, 5 cents a year in clubs of twenty or more.	
Bible Lesson Pictures,	$1.00		

Your patronage will help the Bible, Colportage, Chapel Car, and Sunday-school Work of the denomination.

Baptist Educational and Missionary Convention Of North Carolina.

Next Session will be Held in Charlotte, N. C., October 21, 1897.

Officers 1896-97.

Rev. N. F. ROBERTS, D. D., President, Raleigh
Rev. C. S. BROWN, Secretary, Winton.
J. A WHITTED, Cor. Secretary and General Missionary, Raleigh
A. W. PEGUES, Ph. D., Treasurer, Raleigh.
Rev. G. W. MOORE, Auditor, Fayetteville.

Missionaries.

J. A. WHITTED, General, Raleigh.
Rev. P. F. MALOY, Western District, Greensboro.
Rev. A. B. VINCENT, Central District, Raleigh.
Rev. C. C. SUMMERVILLE, Eastern District, Rocky Mount.

☞ All communications concerning State Work, New Era Institutes, Co-operation, and the Baptist Quarterly, should be directed to the Corresponding Secretary and General Missionary at Raleigh.

REV. JOHN E. WHITE.

Baptist Quarterly.

Vol. 2.   July, 1897.   No. 3.

EDITORIALS.

The interest in the work of co-operation in North Carolina grows with each new course of lectures. We have just now closed the third course and the work was never more telling. Wherever a meeting has been previously held the people better understand the work and are better prepared to take in the lectures.

The people of Charlotte claim that they enter upon the work with new zeal and Charlotte must be made to take the lead in missions. Raleigh, as might have been expected, gave the largest contribution in the last course, one hundred and two dollars and fifty cents.

We can find no fault with the people of any section in which a meeting has been held. Many places are begging us to come back, for they believe the meeting is of untold good to the churches, pastors and people generally. In some places ministers who do not venture into such meetings are staying away, but in every case of such kind the people are taking careful note of it; they themselves are being educated from such leaders, and the minister who would continue to lead the people must not suffer them to be educated away from him. The time is, if we would lead the people we must be prepared to lead them. These meetings are not held to belittle our men to "show them up" as some suppose, but to show up to them that which will enlighten and inspire them to greater work.

It tends also to unify our brethren. The ministerial fraternity of the Baptists of North Carolina stand fully as much in need of unity as they do of knowledge.

When we are reminded of the principles and practices of the Baptist church, it is not surprising that many divisions exist.

Each church is its own sovereign, and where ignorance predominates it is not surprising that this sovereignty should be misleading, and many of our brethren should stand apart.

But now the sun of enlightenment is getting high up in our sky, let us learn to come closer to each other.

Let the stronger bear up and encourage the weaker. Let North Carolina Baptists be a unit in their devotion to the work and their loyalty to each other.

Let us foster the doctrines and principles of our church—founded, as they are, on the Word of God. Let us encourage our institutions of learning, see to it that each and all of our children are educated therein, that they may be thoroughly indoctrinated. See to it that every church and association is represented in our great State Convention, that a greater work may be done in our own land, that a greater work may be done in Africa.

In the town of Weldon, N. C., about a year ago Clifton C. Matthews, who had been a member of the Weldon Baptist church, passed away and left a two story house with an adjoining lot to the church of which he had been a member. This house is now the parsonage for the church, and the adjoining lot and building will be rented and the proceeds will go to the benefit of the church.

We highly commend brother Matthews for his noble gift. Oh, if more of our church members would show their love to their churches, not by what they say, but by what they do for the church, how much more would we see strength and development in Zion.

THERE is a man in Eastern North Carolina claiming to be a moral missionary from Virginia. We hope all the missionaries from Virginia and in Virginia are to lift up the people morally, otherwise they are not missionaries of the Cross, but if the brethren of Virginia have a specialist on this line we would recommend him to stay on the other side. We know that in Virginia, as in North Carolina, all missionaries are regularly appointed, and we wish to warn our brethren against such men constantly rising up, even in the borders of our own State, claiming to be missionaries, deceiving the people. All our missionaries are commissioned, and previously announced in our QUARTERLY. Do not let such men deceive you.

THE Board of Managers have appointed Rev. A. S. Dunston, of Hertford, N. C., as local missionary for Eastern North Carolina and Rev. F. W. Wallace, of Dillsboro, N. C., to labor beyond the Blue Ridge.

Rev. Dunston has already labored a month to the entire satisfaction of the General Missionary and the Board. All we need is more money and men for North Carolina.

When you give to co-operation you simply enable us to do more in the prosecution of the Lord's work in the State and in Africa.

NAMES with the cross mark attached will know they are due for the contribution of the QUARTERLY.

REV. P. S. LEWIS, of Salisbury, N. C., has been appointed District Missionary in Virginia, and he has accepted. Rev. Lewis has been the pastor of the Dixonville Baptist church for upward of ten years, and his work there in every sense has been profitable. He has filled prominent places in our State organizations, and in all has been a success.

North Carolina Baptists are very proud of Rev. Lewis. We deeply regret to have him leave; we recognize the loss we sustain, but greatly appreciate the gain which our Virginia brethren have in him. May God's blessings attend him wherever he goes.

DR. H. L. MOREHOUSE, of New York, the great Field Sec'y of the American Baptist Home Mission Society, has been quite sick for several months, but we praise God in His providence, he is still spared to his noble task. Loved as he is North and South, prayers were offered for his recovery, and his many friends North and South praise God for the answer.

WE are informed that Rev. James M. Young has been called to the First Baptist Church of New Orleans. We feel very proud that other states besides our own find something in our men worthy of honor. Brother Young goes to his new field with the best wishes of our North Carolina brethren.

POSSIBLY at no time in our history have so many changes occurred in one place in so short a time as has in the pastorate of the Baptist churches of Wilmington. Within nine months every church in the city has made a change of pastors. We truly hope we may see God in the entire change. The brethren who have gone have our best wishes, and those who come. Wilmington is a very important point. We give the former pastors great credit for the improvement and development of the past few years; we shall look for a continued development and improvement. To do this the brethren must be united and labor to one common end.

※

SHAW UNIVERSITY has honored Hon. H. P. Cheatham with the degree of LL. D. and with the place of Trustee of that institution. Hon. Cheatham has labored in his sphere as few ever have, and we better see his worth than ever before.

REPORT OF EASTERN DISTRICT.

CONTRIBUTORS.

R. V. James, Cisco, 25; Rev. R. L. Elliott, Cisco, 25; William H. Twine, 25; Edward Dickson, Warsaw, 50; Chas. Branch, Warsaw, 60; Lucy C. Williams, Magnolia, 50; Mrs R. A. Williams, James City, 50; Charles A. Nelson, 25; Margaret Hicks, care Rev. L. P. Martin, Newbern, 50; Francis Skinner, 25; Mrs. Hettie Smith, Newbern, 50; Rev. A. A. Spruill, 25; Rev. W. R. Slade, Newbern, 65; Giles Moyer, Newbern, 50; Rev. A. Wynn, 30; W. T. Bell, 25; Albert Fields, 25; Rev. Moore, 25; Priscilla Smith, 25; Rev. A. F. Bryant, 25; Mrs. C. E. Waugh, 25; Rev. Thomas H. Forbes, James City, 1.25; Rev. W. H. Howard, 25; Dennis Cox, 25; Rev. T. S. Evans, Morehead City, 1.25; Rev. J. E. Everett, Sneeds Ferry, 50; P. J. Lee, 25; Mary J. Peterson, 25; Lucy Slade, Newbern, 50; Julia Benson, 25; Rev. A. T. Foreman, James City, 50; Rev. I. Garrett, 25; Sanders Jones, Newbern, 50; Rev. L. P. Martin, Newbern, 1.25; J. D. Daniels, James City, 50; Hettie Smith, 25; Charles Whitfield, 25.

The above names are the list of subscribers from March 17th to March the 30th.

Yours truly,
C. C. SOMERVILLE.

Wilmington, N. C.—H. Saunders, 25; Rev. W. M. Spicer, 25; Rev. W. T Cowan, 25; W. H. Dudley, Sr., 25; Mrs. E. H. Thomas, No. 606 McCray St. W. 50; Phoebe A. Borden, No. 312 S Eighth St., 50; Miss C. F. Blount, No 1229 Chestnut St, 50; William B. Wheeden, 25; Samson Isler, 25; Gaston Hicks, 25; Rosa. Reynolds No. 607 Red Cross, 25; Richard Ashe, 25; Harriet A. Wheeden, 25; Dianna Johnson, 25; C. A. Jones, 25; W. H. Perry, No. 410, N. Seventh St., 25; Henry Lamb, Burgaw, 50.

Edenton, N. C.—May 12. Rev. S. P. Knight, 1.25; Rev. H. A. Brindley, 75; W. R Capehart, 50; A. S. Dunston, 50; J. H. Barclay, 25; J. D. Yarboro, 2.10; E. W. Whitley, 50; Isadora Halley, 25; Jno. Y. Creasy, 25; L, E. Mabane, 25; Mary Hurton, 25; Horace Bowen, 25; W. H. Barner, 25; David McClease, 75; Rev. G. T. Watt, 55; Samuel Fulton, 25; Eliza Perry, 25; Joseph Bond, 25.

Clinton, N. C.—June 1. Rev. A. A. Smith, Mt. Olive, 1.85; King Pigford, 50; Rev. D. T. Best, 1.00; Rev. E. E. Smith, 25; Rev. A. Moore, 50; Christopher Taylor, 25; W. R. Maynard, 25; A. L. Sumner, 25; Daniel Moore, 25; Alex Moore, 25; G. L. Bissell, 75; O. F. Herring, 25; Abraham Graham. 25; Addie Best, 25; G. W. Sterring, 50; J. L. Holmes, 55; Caldonia Holmes, 25; Lilly Taylor 25; L. B. Berry, 25; W. H. Ashford, 30; Paul J. Sherard 25; Alice Taylor, 25; Emma Robinson, 25; G. W. Faison, 25; T. M. Faison, 25; A. D. Graham, 25; John Moore, 25; Pearl Hicks, 25; Jerry Faison, 25; Moses Jones, 25.

SUBSCRIPTIONS TO QUARTERLY.

Mrs. Delsy Morrow Tillery, 50; Sallie Hunter, 25; Maggie L. Hunter, Tillery, 50; Rev. Z. H. Bury, Elizabeth City, 1.30; Rev. J. S. Sills, Tarboro, 60; Rev. Elijah Turner, 25; Prof. P. W. Moore, 25; Rev. J. W. Faulk, 70; John Sykes, 25; Elizabeth City, J. B. Trotton, Bell Cross, 50; Rev. R. R. Creesy, Columbia, 50; Lizzie V. Skinner, 25; Elijah H. Hatherly, 25; Frank Simons, Elizabeth City, 50; Mary Evans, 25; Charlotte Kearney, 25; J. H. Johnson, 25; Rev. G. W. Williams, Elizabeth City, 50; J. A. Fleming, 25; Penelope Jones, Elizabeth City, 50; Sam Jones, 25; Mrs. S. T. Moore, 50; J. L. Lewis, 50; Rev. J. Archer, 25; Phenia Jones, 25; Geo. D. Griffin, 25; Mrs. J. K. Lamb, Elizabeth City, 50; Jane Oberby, 25; C. W. Murrin, Jr. 25.

Edenton, N. C.—L. A. Green, 50; W. R. Capehart, 50; Richard Wynn, 50; Mrs. C. M. Capehart, 25; W. R. Capehart, 25; W. C. Burk, 25; G. W. Parker, 25; Thomas Jones, 25; Wilson Woodard, 30; W. A. Williams, Whitakers, N. C., 50.

Rocky Mount, N. C.—Rev. G. B. Blacknall, Enfield, 1.00; Rev. S. Hicks, Rocky Mt., 50; Rev. R. T. Vann,

Scotland Neck, 1.00; W. D. Graves, 25; Julia Davis, Rocky Mt., 50; Rev. W. V. Savage, Tarboro, 1.60; Pearl W. Hicks, 25; Moses Jones, 25.

Names sent to the Gen. Missionary from April 20th to June 1st:

J. L. Fennel, Rose Hill, 50 cents; G. B. Harring, 50; A. C. Moore, Wallace, 50; W. T. Cowans, 25; C. D. High, 50; W. H. Alderman, Teacheys, 50; J. C. Murray, Willard, 50; Hannah M. McMillian, 25; Isabella Newton, 25; Hattie Alderman, 25; Peter Murray, 25; Owyn Stovers, 25; N. Moore, Wallace, 50; C. B. McMillan, 25; R. S. Alderman, 25; Sampson Isler, 25; Gaston Hicks, 25; Rosa Reynolds, 607 Red Cross, 25; Richard Ashe, 25; Hurmit A. Wheeden, 25; Dianna Johnson, 25; C. A. Jones, 25; W. H. Perry, No. 110 N. St., 25; Henry Lamb, Burgaw, 50; J. R. Murray, 25; S. H. Murray, 25. J. M. Lewis 25.

Edenton, N. C.—Rev. S. P. Knight, 1.25; Rev. H. H. Brinkley, 75; W. R. Capehart, 1.50; A. S. Dunston, 50; J. H. Barclay, 50; J. D. Yarboro, 2.10; E. W. Whitley, 50; Isadora Holly, 25; John Y. Creasy, 25; L. E. Mebane, 25; Merry Horton, 25; Horace Brown, 25; W. H. Barner, 25; David M. Clash, 75; Rev. G. T. Wall, 55; Samuel Tilton, 25; Eliza Perry, 25; Joseph Bond, 25.

Clinton, N. C.—Rev. A. W. Smith, Mt. Olive, 1.85; King Pigfort, 50; D. T. Best, 1.00; Rev. Moore, 50; Clinton. E. E. Smith, 25; Christopher Taylor, 25; W. R Maynard, 25; A. L. Sumner, 25; Daniel Moore, 25; Alex Moore, 25; G. L. Bissell, 75; O. F. Herring, 25; G. H. Herring, 50; Abraham Graham, 25; Addie Best, 25; J. L. Holmes, 30; Caldonia Holmes, 25; Lally Taylor, 25; L. E. Berry, 25; W. H. Ashford, 30; Alice Taylor, 25; Emma Robinson, 25; G. W. Faison, 25; A. D. Graham, 25; John Moore, 25; Jerry Faison, 25; R. S. Morgan, 25; John W. Freeman, 25; Edward Malone, 25; Henry Ivey, 25; Johnnie Ivey, 25; Rev. H. Pair, 25; James Watkins, 25; Ist an Hunter, 25, J. W. Howard, 25; E. E. Temmons, Rocky Mt., 50; George Parker, Enfield, 1.00; J. W. Joyner, 50; Carter Thorp, 25; Olivia Collins, 25; Milly Whitehead, 25; Cora Taylor, 25; D. W. Winstead, Rocky Mt., 50; John T. Smith, 25; Lucy Arrington, 1.00; J. L. Spencer, 25; T. W. Davis, Rocky Mt., 50; William Pura, 25; Octoria Battle, 50; W. H. Hernis, Rocky Mt., box 44, 50; Isabella Battle, 25; Jessy Wiggins, 25; Mrs. T. E. Heriss, Rocky Mt., box 11, 50; Henry Towler, 25

Names sent to the General Missionary from February 10th to March the 17th:

R. V. James, 25; Wm. Henry Times, 25.

Warsaw, N. C.—Edward Dickson, 50; Charlie Branch, 60; Lucy Williams, Magnolia, 50.

Newbern, N. C.—Mrs. R. A. Williams, James City, 50; Charles Nelson, 25; Margaret Hicks, care Rev. L. P. Martin, 50; Francis Skinner, 25; Mrs. H. Smith, Newbern, 50; Rev. A. A. Spruill, 25; W. R. Slade, Newbern, 65; Giles Mayer, 50; A. Wynn, 30; W. F. Bell, 25; Albert Fields, 25; Rev. Moore, 25; Priscilla Smith, 25; Rev. A. F. Bryant, 25; Mrs. C. E. Waugh, 25; Rev. Thomas Forbes, James City, 50; Rev. W. H. Howard, 25; Dennis Cox, 25; Rev. T. F. Evans, Morehead City, 1.25; J. E. Everitt, 50; R. E. Lee, 25, Mary Peterson, Sneeds Ferry, 25; Lucy Slade, Newbern, 50; Julia Benson 25, Rev. A. F. Foreman, James City 50; Q. Garrett, 25; Sam Jones, Newbern, 50; Rev. L. P. Martin, 1.25; J. D. Daniels, James City, 50; Hettie Smith, 25; Charles Whitfield, 25.

Names sent to the General Missionary from March 17 to March the 30:

Wilmington, N. C.—H. Saunders, 25; Rev. W. M. Spencer, 25, W. T. Cowan, 25; W. H. Dudley, 25; E. H. Thomas No. 606 McCray St, 50; Mrs. C. F. Blount, No. 1229 Charlotte St, 50; William B. Wheeden, 25.

NAME OF CHURCHES VISITED AND AMOUNTS CONTRIBUTED.

February—Galilee, 1.52; Corner Stone, Elizabeth City, 20.31; Gale St., 3.15; Tillery's Chapel, 1.02; Crowell's X Roads, 4.31; Little Zion, Whitaker, 1.00; St. Paul, Enfield, 1.25.

March—New Bethel, Enfield, .15; St. James, Rocky Mount, 70; Union Hill, Nash county, 1.75; First Baptist, Rocky Mt. 18.45; First Baptist, Goldsboro, 8.37; Williamston, 1.01; Zion

Hill, Plymouth 2.55; Spring Garden, Washington, 2 00; Hyde Chapel, 1.50; Triumph, 31.

April — First Baptist, Newbern, 20.62; Shiloh, Wilmington, 50; Bear Swamp, 1 73; Magnolia Baptist, 1.30; Shiloh, 2.05; Burgaw, 2.00; Central Baptist, Wilmington, 25; Ebenezer, Wilmington, 55; Shiloh, Wilmington, 10.06; Cedar Grove, 1.15; Mt. Shiloh, James City, 2.00; St. John, 1.00; Rock Peter, 25.

May—Providence, 17.50; Powellsville, 3.74; Ahoskie, 3.26; Eprew Baptist, 5.50; M. E. Church, 2.50; St. Philip, 5 55; St. James Temple, 3.00.

June—First Baptist, Clinton, 25.00; Mt. Zion, 1.50; First Baptist, Enfield, 1.92; Piney Woods Chapel, 11.36; Sandy Run, Jacksonville, 11.10; Adoram Wallace, 17 50.

REPORTS FROM CENTRAL DISTRICT.

The New Era meeting at Piney Grove Church under the pastorate of Rev. T. O. Fuller was an inspiring and soul-stirring affair.

Rev. J. S. Hardiway, of Oxford, and Rev. J. H. Scott, of Shaw, were at their best, and that of itself means volumes to those who know something of the ability of these eminent and consecrated divines. Biblical Theology, Church History and Discipline, Education, Missions and the Ministry were discussed by these brethren and Missionary Vincent, assisted by the pastor and others.

Although the meeting was held at a very busy season, yet the attendance was good every day. Rev. Scott remarked during the meeting: "This is the best meeting I have visited." Rev. T O. Fuller deserves much credit for the rare leadership evidenced in his church work. He has some very good material to assist him: Deacon John Winstead, Rev. J M. Taylor, T. B. Bobbitt and L. D. Hockaday, all earnest and loyal to the cause of missions. The woman's meeting conducted by sisters J. M. Taylor, Jane Winston and Mrs. L. D. Hockaday and others, was very interesting, and showed a vigorous and healthy indoctrination of Bible teaching. These sisters, all fearless and aggressive in the mission work, and have already put to flight some of our brethren who invaded their territory. The kindness of heart and ample provision for strangers mark these people as a high type of citizens. The white citizens did their part to entertain the white lecturers.

The Womans' Missionary Society donated $5.00 for the benefit of the meeting.

Our minds will often recur with pleasure and interest to the pleasant recollection of the Piney Grove meeting, April 14–16.

Respectfully,

V———.

The New Era meeting held with the Blount St. Baptist Church, April, 6-8, in Raleigh, in many respects, towered above all others yet held. Deep, profound, yet practical thought ran through every lecture. The fundamental gospel truth so graphically set forth by Revs. J. H. Scott, of Shaw University, B. W. Spillman, of the "Biblical Recorder" staff, Editor J. W. Bailey and Prof. W. C. Bruce, Dr. A. W. Pegues, Revs. G. W. Perry, J. J. Worlds and Dr. J. W. Carter, of Raleigh; Rev. J. E. White, Corresponding Secretary of North Carolina Baptists President Charles F. Meserve, of Shaw University, and Rev. O. L. Stringfield, of Raleigh, made the exercises most valuable and excellent in instruction. From beginning to end the speeches were of a high order and had a most edifying influence upon the large and appreciative audience.

The Womans' Meeting, conducted by Miss Emma Miller, of the Missionary Training School, assisted by Mary Hamilton, of Shaw, and Miss Fannie Heck, President of Womans' Work of the Southern Baptist Convention, was unique in its sphere, wholesome and heaven-like in its Christ-like spirit, and crowned this great meeting with an atmosphere of the purest and most glorious anticipations of what this feature of co-operation will bring to the firesides and homes of our people. Many such meetings as this will lift the people of Raleigh into a more elevated realm of Christian thought and activity, and revolutionize churches in Raleigh.

One hundred dollars was raised for the work, and the singing of Mrs. F. R. Howell and the interest of pastor and church deserve special mention. Let us have at last another meeting like this in Raleigh. We will not make invidious comparisons, since all the speeches were good, but Dr. Carter, Revs Jno. E. White, O. L. Stringfield and G. W. Perry were evidently at their best.

V——.

WILSON INSTITUTE. APRIL 30, AND MAY 1--2. 1897.

The New Era Institute held with Rev. W. H. Woodward's church at Wilson was deeply enjoyed by Rev. J. H. Scott, of Shaw University, and A. B. Vincent, Missionary, and J. A. Rood, who delivered the lecture, and all those who attended.

Rev. Woodward is doing a good work at Wilson and evidenced much interest in this meeting; his arrangements were creditable and highly satisfactory in every respect, and the hospitality of his people was most liberal. Possibly no point in Eastern Carolina deserves more recognition than the work of this place. The pastor has labored long and hard in church and school until light is dawning and the future full of promise. This great railway center is one of the strong strategic points of the black belt territory.

Rev. J. H. Scott's talk Sunday night on character and the mission of church members in fitting souls for God's kingdom was a master piece in spirit, thought and delivery. Prof. S. H. Vick assisted the Missionary in raising a collection of over fifteen dollars during the day.

Respectfully,

V——.

NEW ERA INSTITUTE AT SEABOARD, APRIL 22-24.

This meeting was held in the church pastored now by Rev. H. Clements, of Branchville, and those who know the pastor and his congregation at Seaboard, were not surprised when the Institute was enrolled as one of the best yet held. Lectures were delivered by Missionaries Vincent, Whitted, Revs. A. Cree, of the white church of Seaboard; R. G. Kendrick, of Weldon; Dr. N. F. Roberts and President Chas. F. Meserve, of Shaw University. Special mention is made of President Meserve's address on Education, which was one of the best things witnessed during the meeting or heard anywhere on the field. This distinguished educator was practical and simple, at times eloquent, always thoughtful and scholarly. Dr. Roberts' illustrated lecture we learn was a rare jem, and all who heard it considered themselves fortunate, and those who did not were really unfortunate.' Strong and able speeches were made by Revs. A. Cree and R. G. Kendrick, of the white church of Weldon. Both of these brethren were indeed helpful in the meeting.

Rev. A. Cree and some of the whites were kind and liberal in supporting and aiding the Institute.

Special credit and thanks are tendered to the good people of Seaboard, and especially to Profs. W. C Coats and J. N. Coats and deacon Phillps and others for the deep interest and sacrifices in making the occasion pleasant and profitable to all.

We would not forget the sisters missionary meeting, conducted by Mrs. Bettie Young and others, which was full of enthusiasm and interest. Addresses were delivered by the missionaries and Dr Roberts on this phase of the work.

The following are some of the leading brethren who attended:

Rev. Dr. R. I. Walden, Revs. Nick Robinson, Wm. Thompson, C. J. W. Fisher, J. W. Wood, Henderson Peoples, J. K. Ramsey, H. Clements, S. Delooch, J. Norman, W. C. Coats and Seldom Jeffries.

Pleasant recollections of the good people of this section will often recur when our minds turn toward Northhampton county.
V———.

CONTRIBUTIONS FROM CENTRAL DISTRICT.

Mount Moriah Church, Franklin county, Rev. P. T. Hall, pastor, $2.08.
The following gave 25 cents each: P. D. Dunston, Miss E. S. Yarboro, H. P. Perry, George Nichols, Thomas Perry, A. T. Neal. Louisburg.

Forestville Church, Rev. W. A. Jones, pastor, $3.57.

Henry Dunn, George Massenburg, Miss Lenora Jeffreys, 50 cents each; Maggie Dunn, 27; Julia Harris, Sarah Mitchel, Fannie Leggans, Lawrence Dunn, Joseph Alston and David Martin, 25 cents each.

Baptist Church, Elm City, Rev. N. H. Arrington, pastor, $1.25.

G. A. Gaston, Nellie Montgomery, A. W. Williams and Mr. Kelly gave 50 cents each; Home Mission Society, Miss Susan Williams, 1.00 Kittrell Church, 33 cents.

RALEIGH INSTITUTE, BLOUNT STREET CHURCH.

Revs. G. W. Perry, 50 cents; F. R. Howell, $1.00; C. Johnson, 60; D. S. Saulter, 1.00; Raleigh, Rev. H. Pair, Shotwell, 6.82; Rev. T. B. Edwards, 25; Rev. J. J. Worlds, 2.50, Miss Emma Miller, Raleigh, 1.00, : Rev. S. S. Henderson, Greensboro, 50; Prof. L. B. Capehart, 50, Thomas Donaldson, 1.00; Samuel C. Dixon, 50; A. Jenkins, 25; President Chas. F. Meserve 20.00; J. H. Dunston, 50; Rev. Dr. J. W. Carter, 25, Rev. Jno. E. White, 25; Fred. Jenkins, 25; Isaac Cook, 50; Miss Cora J. McDougald, 25; Rev. J. H. Scott, 3.00; Mrs. J. H. Scott, 50; Rev. E. B. Blake, 25; Cato Thornton, 25; Rev. A. G. Davis, 25; Rev. A. Stroud, 25; Dr. A. W. Pegues, 5.00; Mrs. Moses Thompson, 1.50; Dr. N. F. Roberts, 1.00; Dr. N. F. Roberts and Charles Cardwell, 5.00; ($2.50 each,) John. O'Gary, 50; Charles Cardwell, 1.00; Mrs. A. B. Vincent and sister, Mabel Vincent, 4.10; Mrs Cloe Perry, 25; Saddie J. Saunders, 26; Mrs. Lenora Slade, 806 South Wilmington St, 25; C W. Hoover, 25; S. M. R. Slade, (for Quarterly) 25; Rev D. J. Avera, 50; Mrs. Charles Cardwell 60, Joe High 20, Dr Wyche 1.50, Anthony Burns 30, Teachers at Shaw 1.00, Rev J A Whitted 8.00, Rev D T Strayhorn 25, Miss I J Brown, Shaw University 50, Miss Cloe Philips 25, Miss Margaret Hamilton, (Shaw) 50, Merrimon Wortham 25, Robert Evans 55, Professor N C Bruce 1.50, collected by A B Vincent, from A Burton 50, Turner Evans 25, Miss Chanie Alston 25, John T Pullen 1.00, Mrs F R Howell 1.00, W H Dowd 50, J J Weaver 524 Newbern Av 50, B W Hunter, McKimmon's Drug St re 1.50, T S Pierce at Briggs' Hardware Store 25, Wesley Mosely 25, Murphy Alston 25, H G Otey 50, Primus Busbee 50, James A. Briggs Hardware Store 50, S B Norris at Pool's Shoe Store 50, Dr M D Bowens M D 5.00, First Baptist Church Oberlin, 5.00, Prof E A Johnson 3.00. Total contribution, $100.00.

Institute, Clayton—Rev. A. A. Jones, pastor, $24.50.

T. T. Saunders, 55 cts; Bethie Jones, David Saunders, Jane Durham, N. L. Horton, Joseph Banks, A. J. Saunders, Mahalie Brodie, J. W. Campbell, William Nunn, Lewis and Mariah Banks, 25 cts. each. Jessie Banks, Malinda Saunders, A. A. McDonald, Daniel Nunn, A. Saunders Jr., Ida McCullers, Minnie Pattridge, 25 centseach. C. P. Thompson, Prof. O. C. Mial and wife 50 cents each; Rev. J. H. Scott, 40; T. T. Saunders, 60; Ripie Whitley, D. M. Morgan, Elizabeth Morgan, 40 cents each. L. B. McCullers and wife 55; Carrie G. Saunders, 35 cents.

Institute, Piney Grove—Rev. T. O. Fuller, pastor, $19.04.

Revs. J. M. Taylor, L. D. Hockaday, Creedmore; Rev. J. S. Hardiway, Oxford; Henderson Thorp, 50 cents each. Rev. T. O. Fuller, Deacon John Winstead, William Lawrence, Creedmore, 75 cts. each. J. S. T. Mitchell, Rev. J. H. Scott, Isam Rogers, William Beasly, Annie Alston, Jane Winston Hester, Permelia Bobbitt Hester, Calvin Lyons, Creedmore, Lewis Satterwhite Lyons, Andrew Daniel, Knap of Reeds, Charles Bobbitt, Willie Bullock, Andrew Holdman, Knap of Reeds; Julia Rogers Lyons, Otho Taylor, Creedmore; Willie Mitchell, Jane Chavis, Knap of Reeds; Thos. Williamson and Dr. J. F. Sanford, Creedmore; Osborn Perry, Jno. Winston, Willie Bullock, gave 25 cents each. Woman's Missionary Society, Mrs. J. M. Taylor, President, $5.00.

CENTRAL DISTRICT.

Franklin County Sunday School Convention $2.50; Mrs. Nellie Montgomery, Elm City, 25; Flat Swamp Church, Rev. N. B. Durham, pastor, $1.19; Pleasant Grove, Rev. N. B. Durham, pastor, 55.

INSTITUTE AT SEABOARD. APRIL 22.

Amount collected, $20.50. Rev. H. Clements, pastor: The following contributed 25 cts. each:

Revs. Henderson Peeples, Jackson; J. W. Wood, Weldon; J. A. Whitted, Eddie Smith, Gracie Taylor, Elizabeth Coats, W. C. Coats, Miss M. N. Murphy, Mrs. L. E. Powell, Thomas Ramsey, Maggie Smith, Seaboard. President Charles F. Meserve, 1.50; Annie B. Chopell, Josephine Vassar, Panthy Vassar, Callie Sykes, Mary J. Long, Mrs. J. Norman Coats, 50 cts each. Nellie B. Jordan, 35; Addie L. Smith, 29; Mrs. Josie White, 75; Peter Roberts and Wm. Garris, 35 each. Bethlehem Sunday-school, Seaboard, N. C., 50; Harrison Boone, Seaboard, 50. Oaky Grove—Rev A. A. Jones, pastor, 53 cents.

Clayton Baptist Church, 1.53; Baptist Church, Kittrells, 50; Zoor Church, (Rev. A. Clements) 2.00; Kittrell, Hattie Rogers, 1.00; Miranda Hall and Edward Owens 25 each; Williams' Chapel, 70; Piney Grove, Granville, 42; Jackson Baptist Church, (Rev. J. W. Wood) 1.54; Gareysburg Church, through Rev. C. B. Harris, 1.05; Selma Baptist Church, (Rev. E. B. Blake) 77; William Montgomery, 25.

Spring Hill, Cumberland County, June 8-10.—Rev. H. C. McDonald, pastor, 10.37.

Rev. H. C. McDonald, Lumber Bridge, 50; Mrs. Orie Murphy, Hope Mill, 50; Rev. J. D. Lyles, Fayetteville, 25; Rev. A. B. Dunham, 25; Rev. W. H. Andrews, Idaho, 25; G. W. Carver, 25; Martha McKinnon, Hope Mill, 30; J. R. Richardson, Cedar, 50; Viney Wilson, 25; Henry McKinnon, 55; Gertrude Maxwell, 25; Viney Jane McKinnon, 50; Miles McKinnon, 25; Sarah McCoy, 25; Jno. Wilson, 25; Home Mission Secretary, (M. A. McKinnon) 50

WILSON INSTITUTE. APRIL 30. MAY 1-2.

Rev. W. T. H. Woodward, pastor, total contributions, $15.34.

Wilson—Prof. S. H. Vick, 50; J. W. Rogers, 50; Rev. J. A. Hunt 50; W W Stanford, 50; Mrs. Sallie Barber, 50; Alfred Dew, 50; J. S. Jackson, 50; Richard Renfrod, 50. L. A. Moore, 25; Isaac Whitaker, 35 (for QUARTERLY;) Roddie Whitaker, 25; Lonnie Hicks, 25; Clarisa Williams, 25; Julius Price, 25; John Tate, 25; J. T. Davis, 25; G. H. Holden, 25; Isaac Young, 25; Jacob Tucker, 25; A. J. Townsend, 25; Jno. Tate, 25.

THE MISSION OF A NEW TESTAMENT CHURCH.

P. F. MALEY, DISTRICT MISSIONARY, WESTERN N. C.

A New Testament Church is one whose life, labors, faith and practice are all in full conformity to the teachings and doctrines of the New Testament. To form correct ideas about the church, and its responsibilities, it is necessary that all believers, as well as others who do not believe, have, in their minds, a clear definition or conception of a Gospel Church.

We know of no better definition than the one given by Dr. Hiscox, namely: "A Christian Church is a congregation of baptized believers in Christ, worshipping together, associated in the faith and fellowship of the Gospel; practicing its precepts, observing its ordinances, recognizing and receiving Christ as their supreme ruler and lawgiver, and taking His word as their sufficient and exclusive rule of faith and practice in all matters of religion." This definition we believe to be as true as it is full, and true enough for the Son of God. This we regard a logical as well as scriptural solution of the question, and come at once to the question in consideration, "The Mission of a New Testament Church." Through man, at his own will, sin entered into the world; through God it must be condemned, punished and controlled. To this end God has established His church, and laid upon it the burden of will and purpose to overthrow the power of sin, through the blood of His Son. He has ordained that man shall be party to the plan of redemption. The church, therefore, by Christ, Himself, is called salt of the earth, light of the world, and a city on a hill, to save and bring back the lost sheep of the House of Israel. This the church must be and do, or lose the importance of its name.

Sin has committed a great crime in the world, in that it overthrew the first holy state of man, crucified our Lord Jesus Christ, attempted to overthrow, through sinful angels, the very throne of God, and now seeks to doom this world. This giant evil of all ages, and enemy to all that is good and holy, God is gradually, but will finally crush his head. This ardent and divine work is left to the accomplishment of the true, consecrated and regenerated church of God. The pastor of a church is, in a sense, the mediator between God and His people. He is the message-bearer and the expounder of divine truth. He stands between the people and God, to make known the whole will and counsel of God to men, and to feed them with knowl. edge and understanding. "Go teach all nations, and baptize them," is God's command to the shepherd of every fold. No one shepherd is allowed to use his own judgment in what he is to preach, but God has taken to himself the exalted duty of selecting the message of every minister. His orders are, "preach the word;" "teach whatsoever I have commanded you." Here, we observe, that the word, not the will and pleasure of men, is to be preached; the commands of God, not the dictates, creeds and formulas of priests and popes. A Gospel of regeneration, sanctification, perseverance, sacrifice, purity, peace and faith must be preached from every pulpit, stage and platform, by every messenger of God, till sinners, backsliders, lukewarm church members and faith-paralyzed churches everywhere shall know and believe the blessed Gospel of Christ. When this is done the spirit of the Gospel will be to every believer the spirit of missions.

Brother pastors, let us take the stand, along by the side of Paul, the great Apostle. Let us examine ourselves and see if we are forced to answer as he did, "Woe is me if I preach not this Gospel; not the narrow, contracted and selfish manner of preaching it, but let us, if we can, remember it, put the great commission of our Lord in all our preaching, for the true and spiritual development of our members.

We believe that very few of our church members have a full, Godly idea of the *great commission*, hence cannot be in proper sympathy with it. Let us seek a little rest in our boasting of numbers and a proper mode of baptism, and urge, in all our preaching, the importance of a model New Testament Church, ready to every duty and responsibility of service to the master. It is said of the Disciples in Jerusalem, that they continued steadfastly in the Apostles' doctrine; that they were all together and had all things common; that the Lord added unto them daily such as should be saved. This, we believe, was all the outgrowth of a faithful ministry and cultivated membership. This state of things can exist in our day, and should exist, because of the God we serve, and "who is no respecter of persons."

The Jerusalem Church inhaled a pure Gospel atmosphere from her pulpits; the lives and souls of those ministers were baptized in the pool of studying to show themselves approved unto God; workmen that needeth not be ashamed. Laborers were sent out into all lands by this church, and volunteers to the Master's cause entered the church daily and all the time. This church realized its duty and mission to give the Gospel to all men.

The pastor, together with his officers and members, form the stewardship of God's kingdom on the earth. They are equally responsible for the carrying forward of the work of the church. The pastor must teach, plan, push and encourage the work. The officers must co-operate, help, endorse and take the lead in every good work, while the whole congregation, to do the greatest amount of work, should fall in line with every Scriptural obligation undertaken by the church, and do all possible to present the bright side of a true Gospel church. Let every church in the State take on new life, in a fixed purpose to give regularly and with a well-defined system, to all objects of Christian missions.

Let every pastor have a plan that is best suited to himself and people, and begin at once, the new era indeed, of mission, among his flock. Whether little or much be raised, start upon your plan, and let us have your experience and model. The matter of soul-saving and Bible Missions should absorb the whole life and energy of every Christian church. No church should claim to be upon a truly divine mission that fails in these things. A church that is not missionary in its work should lay no claim to the spirit of Christ. The mission of a New Testament Church is to herald the news of salvation to all nations, in all lands, through missionaries, Bibles, tracts and every God-given, available means. Such a church, anywhere, is salt of the earth, and light of the world. Such a church, with such a minister will, indeed, triumph over the enemy of righteousness, and trample down, to rise no more, the bulwarks of Satan, though they be mountain high, and stand complete at last, on the right hand of God to receive the welcome plaudit,. "Well done, good and faithful servant, enter into the joys of thy Lord."

WESTERN DISTRICT.

ROLLS OF HONOR.

At High Point, N. C.—February:
Deacon L. Trainum, 25 cents; Rev. W. Price, 25; Mr. R. C. Charles, 50; Rev. W. H. Graves, 25; Dr. Thomas Carrick, 25; Dr. J. B. Richardson, 25; Rev. J. E. Jackson, 25; Rev. George Trainum, 25; Rev. B. F. Robin, 50; H. Davis, 25; Rev. A. Wilburn, 25; Mrs. L. C. Smith, 25; Mr. M. F. Smith, 25.

March 1:
Rev. P. S. Lewis, 25; Mr. J. Wallace, 25; Rev. W. H. Hairston, 25; Dr. J. O. Crosby, 25; Rev. H. P. Alexander, 25; Deacon Woods, 25; Mrs. Eliza Gasty, 25; Miss A. Miller, 25.

At Charlotte, N. C.—March 23:
Rev. C. F. Davis, $1.00; Rev. C. H. Williamson, 1.25; Rev. J. B. Lee, 25; N. D. Deuiding, 25; Primus Moore, 25; Mrs. Mary Hill, 25; W. L. Killen, 25; H. C. Cogdell, 25; Rev. R. D. Harris, 75; Prof. R. W. Brown, 25; Deacon James Carpenter, 25; Rev. L. D. Holland, 25; Mrs. L. Hasty, 30; Miss E. Robinson, 26; Mrs. Lucy Blakeny, 25; Miss A. Chambers, 42; Mrs. Jessie Butler, 51; Mattie Robinson, 31; Laura Robinson, 25; Mrs. S. A. Blakeny, 1.25; N. B. Blackwell, 30; Lula Rowland, 30; Rev. King, 25; Rev. John Faison, 25; Mrs. A. G. Carter, 45.

At Salisbury, N. C.:
Mrs. R. B. Bruce, 25.

At Monroe, N. C.:
Rev. J. B. Blakely, $2.05; Rev. W. J. Silas (A. M. E. Z. Church), 25; Mariah Roberson, 1.65; Mrs. Caroline Sewell, 25; Mrs. Mary Coban, 1.50; Miss Ida Shadd, 1.75; Mrs. A. Albrooks, 51; Miss M. Shadd, 65; Miss M. Horn, 51; Mrs. M. A. Watts, 1.50.

CONTRIBUTIONS OF CHURCHES, INSTITUTES AND SUNDAY-SCHOOLS.

Thomasville Baptist Church, $3.20; Zion Baptist Church, Salisbury, N. C., 2.02; Dixonville Baptist Church, Salisbury, N. C., 3.06; Emans' Baptist Church, Statesville, N. C., 4.31; St. John's Baptist Church, Statesville, N. C., 1.55.

Sunday-schools February:
Thomasville, 75; Zion Baptist, Salisbury, 80; Statesville, 55; Woman's Missionary Society, First Baptist Church, Salisbury, 1.74; Wo-

man's Missionary Society, Zion Baptist Church, Salisbury, 1.33.

March.—Shady Grove Church, Salisbury, N. C., $2.50; Sunday School, 92; Henderson Grove Church, Salisbury, 2.00; Mt. Carmel Church, Charlotte, N. C., 4.10; Ebenezer Church, Charlotte, 5.00; First Baptist Church, Charlotte, 3.65.

April.—First Baptist Church, Monroe, N. C., $6.88; Mt. Sinai Church, Mt. Holly, N. C., 5.17; Sunday-school, 93.

Institute collections at High Point, N. C., February: $7.54; Salisbury, N. C., March, 9.04; Charlotte, N. C., March, 11.51; Monroe, N. C., April, 18.06.

ASSOCIATIONS: TIME AND PLACE.

Johnston Baptist Association; meets Thursday before the third Sunday in October, 1897; Gallilee Baptist Church. Rev. Wm. Ellerbee, Moderator; Q. C. Mial, Clerk.

Middle District Missionary Baptist Association; meets at Lake Chapel, Pender County, Thursday before the second Sunday in October, 1897. Rev. Wm. Devane, Moderator; Rev. I. M. Powers, Clerk.

Union Baptist Association will be held at ——, October 16, 17 and 18, 1897, N. B. Dunham, Moderator; W. H. Smith, Clerk.

Lane's Creek Union Baptist Association; meets Friday before the third Sunday in July, 1897. Rev. L. W. Wolfe, Moderator; D. J. Evans, Clerk.

Mud Creek Baptist Association; meets with the Green Mountain Church, Thursday before the third Sunday in August, 1897. Rev. C. W. Hemphill, Moderator; H. H. Hemphill, Clerk.

Lumber River Missionary Baptist Association, Rev. A. H. Thompson, Moderator; W. C. Pope, Clerk.

Rowan Baptist Association; meets with the Allison Grove Baptist Church, Concord, N. C., Wednesday before the fourth Sunday in August, 1897. Dr. J. O. Crosby, Moderator; Rev. E. F. Parham, Clerk.

Pee Dee Branch Missionary Baptist Association; Thursday before the second Sunday in October, 1897. Rev. S. W. Dockery, Moderator; Rev. T. A. Lomax, Clerk.

Lake Waccamaw Baptist Association; meets with White Pond Baptist Church, Bogue Swamp, Columbus County, Friday before the third Sunday in October, 1897. Rev. D. J. Moore, Moderator; B. M. Spaulding, Clerk.

Old Eastern Missionary Baptist Association; meets with ——. Rev. T. S. Evans, Moderator; C. C. Forbes, Clerk.

French Broad Baptist Association; meets ——, August 9, 10, 11 and 12, 1897. Rev. R. J. Martin, Moderator; C. A. Hamilton, Clerk.

Roanoke Missionary Baptist Association; meets at Roper, May 19-21, 1897. Rev. S. P. Knight, Moderator; Rev. A. S. Dunston, Clerk.

Neuse River Baptist Association; meets at Zion Hill Church, near Littleton, Tuesday after the fourth Sunday in September, 1897. Rev. W. R. Mason, Moderator; Prof. A. P. Robinson, Clerk.

Baptist State Sunday-school Convention of North Carolina; meets with the Baptist Church and Sunday-school at Louisburg, N. C., on Wednesday before the fourth Sunday in September, 1897. Hon. Jas.

H. Young, President; Rev. T. O. Fuller, A. M., Secretary.

The Western Baptist Sunday-school Convention; meets with the Arden Sunday-school, Friday before the fourth Sunday in July, 1897. J. P. E. Love, President; Miss Rosa E. Love, Secretary.

Albemarle Baptist Sunday-school Convention; meets at Lily of the Valley, near Plymouth, Saturday before the fourth Sunday in April, 1897. G. T. Hill, President; T. I. Blount, Secretary.

Kenansville Eastern Baptist Sunday-school Convention; meets July 16, 17, 18 and 19, 1897; Brown's Chapel, Sampson County. Rev. W. B. F. Kornegay, President; Hon. A. R. Middleton, Secretary.

New Hope Baptist Auxiliary Sunday-school Convention; First Baptist Church, Carthage, N. C., Friday before the first Sunday in August, 1897. Rev. J. H. Caldwell, President; Rev. M. W. Brown, Secretary.

Shiloh Baptist Association; meets at Spring Green Baptist Church, near Warrenton, Tuesday after third Sunday in August, 1897. Rev. I. Alston, Moderator; Hon. M. F. Thurnton, Clerk.

Wake Baptist Association; meets with the First Baptist Church, Franklinton, N. C., Wednesday before the third Sunday in August, 1897. Rev. J. Perry, Moderator; Dr. N. F. Roberts, Clerk.

Atkin's Association; Wednesday before the second Sunday in October, 1897, at Mt. Pleasant Baptist Church, Anson County. Rev. W. Leak, Moderator; S. S. Thomas, Clerk.

Ebenezer Association; meets Thursday before the fourth Sunday in October, 1897. A. Ellis, Moderator, Waco, N. C.

Yadkin and Davie Association; meets Thursday before the second Sunday in August, 1897. P. C. Young, Moderator.

Mt. Pleasant Association; will meet with Mt. Zion Baptist Church, Belmont, N. C., Thursday before the third Sunday in October, 1897. Thomas Barnwell, Moderator.

Mountain and Catawba Association; meets with Clark's Chapel, near Statesville, Thursday before the first Sunday in August, 1897. Rev. G. W. Turner, Moderator.

High Point Educational and Missionary Association; meets at Asheboro, first Thursday in August, 1897. Rev. S. Thomas, Moderator; Rev. F. A. Long, Secretary.

Waynesville Association; meets Thursday before the first Sunday in September.

PLACES AND TIMES FOR FOURTH COURSE OF LECTURES NEW ERA INSTITUTE. WESTERN DISTRICT

Greensboro, July 6, 1897.
Winston, July, 27.
Asheville, August 17,
Reidsville, September, 7.
Wilkesboro, September 28.
Lilesville, October 17.
Dallas, November 9.
Monroe, November 30.

CENTRAL DISTRICT.

Graham, July 20–22.
Wakefield, August 10–12
Hillsboro, Aug. 31, September 1-2
Hubb, September, 21–23.
Greystone, October 12–14.
Pleasant Grove, November 2–4.
Weldon, November 23–25.
Sanford, December 14–16.
Other important meetings in all

the districts—Central, Maxton, Red Springs, Youngsville and Troy.

EASTERN DISTRICT.

Wallace, June 22–24
Harrellsville, July 13–15.
New Hope, August 3–5.
New Sawyer's Creek, August 24 26.
Tarboro, September 14–16.
Windsor, October 5–7.
Jacksonville, October 26–28.
Clinton, November 16–18.

NEW ERA INSTITUTE FOURTE SESSION.

The New Era Institute has proved a great success. It is no longer an experiment. Hundreds of pastors and others are enthusiastic over it, declaring that it is one of the greatest blessings that has ever come to the colored Baptists of this State. They look forward with eager interest to the fourth meeting, the general programme of which is given in this leaflet. We hope to see every pastor and many others who were not at the previous Institutes. Brethren, you cannot afford to miss this rare opportunity.

There will be twelve lectures at each Institute (unless special circumstances prevent), and seventy-two lectures for the entire three-years' course. The subjects will include Biblical Theology, Church History, The Ministry, Christian Education, Missions, The Church and its Work, and other practical matters. It will be a kind of theological school brought nigh to the people. The best of available talent, both white and colored, will be secured for lecturers.

Everybody is invited. Every minister should attend every Institute. It will be of great value to him. It is proposed to publish a "Roll of Honor" of ministers who pursue the entire course of lectures. We look to the pastors to lead their people by word and by example in this new movement that promises so much for our cause in this State. Come, pastors, and bring with you as many of your people as you can.

Each lecture will be followed by a discussion, for about thirty minutes, when members of the conference may ask questions and present their views of the subject.

The following is the outline of lectures for the fourth Institute:

BIBLICAL THEOLOGY—FOUR LECTURES.

1. *The Holy Spirit.* A Person. His manifestations in the old dispensation. Christ's promise of the Spirit. Day of Pentecost and miracles of the Spirit. Titles of the Spirit: Their significance.

2. *The Holy Spirit.* In relation to Christ. The Spirit as author of the Scriptures. Inspiration.

3. *The Holy Spirit.* Regeneration: Its nature and necessity. Evidences of regeneration. Fruits of the Spirit.

4. *Faith.* A condition of salvation. What is faith? Abraham's faith. "The devils believe." Saving faith; assent of mind, consent of heart. Faith and works.

CHURCH HISTORY—TWO LECTURES.

1. *Spread of Protestantism from* 1517. Discovery of printing: The Bible, for the common people. The Lutheran Church. Calvin in Switzerland and Knox in Scotland; the Presbyterian Church. King Henry VIII. of England, head of the

English Episcopal Church. Huguenots in France. Persecutions; Inquisition; wars. Massacre of St. Bartholomew.

2. *Spread of Protestantism from 1517.* The Anabaptists in Holland: Their doctrine and influence. The Puritans in England. Cromwell and the Independents. The Wesleys and Methodism. State Churches. Origin of Sunday-schools.

THE GOSPEL MINISTRY—ONE LECTURE.

1. *Delivery of Sermons.* In a persuasive manner. Not dictatorially. Earnestly, but not boisterously. In the fear of God. The preacher's manner; tones of voice, etc. Practice in reading.

CHRISTIAN MISSIONS—TWO LECTURES.

1. *The Missionary Spirit a mark of the true Church.* Jesus Christ's great mission to earth. His last command to evangelize the world. Duty to go or give. Need of a missionary revival.

2. *Encouragements to faith in the missionary enterprise.* Carey's work and waiting. Judson. The "Lone Star Mission" and Clough. Other instances. The promise of God.

CHRISTIAN EDUCATION—ONE LECTURE.

1. *The History of Baptist Educational work in this State since emancipation.* Beginning by the Home Mission Society. Work of President H. M. Tupper and others. Growth of the work. Its expense to the Society. Number of Schools in the State. Contrast between the intellectual condition thirty years ago and now.

Stereopticon views.

THE CHURCH—TWO LECTURES.

1. *Christian Stewardship.* Teachings of Scripture on the subject. "Not our own." Parable of the talents. Time, talents, possessions to be used rightly for Christ.

2. *Christian Benevolence.* Christ's teachings on the subject. The early Christians. Paul's letters. Duty to get in order to give. Economy and industry a duty. Sinful waste of the Lord's money.

REV. J. A. WHITTED,
Gen. Miss'y, Raleigh, N. C.

PROGRAMME BAPTIST MISSIONARY AND EDUCATIONAL CONVENTION OF NORTH CAROLINA.

EBENEZER BAPTIST CHURCH,
CHARLOTTE, Oct. 19-24, 1897.

Tuesday, 7:30.—Address of Welcome, part of churches, by the pastor, Rev. C. L. Davis. Response by Rev. S. H. Witherspoon, Greensboro. Address on part of the citizens by the Mayor of Charlotte. Response by Dr. J. E. Dellinger, Greensboro.

Introductory Sermon, Rev. P. S. Lewis, Salisbury, N. C.; Alternate, Rev. A. S. Dunston, Hertford, N. C.

Collection announcements.
Adjourn.

Wednesday, 9:30. — Devotional exercises, Rev. S. W. Dockery, Maxton; Rev. S. S. Henderson, Greensboro.

Reading Constitution.

Enrollment of delegates, and payment of representation fees from churches and Associations as names of delegates and churches are enrolled.

Collection.
Adjourn.

2:30.—Devotional exercises, Rev. D. J. Moore and Rev. J. W. Dew, Goldsboro.
Announcement of committees.
Report of Corresponding Secretary.
Co-operation as suited to the needs of the colored people, Dr. I. T. Tichenor, Corresponding Secretary Home Mission Board Southern Baptist Convention; Dr. H. L. Moorehouse, Field Secretary American Baptist Home Mission Society.
7:30.—Missionary sermon, Rev. Joseph Perry, Sunday-school Missionary for North Carolina, Raleigh, N. C.; Rev. C. M. Cartwright, Edenton, Alternate.
The American Baptist Publication Society; what it has done and is doing for the colored people of the South, Rev. S. N. Vass, Secretary Southern States.
Collection for the Society.
Adjourn.
Thursday, 9:30.—Devotional exercises, Rev. D. S. Salter, Raleigh; Rev. A. Wilburn, Trinity College.
10.—Business.
10:30.—Remarks upon the needs and condition of the field's by the district missionaries, twenty minutes each. Local missionaries, ten minutes each.
Relation of Associations and churches to the Baptist State Convention of North Carolina, and how best sustained, Rev. W. R. Mason, Weldon, N. C.; Rev. W. R. Slade, Wilmington, N. C.; Rev. D. T. Best, Clinton, N. C.; Rev. Wm. Devane, Wilmington, N. C.
Collection.
2:30.—Devotional exercises, Rev. S. G. Newsome, Margarettsville; Rev. M. T. Hawkins, Ingleside.
3.—Business.

3:30.—Systematic giving.
Report of committee.
Address, Rev. T. J. Morgan, LL. D., Corresponding Secretary American Baptist Home Mission Society.
Discussion by the brethren.
Collection.
Adjourn.
7:30.—Devotional exercises, Rev. M. D. Matthewson, Tarboro; Rev. L. H. Hackney, Chapel Hill.
Home and Foreign Missions: how may our people be awakened to their importance. Rev. J. E. White, Raleigh; Rev. W. A. Patillo, Oxford; Dr. A. W. Pegues, Raleigh.
Collection for missions.
Adjourn.
Friday, 9:30.—Devotional exercises, Rev. J. R. Nelson, Asheville; Rev. Thomas Sharpe, Harrellsville.
Reports of committees.
Collection for Shaw University.
Adjourn.
2:30.—Devotional exercises, Rev. J. H. Dunston, Morrisville; Rev. Alvis Whitted, Hillsboro.
The progress of the work beyond the Blue Ridge, and western North Carolina, Rev. Hemphill, Hendersonville; Rev. W. T. Minter, Asheville; Rev. G. W. Moore, Reidsville; Dr. Carey, Shelby. Eastern North Carolina, Rev. L. P. Martin, Rev. T. S. Evans.
7:30.—The Baptist ministry and churches of North Carolina: their duty to Shaw University, President C. F. Meserve. To our secondary schools, Rev. T. O. Fuller, Franklinton; Rev. Luke Pearce, Windsor.
Collection for Shaw University.
Saturday, 9:30.—Missionary and Educational Conference, Rev. G. W. Perry, of Raleigh, presiding.
The following ministers are especially requested to fill the churches

of the city Sunday: Rev. J. J. Worlds, Rev. M. C. Ransom, Rev. J. O. Crosby, Rev. T. O. Fuller, Rev. W. A. Patillo, Rev. Luke Pearce, Rev. J. W. Dew, Rev. J. Perry, Rev. N. F. Roberts, Rev. S. H. Witherspoon, Rev. W. H. Woodward, Rev. P. F. Maloy, Rev. A. B. Vincent, Rev. C. C. Somerville, Rev. W. R. Slade, Rev. S. H. Hicks, Rev. M. D. Matthewson.

J. A. WHITTED,
Corresponding Secretary.
N. F. ROBERTS,
Chairman Board Managers.

THE MODEL DEACON.

A deacon is a church officer, chosen to be a minister or servant of others. As to the manner in which he discharges the function of his office he will win for himself, both from God and his brethren, the title of "model." The term, when applied to an individual, is comprehensive and broad, meaning that the person is a standard, for imitation or comparison, a fitting exemplar. His office is to have charge of the sick and needy members, and such temporal affairs of the church as may require his attention; besides, he is to act as counsellor and assistant of the pastor in promoting the interest of the church. There is no department of the church work of more vital concern, and more fully demonstrates "pure and undefiled religion" than the interest shown by the church for its sick and needy. The deacon is the vigil, whose duty it is to look after this class of persons, which, as the meaning of the subject implies, ought to be done by the deacon, without murmuring or complaint. There may be cases where the deacon not only waits to be told his duty, in this respect, but actually waits to be "put on a committee," and when reminded of his plain Christian duty is always ready to say that he has a family to work for. In such a case he is a "model" of stupidity and selfishness. Since he must counsel with the pastor in matters of business, he should, at least, have the qualification recorded in Acts 6:3, "Of honest report, full of the Holy Ghost and wisdom."

Of the three qualifications mentioned in that passage, none is more weighty and serves to a better purpose for the material advancement of the church, than the last. Not, however, at a sacrifice of the two former. Wisdom is the faculty of forming the fittest and truest judgment in any matter presented for consideration, combining the knowledge of men and things gained by experience. The deacon ought to possess sufficient mental powers to be able to aid the pastor upon almost any question that may arise. The question of raising money for the various objects of the church; of advancing the educational interest, looking to the hope of the rising generation; of overcoming friction that may arise from time to time; of how we may best unify our forces to accomplish the most good, are matters that will as certainly confront the church as it is to exist. In anticipation of these conditions, it is obvious the class of men wanted to face them. That church is to be pitied whose only claim for the choice of a deacon is, that he is a "good man." Perish the thought, that I would divorce goodness from wisdom, but repeat, with emphasis, that will go ringing down the ages, that the "model deacon" should possess a happy combination, not to say trinity, of *honesty, fulness of the Holy Ghost, wisdom.*

In these days of rapid transit and endless imitations, it would seem that many of our churches are suffering, just now, from the mania of changing church officers. Ever and anon the question comes up to change the deacon and create a "new board," and it is not infrequently the case that those who are so restless and always clamoring for a change, themselves have an "axe to grind." A life tenure of office as deacon may be as detrimental to the church as the very rapid and constant changes, for, when a deacon gets it in his head that he is chosen for life, and decides to be a sort of Czar, the church will be subjected to the worst kind of tyranny it is possible to imagine. The deacon, who, by his faithful and good works proves that his service is substantial and important, is likely to hold the office as long as he wishes, and if any unforseen event should bring about a change, he can retire with the consciousness that he has done his full duty, with an eye single to the glory of God, and though men may not appreciate his service and worth, he has won from his Master the plaudit, "well done!"

Some things the model deacon will NOT do: He will not hold private caucuses in the church, behind his pastor's back, seeking in each meeting to bring into ill-repute his good name, and hinder his work he came to do. He will not handle improperly the finances that come into his hands, and make a plea to the people from time to time that he needs money for the pastor, and money to carry on the Lord's cause, when at the same time he rarely ever contributes a penny, and a large percentage of the money that goes into the treasury never finds its way out, except as it goes to advance his own personal interest.

He will not criticise his pastor before his enemies, and claiming, at the same time, that he would not "hurt a hair of his head."

The model deacon will not frequent the bar-room, neither will he come reeling before the church, under the pernicious and damnable influence of whiskey.

Things the model deacon will do: If there be a Sabbath school he will attend it, and if no school is organized he will never be contented until one is, and will see to it that his whole family attend, as far as is practicable.

He will take a lead in financial and educational matters, and may be safely counted upon to do his whole duty. He never tires working for his church, and no claim is too heavy or urgent for his prayerful consideration if it means to advance the Master's kingdom. He will pray for and love his pastor.

Many a conversion in the church is traceable, not so much to the preacher's sermon, as to the deacon's prayer. The man who works in harmony and conjunction with his pastor, in the right, may live to see glorious harvest for which his soul will rejoice through all eternity.

The "model deacon" will attend prayer-meetings. That deacon who is almost too busy to be found in the prayer-meetings, but on such nights must go to the "lodge," is happily out of place, and his bishopric should be given to another.

C. C. SOMERVILLE.

SCHOOL OF MISSIONARY TRAINING. SHAW UNIVERSITY. 1897.

Dialogue Commencement—Our Training and our Future.

EMMA L. MILLER.

Mrs. Gibbs: "Just think girls, we have actually come to the last time, probably, that we shall all be together! It does not seem possible that the year is over, and that tonight we must separate. It makes me sad to think of it."

Miss McDougald: "Yes, it makes us all sad to think of that, yet I cannot help being glad to-night, too. I have enjoyed my work every day and thanked God more and more for our school, but now let us go out to help others, and put into practice what we have learned here, and let us go with hope and courage, thanking God for this time of preparation we have had together."

Miss Ingram: "Yes, that is the way we ought to feel, and I believe our vacation will have some good lessons for us all. As I look back over our school year, I don't know what to be most grateful for, or what I have enjoyed most. Suppose we each tell what we have enjoyed and what has been most helpful to us?"

Miss Edwards: "If I should try to tell what I have enjoyed most, I am sure I should not be able, but I know what has been most helpful, and that is the Bible study. When I came here I did not really know what it meant to study the Bible, but now I think I have some idea of what it means. I am sure it is a new book to me, and the more I have studied it the more I long to have a better knowledge of it."

The study of Bible geography and history has brought the places and people nearer to me, and I have seen the unity of the Old Testament and its connection with the New Testament as never before. When we came to study the life of Christ I gained a new view of God's wonderful plan of redemption. That life of our Savior has grown more real, more beautiful, more human and more divine. As that life has been held up before us day by day, and its true meaning has dawned upon us, I am sure we must have felt how much it means to be a follower of Christ—a Christian. Then, too, I have much enjoyed the study of the Acts and some of the Epistles, and have seen in them the development of Chrtstianity.

O, the Bible is truly a new book to me, and I love it more dearly than ever before."

Miss McDougald: "I wonder if you have all enjoyed our lectures as much as I. Our medical lectures have been a help to us in many ways, and I am sure we will be better able to help the sick than we would have been without them. We shall often be called upon to visit and care for the sick, and then we will have an opportunity to help them spiritually, that we could have in no other way. The lectures by Miss Wyche on nursing were full of common sense and practical suggestions. Since Mr. Spilman gave his lectures on Baptist history I have had a great desire to study the subject farther. Dr. Carter is always interesting and instructive, and we were very sorry when his lectures were over. I think Mr. Broughton is an enthusiastic Sunday-school worker, and his talks made us long to have everybody in a good, live Sunday-school. It is very kind of these friends to give this service to the school, and I think we should show our appreciation in every possible way. There are others also among our own faculty to whom we are indebted for helpful talks upon various topics. I tell you, girls, there are very few among our people who have the privileges we enjoy; I only hope we make good use of them."

Miss Lee: "Well, I don't think any of you have enjoyed our class-room work more than I, but suppose that was all we had gained, would we be ready to go out knowing *what* to do and *how* to do it? I am sure I would not. I think our practical training in field work has been quite as helpful as anything else. If we had not been trained in industrial school work, how could we hope to go out prepared to do that work with the children? And how much we will be able to help them in this way. Then there are the women's meetings and the childrens' meetings that we have conducted this year, five each week. I am sure if they have not helped other people, they have helped us. I have gained a new idea of Sabbath-school work from the primary Sunday-school which we have carried on. I am sure we shall be able from what we have learned in this way, to help in Sabbath-school work, wherever we may be. In our house-to-house visiting, I have realized more than ever in my life, how much our people need help, and how little they know of the Word of God, and what it means to be a Christian, and if this is the condition here, in Raleigh, where so much missionary work has been done, what must it be in many other places that have not been reached by such influence? I have been thinking all the year that this is just the kind of work our people need."

Miss Allen: "I have been wondering if no one was going to say a word about our house-work. I think that is too important to be omitted, for if we cannot help the members in the homes, where many of them need help so much, we shall fail of doing a very important work. I believe every woman should know how to cook, sew, wash, iron and keep house well; she ought to know how to do these things, whether she ever intends to do them or not, and there are very few women who do not need either to do them themselves or to teach other people how to do them. Just think of it, girls: there is not a lady teacher in Shaw University who cannot go into the kitchen in the mansion and get as good a meal and serve it in as fine style as you will find in any elegant home. They can make as nice cake as anybody in Raleigh, and a while ago, when their cook was sick, they did not have to rush frantically after another girl, or starve until some one came to the rescue. No, they did the work themselves, and enjoyed doing it, too, just as any woman enjoys doing anything she knows how to do *well*. Do you know why some vain, proud women look down upon house-work as drudgery? It is because they do not know how to do it *well*. I never saw a woman yet who despised to do anything she could do beautifully. I am glad we have been taught all kinds of house-work at the Training School; I know I needed it and think if you would all confess the truth, you would say you needed it too. I am not the only one who did not know how to make bread."

Mrs. Williams: "I am glad to hear Miss Lee and Miss Allen speak as they have, about our practical training, and am glad that during the past two years the plan of the school has been enlarged, so as to put more of this work into it. I can tell you, girls, when you go out in your mission work, as I have been doing for years, you will need to know all these things, that you may be able to help our people; you will need to know just what to do and how to teach other people to do it."

Miss Gray: "You girls who were not here last year don't know how to appreciate the improvements that have been made in our Training School home this year; new paper, paint, whitewash, carpets, rugs, curtains, pictures, table covers, bed spreads, toilet articles, tidies, hanging-lamps and many other little things that made home pleasant and attractive. We had none of these things last year; we did not have our reading-room fitted up, either, and had no books to read for pleasure or for study. Then, how much more cheerful our class-room and library are since glass doors have been put in, and how proud we are of that fine book case Mr. Tolman has made for us. I tell you, girls, you don't know how to appreciate all these improvements."

Miss Lee: "Well, I presume we had not thought very much about that, or where all these things came from, but we have enjoyed them, I'm sure. I wonder if, when we come back next year, we shall find any more improvements in our home?"

Miss Jordan: "No doubt you will, for our preceptress will never rest until she gets the things that are needed. She is not one to sit down and wait for things to come to her, either. If she don't find what she wants, she gets it or makes it, or gets some one else to get it or make it. I believe she could build a house and make the furniture for it if she should try, and if she doesn't get a new class-room before long I expect to see her with lumber, hammer and nails, making one. Don't you suppose if she should start it the President would see that it was finished? Let's help her start it and see."

Miss Ingrom: "I am sure I would be willing to do my part, for I can drive a nail without hitting my finger, and that's more than some women can do."

Miss Edwards: "How nice it would be, if we had a good, large, airy class-room. I believe we could do better work, and then, when we had company, we would not have to crowd them into a corner for lack of room, and we would not have to open the outside door every few minutes to get a breath of air. I do hope we can have a new class-room before another year."

Mrs. Gibbs: "Well, now, we have been looking back over our school life, and I know we are grateful for it all, but I can't help looking into the future to-night, and wondering what our lives will be and where they will be spent."

Miss McDougald: "I hope most of us can come back for another year—I'm sure I mean to, and I am going to work through the summer to earn money to come with. I think if we work for our education we will appreciate it far more than we would if some one gave it to us."

Miss Ingrom: "So do I, and I always did. I would rather work my finger nails off than give up coming back next year."

Miss Lee: "Yes, I hope most of us can come back, but we know Miss Jordan and Miss Gray will not return, and I think it would be nice to have them tell us what they want most to do, now that their school life is over. Miss Jordan, would you mind telling us what your plans are for the future?"

Miss Jordan: "It is not an easy matter for me to decide where to work. When I gave my life to the Savior, I said, 'I will do whatever my hands find to do.' I am interested in the Lord's work everywhere, and want, most of all, to go where He leads me. I have often repeated to myself the first verse of the class hymn for last year.

"Submission to my lot, what'er it be,
Teach me, O Lord, to know, Thy hand to see
In every path of life, still guiding me."

If I thought the Lord wanted me to go to Africa I would be willing to go. When, as a child, I heard of the terrible condition of the brethren, and that this was because they knew nothing of Jesus, I wanted to send them my Bible story-books. When I became a Christian my interest in Africa increased, and although I do not feel sure that the Lord wants me to go, I mean to hold myself willing, should the way be made plain to me. I do think we ought to do all we can to interest our people in Africa, and am glad that Shaw University has sent some workers there.

I once read of a man who was condemned to die; his last day had come. While the warden was making merry with some friends a package was handed him, but he tossed it aside unopened. The prisoner was led forth to his doom, and the warden returned to the prison to open the package, which was found a pardon for the condemned man. We have in our hand a message of pardon from God; shall we not gladly carry it to those who know not of it, ere it is too late? I should like to carry the news of this pardon to Africa."

Miss Edwards: Well, if you do go, I'm sure we will bid you God speed on your mission. Our Training School is already represented in Africa, and one of last year's graduates expects to go soon. How pleasant it would be, if you could go together.

Now, Miss Gray, where do you think the Lord is leading you?

Miss Gray: "Africa is a needy field, I know, and I am glad Miss Jordan wants to go there, but I believe the Lord has called me to work among our own people in this country. From a child I have wanted to be a missionary. You know I was brought up in the North, and did not have a chance to see our people in their worst condition, and yet as I read about them and heard about them from my mother and many others who came North, a strong desire came into my heart to share with them some of the rich blessings God has given me. My mother cheerfully gave me to this work. I feel that the Lord has called me to it, and gladly answer, 'Here am I, send me.' Since I came South and learned more of the great needs of our people, my desire to help them has been strengthened. When I think of all the work that the Woman's Baptist Home Mission Society has done for our people during the last twenty years, and how this year they are supporting fifty-two workers, besides carrying on three Training Schools to fit us for this work," I feel that it is high time we were giving ourselves to it, as they have given themselves. I wish we might see a score or more of earnest, educated, consecrated young women from among our people in our own school for this work."

Mrs. Gibbs: "Yes, Miss Gray, I think so too. I felt when I came here, and saw what privileges we had, that I could not bear to see so small a class enjoying them. I know our teachers take as much pains to teach us as though there were fifty of us. But I want to see more in our school preparing to carry the glad tidings. And now, my dear class-mates, let us go out and try to win others, not only to come to Christ, but to give themselves to His service."

Miss Allen, have you not a closing word before we separate?

Miss Allen: "Does it fall to me to say the last words? I am glad we have had this talk together, and cannot think of anything better to say, as we part, than one of the verses of our last year's class song. I have thought of it many times this year, and tried to live it too:"

"Where Thou dost lead, O Lord, I fain would go,
And gladly would submit, content to know,
That Thou art leading through this vale below."

SKETCHES OF BAPTIST HISTORY AND BIOGRIPHY.

Rev. Benjamin F. Watts, of Hickory, N. C., and of the Mountain and Catawba Association, is one of the foremost Western North Carolina Baptist, and a venerable hero in the faith and practice of the Baptist churches in Western North Carolina. He is now sixty-three years old, was ordained to the Gospel ministry November 27, 1867, by two white ministers, Elijah Allison and William Pool, both of Alexander county, and of the old Catawba Association (white). He has labored zealously in the ministry for more than thirty successive years, nearly one-half of his whole life. He has baptized and added to the church through his direct ministry 1,617 souls, organized twenty or more churches, all of which are now in existence, and some of them the strongest in the west. These churches are located in the counties of Wilkes, Alexander, Gaston, Cleveland, N. C., and Spartanburg, Union and York counties, S. C. He has, with wonderful success as an evangelist, traveled and preached in the States of North Carolina, South Carolina, Tennessee and Georgia. He organized the Mountain and Catawba Association, assisted by some three or four other ministers. He said he had preached more than one sermon in a low, whispering voice, that the white people might not know of the service. He said in most of the secret services the singing would be but a humming sound through the nose.

He still preaches the Gospel with great zeal and earnestness, and holds one or two churches. He exhorts the young men to lead more souls to Christ, and talk less about high salaries; to get off the railroads and come into the backwoods and preach a soul-saving Gospel. He will go to the State Convention.

Rev. Thomas Barnwell, of Belmont, N. C., and of the Mount Pleasant Association, is another of our venerable fathers in the Gospel among North Carolina Baptists. He is sixty-one years old, and is still active in the ministry. He has baptized nearly one thousand souls during his life in the ministry; has organized churches from Charlotte to Spartanburg, S. C. His work for the most part has been in this State, and in the counties of Cleveland, Gaston, Washington and Lincoln. He was born in Charleston, S. C., and was brought to this State in slavery times by his former master. He began to preach in prayer meetings in 1861-'62, and though threatened a number of times for his attempt to teach his people the word of life, he never stopped. Many were converted under this plan of his preaching. He helped to organize the Western Shiloh Association, the Western Missionary Union and the Mount Pleasant Associations, of which he is now Moderator, and many of the Sunday-school unions and district conventions of the west.

Rev. Barnwell is held in high esteem in Baptist circles, and by all who know him, as a Gospel minister and leader of his people, and is honored among them as a Baptist leader of no little importance.

Long live these venerable fathers of our Church principles and the Gospel, as monuments of truth and good works and fit examples to men.

Rev. Barnwell believes that the Baptist Church is the mother church, and that she will on some day see all her children together, as did Jacob of old break down with joy in the presence of his once separated family.

JOTTINGS FROM WESTERN NORTH CAROLINA.

ASHEVILLE.

Editor Baptist Quarterly:

DEAR SIR:—Thinking the brethren of the State would like to know something of the work in this section of the State, I note these jottings for their benefit.

Western North Carolina is a distinct section, not because it is the western part of the State, but because its mountainous character distinguishes it in climate, resources and population from the rest of North Carolina. It is a section of ever-varying and never-ending interest, especially to the student of nature, the tourist, the health-seeker and the lover of forest sports. Now it has on its most charming smile, so to speak, in welcome to the thousands of people all over the South who annually seek rest and refreshment amid its enchanting scenes. Great numbers from the North and West come here as a refuge from the blizzards and severities of winter. Asheville, the metropolis, is located in the very heart of this famous region.

Asheville is situated at the confluence of the Swannanoa and French Broad rivers, among the foot hills of the Black Mountain range, thirteen peaks of which pierce the clouds at an altitude above that of Mount Washington.

Like this section of country, the churches in their work for Christ and humanity are ever-varying in interest, beauty and growth. Since the coming of Rev. P. F. Maloy, A. B., our district missionary last year, with the New Era Institute and Plan of Co-operation, all our churches seem to have taken on new life. Revivals have been held in almost all our churches, and much success reported as the result of them.

Five churches are reported without pastors. We need some good and true Baptist preachers, who are willing to sacrifice, wait and trust in God out here.

I must commend Rev. J. A. Whitted, General Missionary, and Rev. P. F. Maloy, our District Missionary, for their yeoman efforts in securing for us through the State Board a local missionary. We gratefully acknowledge the appointment as God sent.

Rev. F. W. Wallace began his work here on Saturday, July 10th. We expect great things of him for God and the Baptists. Our motto is: *"The world for God and the Baptist Church."*

The churches in Asheville are in harmony and moving on nicely. Rev. Mr. Nelson is meeting with some success in raising money to cancel the mortgage on the church lot.

The First Church is still moving on. The foundation for the new edifice is completed, and the cornerstone is to be laid on Saturday before the third Lord's day in this month. Rev. P. F. Maloy has been invited to be present and officiate. He has accepted, and signified his intention to be present, and a red-letter day is anticipapted among the Baptists. This church edifice has already been published as being planned the most modern and largest in Western North Carolina when complete.

Yours for God, the race, and the success of the Baptist everywhere,

W. T. MINTER.

OFFICE CORRESPONDING SECRETARY OF THE BAPTIST STATE SUNDAY-SCHOOL CONVENTION AND SUNDAY-SCHOOL MISSIONARY OF THE AMERICAN BAPTIST PUBLICATION SOCIETY FOR NORTH CAROLINA.

Dear Brethren and Sisters:

I take this method to inform you somewhat of our Sunday-school work in the State. The field is inviting to the missionary. While something, and, indeed, a great deal, has been done in this line, there yet remains vastly more to be accomplished by the great Baptist brotherhood and sisterhood of the State. New schools are being organized almost every week, and being supplied with literature for three months free of charge by the American Baptist Publication Society, after which they are expected to be able to purchase for themselves. There are neighborhoods in this State where we have no Baptists competent to conduct a Sunday-school. In these regions our people are held up as insignificant by other denominations. It is quite hard to establish schools in most of these places, but I can rejoice over the fact that light is softly but surely creeping in in most of these dark corners. There are also regions where the people will not attend church, and we are making an effort to take the church to them, in that we visit them, and read the Bible and explain it to them, sing and pray with them, trying to stimulate a spirit of Christian service.

This Sunday-school colportage missionary work is truly missionary in the highest degree. It is demonstrating very clearly the spirit of the Master, who went about doing good. The time to care most particularly for the orchard is while that orchard is a nursery. The best time to care for the garden is when the plants are young. The time to be very careful about the flock is when there are lambs, for negligence to the lambs is the most of serious all negligence. The time to lavish the treasure of the heart, such as loving-kindness and tender care of your children, is when they are young, while you have full control, to direct as you wish; while they are dependent upon you for all.

This likeness exists between the church and the Sunday-school. Every church should strive to have the most excellent school, for such a church will have the most excellent membership. In the Sunday-school we have the opportunity of opportunities to indoctrinate our membership into the principles of the Baptist Church, which we believe to be Christian. This is one of the labors of the church, to which each member should stand: "Yea, altogether, as one man," and contribute whatever in his power, of money, time and influence to make it a success. Many of these churches, of which we boast, came from Sunday-schools.

O, my brother, my sister, have you ever considered these facts: That a Sunday-school, where there is no church, means a church in that place in the near future; where there is a church it means a feeder; that all of the great, honorable, influential men and women in the walks of life, have trodden the path which leads through the Sunday-school, that they might gather flowers, jewels and "gems of purest rays serene," to adorn their lives and characters, that, as they come to their station, they might be loaded with honor and fitness. To this source the world is looking for men and women in the future, as in the past. We must be prepared.

One of the ways by which we can help in this great work is to unify our forces and stand as one man to the American Baptist Publication Society, who has been our friend and helper in North Carolina ever since freedom was proclaimed.

Before the din of war had entirely died away the voice of the Society's missionary was heard blowing the trump of God, which was heard on every plantation, and, in every town. He came, pressing his way through the smoke of battle and the blackness of ignorance, with Bibles, papers and tracts in hand, crying, "Let there be light," and, as a result, there was light. This light is descending to the valley, leaping the mountain-peaks, stealing its way through the log-cabins, making sun-beams, before which the darkness of sorrow and ignorance flee away, dance upon the floor, thereby creating joy and light for the indweller.

This is some of the work done by the American Baptist Publication Society: More than five hundred millions of books, tracts and periodicals have been circulated; more than half a million of Bibles given to the needy; six thousand needy Sunday-schools received grants; ten thousand pastors and ministers given good working libraries; three hundred thousand dollars worth of grants have been made; sixty thousand dollars given for Bible work in foreign lands; more than a million two hundred and eighty thousand families visited by its missionaries; ten thousand Baptist Sunday-schools have been organized; one thousand Baptist churches constituted; twenty thousand believers baptized; five chapels are put on wheels, going to destitute parts; the blind, those unfortunate individuals, are supplied with the international lessons. This is the kind of work it is still doing. What will you do to help this great work? Let every convention, association, church, Sunday-school and individual send in contributions regularly. Stand by this Society as you do every object of our denomination. Let every missionary society contribute something. Buy all your books and papers and periodicals from it. They sell cheaper than anyone else, and sell the best. Let the churches and the Sunday-schools make arrangements for the missionary to hold institutes, that will benefit all. All schools who have not observed "Children's Day" we hope will write for programs; Dr. R. G. Seymour 1632, Chestnut Street, Philadelphia, Pa., will send them free, if, when used, you take a collection for the Society. Stand by the old A. B. P. Society. Don't go after strangers. A friend in need is a friend indeed. Such has this Society been to us. Pastors will please read this to their churches.

Yours truly,
JOSEPH PERRY,
Sunday-school Missionary.

Let every Sunday-school and County Convention be represented in the Baptist Sunday-school Convention, which convenes in Louisburg, N. C., September 11, 1897. For information, write to Joseph Perry, Corresponding Secretary, Raleigh, N. C.

WOMAN'S MEETING IN CONNECTION WITH NEW ERA INSTITUTE WORK.

A Woman's Missionary Meeting, of unusual interest, was held in connection with the New Era Institute, at Raleigh.

The subject was "Woman's Work in the Home, Church and Missions."

Miss Miller, of the Training School, presided, and made a brief address upon woman's present opportunities.

Miss Fannie Jordan gave a Bible reading upon woman's work in the *New York Times.*

Mrs. Gibbs gave an address on her work in the home.

Miss May Hamilton spoke on her work in the church.

Miss Fannie Heck reviewed what woman had done, and is doing, in missions.

The addresses were of a high order, and the church was filled to the doors with an appreciative audience, one-third of which consisted of the brethren, who meekly took the back seats.

The exercises were interspersed with excellent music, led by the choir of the University.

The spirit of the meeting was devotional and inspiring.

We trust that henceforth every one of the institutes will have a woman's meeting as a part of the regular program.

A LISTENER.

Such as the above-mentioned Women's Meetings have been held with great profit, in connection with our New Era Institutes, in a great many parts of North Carolina.

One of the greatest developments of the age is the place woman is given in the churches and elsewhere.

It is hoped that some efficient woman may be appointed in connection with missionaries to do this kind of work.

Such a stimulus as this movement would give would be felt in untold good, and especially among the women.

SHAW DAY.

For BAPTIST QUARTERLY.

After consulting with prominent members of the denomination in various parts of the State, I have, with the approval of the officers of the American Baptist Home Mission Society, decided to ask the churches to consider the first Sabbath in November as "Shaw Day." Shaw University is in need of a large sum of money to enlarge its work and provide means for more efficiently carrying it on. Large sums of money in the last few years have come from the North, but comparatively little has been received from North Carolina. The work at Shaw is now in such a progressive and successful condition, particularly in the Theological Department, that a few hundred dollars, contributed by the denomination throughout the State, will enable us to put into operation plans that have been thoroughly and carefully matured. If Shaw can receive on the average a contribution of $5 from each church in the State, it will enable us to strengthen the work and carry forward plans that will bear rich fruit for the Master's cause. We earnestly ask the pastors, deacons, and all other members of the great Baptist denomination throughout the State, to come nobly to the rescue and make "Shaw Day"

a red letter day in the educational history of the race. All funds contributed should be sent to the President, Shaw University, Raleigh, N. C., who will forward a receipt for same, and see that the money is properly expended.

CHAS. F. MESERVE,
Prest. Shaw University.
Raleigh, N. C.
July, 1897.

The Board of Managers has unanimously voted the above named "Day" to Shaw University, and it is earnestly hoped that every church in North Carolina may respond to this worthy cause. Pastors, begin now to speak of the first Sabbath in November to all your churches, and let our worthy institution and its worthy president realize a good collection.

J. A. WHITTED,
Cor. Secretary Baptist Educational and Missionary Convention of North Carolina.

LETTER FROM AFRICA.

The following was received by a friend in this city from Mr. Stephens, now in Africa, which will be interesting to many of our readers:

MBANYA MANTEKE, A. B. M. U.,
SOUTHWEST AFRICA, May 8, '97.

Dear Friend and Sister:—I do thank the heavenly Master, who has given me this blessed privilege of sending you a few lines, after my long silence since I left America for my native land. You are still fresh in my memory, and I often speak to my people of you. The reason you have not heard from me is because I have been very busy, making many visits to the "out schools" and churches, encouraging my fellow native co-workers in the Lord and the work which we have before us daily. Some of them are very able men. The Spirit of the Lord is at work among the sons and daughters of Africa; they have brought many souls to the feet of Jesus in the little they know of the way to salvation.

One of the places visited last year is Mukinkanya. I don't think there were over twenty converts; but when visited the second time six or seven hundred people were on the Lord's side.

There are nineteen out-schools. I should have visited them all, but only had sufficient time to see part of them. Then, at that time, our Evangelist School was opened, and I had to stay at home and teach.

It was week before last I went to meet my sister, at Matadi, who just came down for a change from the heart of the Congo, or what I would call the jungles of the Congo Valley. She had been up there a year helping Dr. L. C. Fleming in the work of the Master. She will be going up again in a few days.

The civilization is fast coming in, but the white man carries his evils wherever he goes—that is liquor, etc.

My wife gave birth to a little boy on the 18th of January, 1897, whose name is Ralph. He is very pretty.

Write me all the news. Love to you from Mrs. Stephens. Please so remember me to all friends, and accept mine.

Yours truly,
H. M. STEPHENS.

REV. JOHN E. WHITE.

As long as a man is alive and at work, the question of his age and birth-place is of the least importance.

John E. White is the son of a sturdy Baptist preacher, Rev. J. M. White, who is yet in his prime, and doing as much work as any preacher in the State. On his mother's side he is the grandson of one of the pioneer preachers of North Carolina, Rev. John Ellington, who was one of the most useful preachers of all the host whose labors have blessed our Zion. His step-mother is a daughter of the sainted Patrick Dowd. He was educated by his father; and then he attended Wake Forest College four years, and graduated.

So heredity and environment continued to lead him into the ministry. But he entered life, as is frequently the case, with no such intention. He went to Western North Carolina to teach, and it was in this work that he saw the door opened, and determined to enter into the larger field. As he tells it, he was helping Elder Sams in a meeting, as a layman; and the old man, temporarily breaking down, he took up his work, carried the meeting on, and thenceforth preached the Gospel. He is not the first prophet who heard the voice of God on the mountains.

He let go ambition for the law, gave up his school work, and went to preaching with a will, at first, in meetings, and then as supply. In this work the winning of souls gave proof of his ministry. Called to the pastorate at Wilson, he built up our cause there, and made a reputation as a pulpit orator, and as a pastor. When he left, to accept the call to

Edenton, it was greatly to the regret of the people of Wilson and that section, regardless of denominations. At Edenton he developed rapidly, and became a power in that great Baptist country. He became known through the denominational press to all our people, and began to be felt in our State Conventions. Still, when the brethren in Convention, at Greensboro, called him to take up the work of the lamented Durham, he was surprised more than all.

But his spirit of loyalty and his faith in God and the brethren moved him to accept. It was a crisis in our history. We had all depended so largely on Durham that when he was suddenly taken, we knew not what to do.

But no mistake was made. The fresh strength, the splendid physical powers, the eloquence in speech, the conservatism and caution, the indomitable ability to work, day and night, and the faith of Secretary White, have stood us in good stead. Raised in the central section of North Carolina, having begun life in the western mountains, having ripened his ministry in the central and the extreme east, he is the only young preacher we had who knows the people and their ways in all sections. And he has made wonderful progress with them in the twenty months he has been Secretary. He has lived in their homes almost constantly. They have learned to love him. And not only the people, but their pastors, stand by him, and the missionaries love him. The old men have gathered around him for the work's sake; the young men have been drawn to him as if by gravitation.

So far he has managed the work well. He is giving his time, not only to missions, but to education, and all our objects; and his executive ability promises to re-create our Baptist book-store, in a business way. He still preaches nearly every Sunday. But, with all his work, his health is ideal.

Secretary White is a friend of the Negro race. He has never failed to give his best efforts in the co-operative work. As does anyone else, who can speak well, he loves to preach to or address a large congregation of the colored people.

We should all be very thankful that we have such a man as he in the arduous and exacting position of Corresponding Secretary of the Baptist State Convention.

To close without a word about his home, and an apology, would be unjust to him and the writer. Secretary White has a help-meet indeed. She makes his home happy, and they have two children, who are the joy of their lives. There is nothing more beautiful than his domestic relations. And for the apology, this writer has written these lines while waiting for a train, and about ten good brethren have interrupted him in the short hour at his disposal.

Rev. J. A. Whitted, Corresponding Secretary and General Missionary, Raleigh, N. C., U. S. A.:

VERY DEAR BROTHER: Your communication of May 8, 1897, is just received, and contents carefully noted.

As I will not have time to prepare an article for the BAPTIST QUARTERLY until after my return from the Union Meeting, on account of press of work, I beg to offer as a substitute the following letter, which I was writing at the time I received your letter:

BREWERVILLE, LIBERIA,
June 8, 1897.

To the First Baptist Church, Caresburg:

DEAR BRETHREN: This comes to inform you that yours of May 17th, requesting me to preach the dedication sermon for you on the fourth Sunday in this month, at 11 o'clock A. M., during the Union Meeting with you, was received a day or two ago.

In reply, I beg to say, up to this writing, I have discovered no reason why I should not accept the request.

Therefore, if, in the providence of God, I attend the meeting, as I purpose to, and find it the mutual consent of both you and your pastor that I should preach the dedication sermon, I will endeavor to do so, *in His name*.

I suppose you have a program for the occasion, which designates a brother to take care of the singing, one to offer the dedication prayer and another to read the Scriptures. This I advise.

"The grace of our Lord Jesus Christ be with you."

I am truly yours,
JAS. O. HAYES.

P. S.—As I have not seen a North Carolina newspaper for a number of years, and have never had the pleasure of seeing a copy of the BAPTIST QUARTERLY, have the kindness to send me a copy, for Africa's redemption.

I am truly yours,
J. O. H.

All contributions sent to the BAPTIST QUARTERLY for Rev. J. O. Hayes will be gladly received and forwarded directly to him.

J. A. WHITTED,
Corresponding Secretary

CONSTITUTION
Baptist State Convention of North Carolina.

We, the ministers and delegates from various Baptist churches in North Carolina, met in the town of Goldsboro, N. C., on the 1st of October, 1867, for the purpose of considering the propriety of entering into some general organization for our mutual improvement, and the diffusion of the principles of the Gospel, and agreed to the following rules of fundamental principle:

(*Revised October 23, 1889.*)

ARTICLE I. This convention shall be known as the "Baptist Educational and Missionary Convention of North Carolina."

ARTICLE II. It shall be the object of this convention to encourage and assist Shaw University and other Baptist schools approved by this convention, to educate young men called of God to the ministry and approved by the church to which they belong; to encourage education among all the people of the State, to support the Gospel in all destitute sections of the State, to send the Gospel to Africa, to encourage the distribution and study of the Bible and sound religious literature, to assist Baptist churches in the erection of suitable houses of worship, to encourage the proper care of indigent orphan children and destitute and aged ministers of the Gospel and co-operate with the Foreign Mission Convention of the United States and the American Baptist Home Mission Society.

ARTICLE III. Sec. 1. This convention shall be composed of Baptist Associations of North Carolina, regular Baptist churches, and all Baptist societies of a missionary nature or character, and members of good standing in regular Baptist churches.

Sec. 2. Any person may become a life member by the payment of $5.00, and an annual member by the payment of $1.00. Any association may be represented by the payment of 50 cents per church, and may send one delegate for every ten churches or fraction thereof. Any Baptist church in good standing may be represented by the payment of $1.00. Ministers in charge of regular Baptist churches in the State will be considered honorary members.

ARTICLE IV. Sec. 1 We recommend that Art. IV, sec. 1, be so amended as to read as follows: The officers of this convention shall be a president, vice-president from each association represented, a secretary, a corresponding secretary, a treasurer and an auditor, and a board of managers, consisting of nine members, of whom the president, corresponding secretary and treasurer shall be *ex-officio* members.

Sec. 2. The president shall preside at all meetings of the convention, and sign all orders upon the treasurer. One of the vice-presidents shall perform the same duties in the absence of the president.

Sec. 3. The recording secretary shall keep a faithful record of the proceedings of the convention. He shall prepare intelligence for the press, making appeals and statements in behalf of the convention. He shall prepare the minutes for the press; his stationery and postage must be furnished by the board of managers.

Sec. 4. The treasurer shall hold all moneys and valuable bonds and notes belonging to the convention, and shall pay all orders for money signed by the president and recording secretary. His books shall be open for inspection by any member of the board of managers. He shall keep an accurate account of all donations, and shall give such bond as the board of managers may determine. He shall present quarterly reports to the board and annual reports to the convention.

Sec. 5. The corresponding secretary shall take charge of the correspondence of the convention with other bodies and corporations. He shall report to the board of managers at their meetings and report all contributions received. The money from all churches, associations and societies must be sent to him.

Sec. 6. The auditor shall, before each annual meeting of the convention, examine carefully the receipts, disbursements, vouchers, papers and books of the treasurer, and his certificate to the facts in the case shall be attached to the treasurer's report.

ARTICLE V. Sec. 1. The board of managers shall secure and hold the title to any and all property belonging to, or which may be acquired by, the convention and take a sufficient bond of the treasurer. They shall have full power to carry out the objects of the convention. They shall employ missionaries, appoint their field of labor and fix their salaries. They shall prepare a program and appoint speakers for the annual sermons on the objects of the convention.

Sec. 2. Seven members of the board shall constitute a quorum.

Sec. 3. The board shall make an annual report to the convention, giving a full account of its transactions during the year.

Sec. 4. The actual traveling expenses of the board to and from quarterly meetings shall be taken out of the general fund.

ARTICLE VI. All officers, managers and missionaries of the convention must be members in good standing in regular Baptist churches.

ARTICLE VII. The funds of this convention shall be educational and general. The first is to provide for ministerial education, the second for the payment of missionaries, home and foreign, and general expenses. These funds shall be kept distinct and the money contributed to either must be applied to it. Unless otherwise directed all money collected shall pass into the general fund.

ARTICLE VIII. The officers of this convention, except the managers, who shall serve during the pleasure of the convention, shall be elected annually.

ARTICLE IX. The convention shall meet annually on Tuesday after the third Sunday in October.

ARTICLE X. The convention may change this constitution, and at any annual meeting, by the vote of two-thirds of the delegates present.

Persons whose Quarterly has on it the (X) cross mark will know their subscription ends with this issue and are kindly requested to renew it.

www.ingramcontent.com/pod-product-compliance
Lightning Source LLC
Chambersburg PA
CBHW032228230426
43666CB00033B/1643